Understanding Pointers In C

Yashavant P. Kanetkar

BPB PUBLICATIONS

B-14, CONNAUGHT PLACE, NEW DELHI -110001.

FIRST EDITION 2001, REPRINTED 2008

Distributors:

MICRO BOOK CENTRE
2, City Centre, CG Road,
Near Swastic Char Rasta,
AHMEDABAD-380009 Phone: 26421611

COMPUTER BOOK CENTRE
12, Shrungar Shopping Centre, M.G. Road,
BANGALORE-560001 Phone: 5587923, 5584641

MICRO BOOKS
Shanti Niketan Building, 8, Camac Street,
KOLKATTA-700017 Phone: 22826518, 22826519

BUSINESS PROMOTION BUREAU
8/1, Ritchie Street, Mount Road,
CHENNAI-600002 Phone: 28410796, 28550491

DECCAN AGENCIES
4-3-329, Bank Street,
HYDERABAD-500195
Phone: 24756400, 24756967

MICRO MEDIA
Shop No. 5, Mahendra Chambers,
150 D.N. Road, Next to Capital Cinema
V.T. (C.S.T.) Station,
MUMBAI-400001 Ph.: 22078296, 22078297

BPB PUBLICATIONS
B-14, Connaught Place, **NEW DELHI-110001**
Phone: 23325760, 23723393, 23737742

INFO TECH
G-2, Sidhartha Building, 96 Nehru Place,
NEW DELHI-110019
Phone: 26438245, 26415092, 26234208

INFO TECH
Shop No. 2, F-38, South Extension Part-1
NEW DELHI-110049
Phone: 24691288, 24641941

BPB BOOK CENTRE
376, Old Lajpat Rai Market,
DELHI-110006 PHONE: 23861747

Price : Rs. 225/-

ISBN 81-7656-358-7

Published by Manish Jain for BPB Publications, B-14, Connaught Place, New Delhi-110 001 and Printed by him at Akash Press, Delhi.

Dedicated to

Seema and Aditya

About the Author

Yashavant Prabhakar Kanetkar obtained his B.E. from VJTI Bombay and his M. Tech. from IIT Kanpur. A Mechanical Engineer by education, he switched to computers a decade ago and hasn't looked back since. Mr. Kanetkar is author of several books including *Let Us C, C Projects, Unix Shell Programming, Let Us C++, Visual C++ Programming, Visual C++ Projects* and *VC++, COM and Beyond* published by BPB Publications and Tech Publications, Singapore. Today Yashavant divides his working hours among writing articles for Express Computer, teaching classes and conducting training seminars in C/C++/VC++/Java/COM. Since 1987 he has been Director of KICIT, a training company that he has set up at Nagpur.

Acknowledgments

During the entire project of writing this book I have received endless help from Niranjan Bakre and Pravin Bagde, right from deciding topics, finalising the method of presentation, framing the exercises, developing the cover idea and what not...

While working with pointers my computers crashed several times. And at all such times I always found Niranjan smiling. He more often than not knew why it crashed and could explain it logically in his inimitable style. Life for him is C and pointers!

Having done DTP of my earlier book Pravin Bagde was ready to take this one head on. He knows only one way of working - clean and efficient. He set a really hot pace for this book and I confess that he almost always won hands down.

The best way to have a good idea is to have a lot of ideas. And Manish Jain of BPB has them in plenty. More importantly he implements most of them. The book that you are holding in your hands is the result of one such idea.

Thanks also to Shakil Ali who wrote and tested most of the programs on Data Structures. The speed at which he is absorbing things I am sure he would go far in life.

N. Kamleshwar Rao was instrumental in designing and executing most of the programs that have been added in this edition. I am confident that the computer world would hear more about him in time to come.

Table of Contents

Preface to Third Edition

In all walks of life anything can be done better the next time around. I realised this more emphatically when I completed the third edition of this book. Thus, the so-called 'perfect' chapters of the second edition had to be redone for more clarity and simplicity.

For quite some time now I have been getting requests from readers that the chapter on 'Pointers and Data Structures' be made more elaborate and exhaustive. I have completely overhauled this chapter. Now it also includes binary trees and graphs.

While reading the first draft of this edition I felt that something is missing in this book. It was only when I was through with the final draft I realised that the missing link (pointer) was a chapter on applications of pointers in real-world programming. After all, no amount of theory is useful unless you can put it into practice. So the final draft became semifinal since I decided to add this chapter to the book. And now I am presenting you the edition which I feel is complete in all respects. And I am praying that I won't be required to write another edition of this book. Any author would testify that writing a new edition is always more pain in the neck than writing a fresh title.

Introduction to Second Edition

Why a book dedicated to one specific topic in C? That's the question that would occur to everyone on reading the title of this book. Two reasons. Firstly, almost all new programmers (and even many seasoned ones) find the topic of pointers quite baffling. Secondly, though introductory text on this topic is available in almost all C books, hardly any has as exhaustive a treatment of pointers as they deserve. My idea here is to present pointers in all their garbs such that the reader gets a true perception of their power.

The chapters in the book have been organised such that the first one explains the concept and rationale of pointers in simplest possible terms avoiding all the jargon that is usually associated with pointers. The next three chapters explore the relationship between pointers and arrays, pointers and strings and pointers and structures. In chapter 4 the usage of pointers in maintaining popular data structures like stacks, queues and singly and doubly linked lists is also discussed at length. Chapter 5 is a new addition to this edition. It deals with the standard data structures like circular linked lists, binary trees, threaded binary trees, etc. and how they can be implemented using pointers. Chapter 6 covers the miscellaneous issues in usage of pointers like near, far and huge pointers, pointers to functions, pointers and variable argument lists etc.

At the end of every chapter several solved and unsolved exercises are given. An attempt to solve them yourselves would help you gain confidence and by the end you would start using pointers with such finesse and grace as if you have been using them since you were knee high in computers.

After going through the book if you think there's something missing or something I could have done better, write to me at:

Yashavant P. Kanetkar,
C/o BPB Publications,
20, Ansari Road,
Daryaganj, New Delhi 110002
Email: kanet@nagpur.dot.net.in
Web: www.funducode.com

Though like all human beings I hate to be corrected, I would answer your letters. And after I sulk for a while, I will surely fix what has gone wrong in the next edition of this book.

Pointers can be made to work if you fiddle with them long enough. If you fiddle with anything long enough you will ultimately mess it.

1 An Introduction to Pointers

Which feature of C do beginners find most difficult to understand? The answer is easy: pointers. Other languages have pointers but few use them so freely, with such abandon, as C does. And why not? It is C's clever use of pointers that makes it the excellent language it is.

The difficulty beginners have with pointers has much to do with C's pointer terminology than the actual concept. For instance, when a C programmer says that a certain variable is a "pointer", what does that mean? It is hard to see how a variable can point to something, or in a certain direction.

It is difficult to get a grip on pointers just by listening to programmer's jargon. In our discussion of C pointers, therefore, we will try to avoid this difficulty by explaining them in terms of simple programming concepts. The first thing we want to do is explain the rationale of C's pointer notation.

The & and * Operators

Consider the declaration,

int i = 3 ;

This declaration tells the C compiler to:

(a) Reserve space in memory to hold the integer value.
(b) Associate the name **i** with this memory location.
(c) Store the value 3 at this location.

We may represent **i**'s location in the memory by the following memory map:

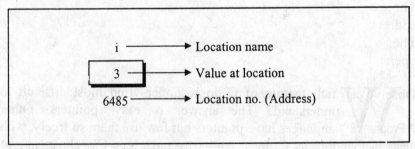

Figure 1.1

We see that the computer has selected memory location 6485 as the place to store the value 3. This location number 6485 is not a number to be relied upon, because some other time the computer may choose a different location for storing the value 3. The important point is, **i**'s address in memory is a number.

We can print this address through the following program:

```
/* Program 1 */
main( )
{
    int i = 3 ;

    printf ( "\nAddress of i = %u", &i ) ;
    printf ( "\nValue of i = %u", i ) ;
}
```

The output of the above program would be:

```
Address of i = 6485
Value of i = 3
```

Look at the first **printf( )** statement carefully. The '&' operator used in this statement is C's 'address of' operator. The expression **&i** returns the address of the variable **i**, which in this case happens to be 6485.

The other pointer operator available in C is '*', called 'value at address' operator. It returns the value stored at a particular address. The 'value at address' operator is also called an 'indirection' operator.

Observe carefully the output of the following program:

```
/* Program 2 */
main( )
{
    int i = 3 ;
    printf ( "\nAddress of i = %u", &i ) ;
    printf ( "\nValue of i = %d", i ) ;
    printf ( "\nValue of i = %d", *( &i ) ) ;
}
```

The output of the above program would be:

Address of i = 6485
Value of i = 3
Value of i = 3

Note that printing the value of *(&i) is same as printing the value of i.

Pointer Expressions

Let us now see what are pointers and how they can be used in various expressions. We have seen in the previous section that the expression **&i** returns the address of **i**. If we so desire, this address can be collected in a variable by saying,

j = &i ;

But remember that **j** is not an ordinary variable like any other integer variable. It is a variable, which contains the address of another variable (**i** in this case).

Since **j** is a variable the compiler must provide it space in memory. Once again, the following memory map would illustrate the contents of **i** and **j**.

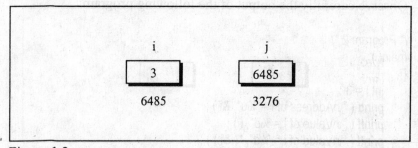

Figure 1.2

As you can see, **i**'s value is 3 and **j**'s value is **i**'s address.

But wait, we can't use **j** in a program without declaring it. And since **j** is a variable, which contains the address of **i**, it is declared as,

int *j ;

This declaration tells the compiler that **j** will be used to store the address of an integer value - in other words **j** points to an integer. How do we justify the usage of * in the declaration,

int *j ;

Let us go by the meaning of *. It stands for 'value at address'. Thus, **int *j** would mean, the value at the address contained in **j** is an **int**.

Here is a program that demonstrates the relationships we have been discussing.

```
/* Program 3 */
main( )
{
    int i = 3 ;
    int *j ;

    j = &i ;
    printf ( "\nAddress of i = %u", &i ) ;
    printf ( "\nAddress of i = %u", j ) ;
    printf ( "\nAddress of j = %u", &j ) ;
    printf ( "\nValue of j = %d", j ) ;
    printf ( "\nValue of i = %d", i ) ;
    printf ( "\nValue of i = %d", *( &i ) ) ;
    printf ( "\nValue of i = %d", *j ) ;
}
```

The output of the above program would be:

Address of i = 6485
Address of i = 6485
Address of j = 3276
Value of j = 6485
Value of i = 3
Value of i = 3
Value of i = 3

Work through the above program carefully, taking help of the memory locations of **i** and **j** shown earlier. This program summarises everything we have discussed so far. If you don't understand the program's output, or the meaning of the expressions **&i**, **&j**, ***j** and ***(&i)**, re-read the last few pages. Everything we say about pointers from here onwards will depend on your understanding of these expressions thoroughly.

Look at the following declarations,

```
int *alpha ;
char *ch ;
float *s ;
```

Here, **alpha**, **ch** and **s** are declared as pointer variables, i.e. variables capable of holding addresses. Remember that, addresses (location nos.) are always going to be whole numbers, therefore pointers always contain whole numbers. Now we can put these two facts together and say—pointers are variables that contain addresses, and since addresses are always whole numbers, pointers would always contain whole numbers.

The declaration **float *s** does not mean that s is going to contain a floating-point value. What it means is, **s** is going to contain the address of a floating-point value. Similarly, **char *ch** means that **ch** is going to contain the address of a **char** value. Or in other words, the value at address stored in **ch** is going to be a **char**. The

concept of pointer can be further extended. Pointer we know is a variable, which contains address of another variable. Now this variable itself could be another pointer. Thus, we now have a pointer, which contains another pointer's address. The following example should make this point clear.

```
/* Program 4 */
main( )
{
    int i = 3 ;
    int *j ;
    int **k ;

    j = &i ;
    k = &j ;

    printf ( "\nAddress of i = %u", &i ) ;
    printf ( "\nAddress of i = %u", j ) ;
    printf ( "\nAddress of i = %u", *k ) ;
    printf ( "\nAddress of j = %u", &j ) ;
    printf ( "\nAddress of j = %u", k ) ;
    printf ( "\nAddress of k = %u", &k ) ;

    printf ( "\n\nValue of j  = %u", j ) ;
    printf ( "\nValue of k  = %u", k ) ;
    printf ( "\nValue of i  = %d", i ) ;
    printf ( "\nValue of i  = %d", *( &i ) ) ;
    printf ( "\nValue of i  = %d", *j ) ;
    printf ( "\nValue of i  = %d", **k ) ;
}
```

The output of the above program would be:

```
Address of i = 6485
Address of i = 6485
Address of i = 6485
Address of j = 3276
```

Address of j = 3276
Address of k = 7234

Value of j = 6485
Value of k = 3276
Value of i = 3
Value of i = 3
Value of i = 3
Value of i = 3

The following memory map would help you in tracing out how the
program prints the above output.

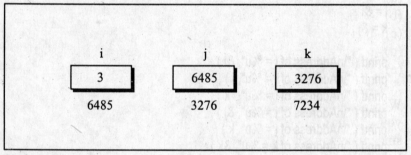

Figure 1.3

Observe how the variables **i**, **j** and **k** have been declared,

```
int i ;
int *j ;
int **k ;
```

Here, **i** is an ordinary **int**, **j** is a pointer to an **int**, whereas **k** is a
pointer to a pointer. In principle, there could be a pointer to a
pointer to a pointer, or a pointer to a pointer to a pointer to a
pointer. There is no limit on how far can we go on extending this
definition. Possibly, till the point we can comprehend it. And that
point of comprehension is usually a pointer to a pointer. Beyond

this, one rarely requires to extend the definition of a pointer. But just in case...

The Jargon of Pointers

Consider the following program segment:

```
int a = 35 ;
int *b ;
b = &a ;
```

Now can you guess which of the following statements are correct:

(a)   **b** contains address of an **int**.
(b)   Value at address contained in **b** is an **int**.
(c)   **b** is an **int** pointer.
(d)   **b** points to an **int**.
(e)   **b** is a pointer which points in the direction of an **int**.

Well, all these statements are correct. That's pointer jargon for you. All the statements are trying to establish the same fact: that since **b** contains address of an **int** it's an **int** pointer. Likewise, had **b** contained an address of a **float** it would have become a **float** pointer. With the same argument if we have three pointer variables first containing address of an array, second containing address of a structure and third containing address of a function then it would be appropriate to call these as an array pointer, a structure pointer and a function pointer respectively.

char, *int* and *float* Pointers

Consider the following program:

```
/* Program 5 */
main( )
{
    char c, *cc ;
    int i, *ii ;
```

```
    float a, *aa ;

    c = 'A'  /* ascii value of A gets stored in c */
    i = 54 ;
    a = 3.14 ;
    cc = &c ;
    ii = &i ;
    aa = &a ;
    printf ( "\nAddress contained in cc = %u", cc ) ;
    printf ( "\nAddress contained in ii = %u", ii ) ;
    printf ( "\nAddress contained in aa = %u", aa ) ;
    printf ( "\nValue of c = %c", *cc ) ;
    printf ( "\nValue of i = %d", *ii ) ;
    printf ( "\nValue of a = %f", *aa ) ;
}
```

And here is the output...

```
Address contained in cc = 1004
Address contained in ii = 2008
Address contained in aa = 7006
Value of c = A
Value of i = 54
Value of a = 3.140000
```

Note that in the **printf( )**s the addresses of **char**, **int** and the **float** all have been printed using the format specifier **%u**. Sometimes the address may turn out to be a number smaller than 32767. In such a case we may use the format specifier **%d** to print the address. Also observe that though the integer variable **i** occupies two bytes in memory the statement **ii = &i** stores only the address of the first byte, 2008 in **ii** (refer Figure 1.4). Similarly, **aa = &a** stores only the address of the first byte (7006) out of four bytes occupied by the **float** variable **a**.

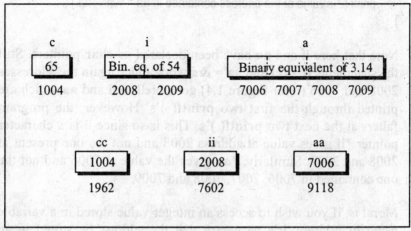

Figure 1.4

The address of first byte is often known as the base address. Though **ii** and **aa** contain only the base addresses, the expressions *ii and *aa allow access to all the bytes occupied by the integer **i** and **a** respectively. This is because **ii** and **aa** have been declared as **int** and **float** pointers respectively. Since **ii** is an **int** pointer, *ii must fetch an **int**. Similarly, since **aa** is a **float** pointer *aa must fetch a **float**.

Do you think the following program would work? And if it does what would be its output?

```
/* Program 6 */
main( )
{
    int i = 54 ;
    float a = 3.14 ;
    char *ii, *aa ;

    ii = ( char * ) &i ;
    aa = ( char * ) &a ;
    printf ( "\nAddress contained in ii = %u", ii ) ;
    printf ( "\nAddress contained in aa = %u", aa ) ;
    printf ( "\nValue at the address contained in ii = %d", *ii ) ;
```

```
        printf ( "\nValue at the address contained in aa = %d", *aa ) ;
}
```

Note that here **ii** and **aa** have been declared as **char** pointers. Still the statements **ii = &i** and **aa = &a** work. Once again the addresses 2008 and 7006 (refer Figure 1.4) get stored in **ii** and **aa** which are printed through the first two **printf( )**'s. However, the program falters at the next two **printf( )**'s. This is so since **ii** is a character pointer *ii gives value at address 2008 and not the one present at 2008 and 2009. Similarly, *aa gives the value at 7006 and not the one contained in 7006, 7007, 7008 and 7009.

Moral is, if you wish to access an integer value stored in a variable using its address, it's necessary that the address be stored in an integer pointer. Likewise, if you wish to access a float value stored in a variable using its address, it's necessary to store the address in a float pointer.

Passing Addresses to Functions

Arguments are generally passed to functions in one of the two ways:

(a) sending the values of the arguments
(b) sending the addresses of the arguments

In the first method the 'value' of each *actual* argument in the calling function is copied into corresponding *formal* argument of the called function. With this method, changes made to the formal arguments in the called function have no effect on the values of the actual arguments in the calling function.

The following program illustrates the 'Call by Value'.

```
/* Program 7 */
main( )
```

```
{
    int a = 10 ;
    int b = 20 ;

    swapv ( a, b ) ;
    printf ( "\na = %d", a ) ;
    printf ( "\nb = %d", b ) ;
}

swapv ( int x, int y )
{
    int t ;
    t = x ;
    x = y ;
    y = t ;

    printf ( "\nx = %d", x ) ;
    printf ( "\ny = %d", y ) ;
}
```

The output of the above program will be:

```
x = 20
y = 10
a = 10
b = 20
```

Note that values of **a** and **b** remain unchanged even after exchanging the values of **x** and **y**.

In the second method (call by reference) the addresses of actual arguments in the calling function are copied into formal arguments of the called function. This means that using the formal arguments in the called function we can make changes in the actual arguments of the calling function. The following program illustrates this fact.

```
/* Program 8 */
main( )
{
    int a = 10 ;
    int b = 20 ;

    swapr ( &a, &b ) ;
    printf ( "\na = %d", a ) ;
    printf ( "\nb = %d", b ) ;
}

swapr ( int *x, int *y )
{
    int t ;

    t = *x ;
    *x = *y ;
    *y = t ;
}
```

The output of the above program would be:

```
a = 20
b = 10
```

Using 'call by reference' intelligently we can make a function return more than one value at a time, which is not possible ordinarily. This is shown in the program given below.

```
/* Program 9 */
main( )
{
    int radius ;
    float area, perimeter ;

    printf ( "\nEnter radius of a circle " ) ;
    scanf ( "%d", &radius ) ;
```

```
    areaperi ( radius, &area, &perimeter ) ;
    printf ( "Area = %f", area ) ;
    printf ( "\nPerimeter = %f", perimeter ) ;
}

areaperi ( int r, float *a, float *p )
{
    *a = 3.14 * r * r ;
    *p = 2 * 3.14 * r ;
}
```

And here is the output...

```
Enter radius of a circle 5
Area = 78.500000
Perimeter = 31.400000
```

Here, we are making a mixed call, in the sense, we are passing the value of **radius** but, addresses of **area** and **perimeter**. And since we are passing the addresses, any change that we make in values stored at addresses contained in the variables **a** and **p**, would make the change effective even in **main( )**. That is why when the control returns from the function **areaperi( )** we are able to output the values of **area** and **perimeter**.

Thus, we have been able to return two values from a called function. This helps us to overcome the limitation of the **return** statement, which can return only one value from a function at a time.

Functions Returning Pointers

The way functions return an **int**, a **float**, a **double** or any other data type, it can even return a pointer. However, to make a function return a pointer it has to be explicitly mentioned in the calling function as well as in the function definition. The following program illustrates this.

```
/* Program 10 */
main( )
{
    int *p ;
    int *fun( ) ;   /* prototype declaration */
    p = fun( ) ;
    printf ( "\n%u", p ) ;
    printf ( "\n%d", *p ) ;
}

int *fun( ) /* function definition */
{
    int i = 20 ,
    return ( &i ) ;
}
```

This program shows how a pointer can be returned from a function. Note that the prototype declaration tells the compiler that **fun( )** is a function which receives nothing but returns an integer pointer. The first **printf( )** would output the address contained in **p** (address of **i**). Can you guess what the second **printf( )** would output? No, it won't print 20. This is because, when the control comes back from **fun( )**, **i** dies. So even if we have its address in **p** we can't access **i** since it is already dead. If you want **i** to survive and ***p** to give 20 then make sure that you declare **i** as **static** as shown below:

static int i = 20 ;

Solved Problems

[A] What will be the output of the following programs:

(1) main( )
```
main( )
{
    int i = -5, j = -2 ;
    junk ( i, &j ) ;
    printf ( "\ni = %d j = %d", i, j ) ;
}

junk ( int i, int *j )
{
    i = i * i ;
    *j = *j * *j ;
}
```

Output

```
i = -5 j = 4
```

Explanation

One doubt immediately comes to the mind—can we use same variable names in different functions? Yes, by all means, without absolutely any conflict. Thus, the two sets of **i** and **j** are two totally different sets of variables. While calling the function **junk( )** the value of **i** and the address of **j** are passed to it. Naturally, in **junk( )** **i** is declared as an ordinary **int**, whereas, **j** is declared as a pointer to an **int**.

Even though the value of **i** is changed to 25 in **junk( )**, this change will not be reflected back in **main( )**. As against this, since **j**'s address is being passed to **junk( )**, any change in **junk( )** gets reflected back in **main( )**. Hence *j * *j, which evaluates to 4 is reflected back in **main( )**.

(2)
```
#include "stdio.h"
main( )
{
    int a, b = 5 ;
    a = b + NULL ;
    printf ( "%d", a ) ;
}
```

Output

5

Explanation

NULL has been defined in "stdio.h" as follows:

#define NULL 0

Hence, during preprocessing NULL will be replaced by 0, resulting into 5 getting stored in **a**.

(3)
```
#include "stdio.h"
main( )
{
    printf ( "%d %d", sizeof ( NULL ), sizeof ( "" ) ) ;
}
```

Output

2 1

Explanation

While finding out size of NULL, we are truly speaking finding out size of 0. This is an integer, hence its size is reported as 2 bytes.

Even though the string "" is empty it still contains the character, '\0'. Hence its size turns out to be 1 byte.

(4)
```
main( )
{
    float a = 7.999999 ;
    float *b, *c ;
    b = &a ;
    c = b ;
    printf ( "\n%u %u %u", &a, b, c ) ;
    printf ( "\n%d %d %d %d", a, *( &a ), *b, *c ) ;
}
```

Output

```
4200 4200 4200
0 24576 -3 16415
```

Explanation

b contains the address of variable **a**. Since **a** is a **float**, **b** must be a **float** pointer. The same address is then assigned to **c**. Therefore **c** has also been declared as a **float** pointer. The first **printf( )** prints the address of **a** in three different ways. No problem there. What is surprising is the output of the second **printf( )**. Through this **printf( )** we are attempting to print 7.999999 by applying pointer operators on **a**, **b** and **c**. **a**, *(&a), *b, *c all yield 7.999999 but when they are printed using **%d**, **printf( )** blows it up as the output above would justify.

So always remember to use **%f** to print floating point values. Don't rely on **printf( )** to truncate a **float** value to an integer during printing by using a **%d**. Vice versa also it is true. The following statements would not print 7.000000. Don't be surprised if you get some odd value. In that sense **%d** and **%f** are a little unreliable.

```
int i = 7 ;
printf ( "%f", i ) ;
```

(5)
```
main( )
{
    int *c ;
    c = check ( 10, 20 ) ;
    printf ( "\nc = %u", c ) ;
}

check ( int i, int j )
{
    int *p , *q ;
    p = &i ;
    q = &j ;
    if ( i >= 45 )
        return ( p ) ;
    else
        return ( q ) ;
}
```

Output

Error message: Non portable pointer assignment in main

Explanation

The reason for the error is simple. The integers being passed to **check( )** are collected in **i** and **j**, and then their addresses are assigned to **p** and **q**. Then in the next statement the conditional operators test the value of **i** against 45, and return either the address stored in **p** or the address stored in **q**. It appears that this address would be collected in **c** in **main( )**, and then would be printed out. And there lies the error. The function **check( )** is not capable of returning an integer pointer. All that it can return is an ordinary integer. Thus just declaring **c** as an integer pointer is not sufficient. We must make the following modifications in the program to make it work properly.

```
main( )
{
    int *c ;
    int *check ( int, int ) ;
    c = check ( 10, 20 ) ;
    printf ( "\nc = %u", c ) ;
}
int *check ( int i, int j )
{
    .....
    .....
}
```

(6) ```
main( )
{
    float *jamboree (float *) ;
    float p = 23.5, *q ;
    q = &p ;
    printf ("\nq before call = %u", q) ;
    q = jamboree (&p) ;
    printf ("\nq after call = %u", q) ;
}

float *jamboree (float *r)
{
    r = r + 1 ;
```
```

```
        return ( r ) ;
}
```

Output

q before call = 5498
q after call = 5502

Explanation

In **main( )**, **q** has been declared as a **float** pointer. It means **q** is a variable capable of holding the address of a **float**. Through **q = &p** the address of **p**, a **float**, is stored in **q** and then printed out through the **printf( )**. This is the value of **q** before **jamboree( )** is called. When **jamboree( )** is called the address of **p** is sent to it and is collected in **r**. At this juncture **r** contains 5498 (when we ran the program it was 5498; when you execute the program this may turn out to be some other address). When **r** is incremented it would become 5502. Why a step of 4? Because **r** is a **float** pointer and on incrementing it by 1 it would point to the next **float** which would be present 4 bytes hence, since every **float** is 4 bytes long. The **return** statement then returns this address 5502 back to **main( )**.

Since a **float** pointer is being returned, a declaration **float *jamboree (float *)** is necessary in **main( )**, which tells the compiler that down the line there exists a function called **jamboree( )**, which will receive a **float** pointer and will return a **float** pointer.

[B] Answer the following:

(1) Can you write another expression which does the same job as ++*ptr?

Explanation

(*ptr)++

(2) In the following program add a statement in the function **fun( )** such that address of **a** gets stored in **j**.

```
main( )
{
    int *j ;
    void fun ( int ** ) ;

    fun ( &j ) ;
}
void fun ( int **k )
{
    int a = 10 ;
    /* add statement here */
}
```

Explanation

*k = &a ;

(3) Are the expressions ***ptr++** and **++*ptr** same?

Explanation

No. ***ptr++** increments the pointer and not the value pointed by it, whereas, **++*ptr** increments the value being pointed to by **ptr**.

(4) Where can pointers be used?

Explanation

At lot of places, some of which are:

- Accessing array or string elements
- Dynamic memory allocation
- Call by reference
- Implementing linked lists, trees, graphs and many other data structures

(5) Would the following program give a compilation error or warning? <Yes/No>

```
main( )
{
    float i = 10, *j ;
    void *k ;
    k = &i ;
    j = k ;
    printf ( "\n%f", *j ) ;
}
```

Explanation

No. Here no typecasting is required while assigning the value to and from **k** because conversions are applied automatically when other pointer types are assigned to and from **void ***.

(6) Would the following program compile?

```
main( )
{
    int a = 10, *j ;
    void *k ;
    j = k = &a ;
    j++ ;
    k++ ;
    printf ( "\n%u %u", j, k ) ;
}
```

Explanation

No. An error would be reported in the statement **k++** since arithmetic on **void** pointers is not permitted unless the **void** pointer is appropriately typecasted.

(7) Would the following program give any warning on compilation?

```
#include "stdio.h"
main( )
{
    int *p1, i = 25 ;
    void *p2 ;
    p1 = &i ;
    p2 = &i ;
    p1 = p2 ;
    p2 = p1 ;
}
```

Explanation

No

(8) Would the following program give any warning on compilation?

```
#include "stdio.h"
main( )
{
    float *p1, i = 25.50 ;
    char *p2 ;
    p1 = &i ;
    p2 = &i ;
}
```

Explanation

Yes. The warning would be "Suspicious pointer conversion in function **main( )**".

(9) What is a null pointer?

Explanation

For each pointer type (like say a **char** pointer) C defines a special pointer value that is guaranteed not to point to any 'bject or function of that type. Usually, the null pointer constant used for representing a null pointer is the integer 0.

(10) What's the difference between a null pointer, a NULL macro, the ASCII NUL character and null string?

Explanation

A null pointer is a pointer, which doesn't point anywhere.

A NULL macro is used to represent the null pointer in source code. It has a value 0 associated with it.

The ASCII NUL character has all its bits as 0 but doesn't have any relationship with the null pointer.

The null string is just another name for an empty string "".

(11) In which header file is the NULL macro defined.

Explanation

In files "stdio.h" and "stddef.h".

(12) Is the NULL pointer same as an uninitialised pointer? <Yes/No>

Explanation

No

(13) What does the error "Null Pointer Assignment" mean and what causes this error?

Explanation

The Null Pointer Assignment error is generated only in small and medium memory models. This error occurs in programs, which attempt to change the bottom of the data segment.

In Borland's C or C++ compilers, Borland places four zero bytes at the bottom of the data segment, followed by the Borland copyright notice "Borland C++ - Copyright 1991 Borland Intl.". In the small and medium memory models, a null pointer points to DS:0000. Thus assigning a value to the memory referenced by this pointer will overwrite the first zero byte in the data segment. At program termination, the four zeros and the copyright banner are checked. If either has been modified, then the Null Pointer Assignment error is generated. Note that the pointer may not truly be null, but may be a wild pointer that references these key areas in the data segment.

(14) How do we debug a Null Pointer Assignment error?

Explanation

In the Integrated Development Environment set two watches—one pointing to the bottom of the data segment and another pointing to the banner (refer (13) above for details).

These watches, and what they should display in the watch window, are:

```
*(char *)4,42MS      "Borland C++ - Copyright 1991 Borland Intl."
(char *)0            NULL
```

Of course, the copyright banner shown above will vary depending on your version of the Borland C/C++ compiler.

You can type the following program and step through your program using F8 or F7 and monitor these values in the watch window. At the point where one of them changes, you have just executed a statement that uses a pointer that has not been properly initialized.

```c
#include "dos.h"
#include "stdio.h"
#include "string.h"

main( )
{
    char *ptr, *banner ;

    ptr = ( char * ) MK_FP ( _DS, 0 ) ;
    banner = ( char * ) MK_FP ( _DS, 4 ) ;

    strcpy ( ptr, "hi" ) ;
    strcpy ( banner, "hello" ) ;
    printf ( "\nGood Morning" ) ;
}
```

Note that a Null Pointer Assignment error is not generated in all models. In the **compact**, **large** and **huge** memory models, **far** pointers are used for data (Refer Chapter 6 for more information about memory models and **far** pointers). Therefore, a null pointer will reference 0000:0000, or the base of system memory, and using it will not cause a corruption of the key values at the base of the data segment. Modifying the base of system memory usually causes a system crash, however. Although it would be possible that a wild pointer would overwrite the key values, it would not indicate a null pointer. In the tiny memory model, DS = CS = SS. Therefore, using a null pointer will overwrite the beginning of the code segment.

(15) Can anything else generate a Null Pointer Assignment error?

Explanation

Yes, using a wild pointer that happens to reference the base area of the data segment may cause the same error since this would change the zeros or the copyright banner. Since data corruption or stack corruption could cause an otherwise-valid pointer to be corrupted and point to the base of the data segment, any memory corruption could result in this error being generated. If the pointer used in the program statement that corrupts the key values appears to have been properly initialized, place a watch on that pointer. Step through your program again and watch for its value (address) to change.

[C] What do the following declarations stand for?

```
int ***i ;
float **j ;
char ****k ;

void f ( int *, char * ) ;
float * g ( float *, float ** ) ;
int ** h ( float *, char ** ) ;
```

Explanation

i is a pointer to a pointer to a pointer to an **int**.

j is a pointer to a pointer to a **float**.

k is a pointer to a pointer to a pointer to a pointer to a **char**.

f is a function which receives an **int** pointer and a **char** pointer and returns nothing.

g is a function which receives a **float** pointer and a pointer to a **float** pointer and in turn returns a **float** pointer.

h is a function which receives a **float** pointer and a pointer to a **char** pointer and in turn returns a pointer to an **int** pointer.

Exercise

[A] What will be the output of the following programs:

```
(1)   main( )
      {
            int a, *b, **c, ***d, ****e ;

            a = 10 ;
            b = &a ;
            c = &b ;
            d = &c ;
            e = &d ;
            printf ( "\na = %d  b = %u  c = %u  d = %u  e = %u", a, b, c, d, e ) ;
            printf ( "\n%d %d %d", a, a + *b, **c + ***d + ****e ) ;
      }
```

```
(2)    main()
       {
            char c, *cc ;
            int i ;
            long l ;
            float f ;

            c = 'Z' ;
            i = 15 ;
            l = 77777 ;
            f = 3.14 ;
            cc = &c ;
            printf ( "\nc = %c  cc = %u", *cc, cc ) ;
            cc = &i ;
            printf ( "\ni = %d  cc = %u", *cc, cc ) ;
            cc = &l ;
            printf ( "\nl = %ld  cc = %u", *cc, cc ) ;
            cc = &f ;
            printf ( "\nf = %f  cc = %u", *cc, cc ) ;
       }
(3)    main( )
       {
            int c = 10, d = 20 ;

            printf ( "\nWe are in main( )...." ) ;
            printf ( "\nAddress of c = %u  Address of d = %u", &c, &d ) ;
            printf ( "\nBefore swap( ),   c = %d  d = %d", c, d ) ;
            swap ( c, d ) ;
            printf ( "\nBack to main( )...." ) ;
            printf ( "\nAfter swap( ),  c = %d  d = %d", c, d ) ;
       }

       swap ( int c, int d )
       {
            printf ( "\nWe are in swap( )...." ) ;
            printf ( "\nAddress of c = %u  Address of d = %u", &c, &d ) ;
            printf ( "\nBefore change( ), c = %d  d = %d", c, d ) ;
```

```
        change ( c, d ) ;
        printf ( "\nBack to swap( )...." ) ;
        printf ( "\nAfter change( ),  c = %d  d = %d", c, d ) ;
    }

    change ( int c, int d )
    {
        int t ;

        printf ( "\nWe are in change( )...." ) ;
        printf ( "\nAddress of c = %u  Address of d = %u", &c, &d ) ;
        printf ( "\nBefore interchanging, c = %d  d = %d", c, d ) ;
        t = c ;
        c = d ;
        d = t ;
        printf ( "\nAfter interchanging,  c = %d  d = %d", c, d ) ;
    }

(4) main( )
    {
        int c = 10, d = 20 ;

        printf ( "\nBefore swap, c = %d  d = %d", c, d ) ;
        swap ( &c, &d ) ;
        printf ( "\nAfter swap,  c = %d  d = %d", c, d ) ;
    }

    swap ( int *cc, int *dd )
    {
        exchange ( &cc, dd ) ;
    }

    exchange ( int **cc, int *dd )
    {
        int t ;

        t = **cc ;
        **cc = *dd ;
```

```
        *dd = t ;
    }

(5)  main( )
    {
        int a = 5, *aa ;

        aa = &a ;
        a = power ( &aa ) ;
        printf ( "\na = %d  aa = %u", a, aa ) ;
    }

    power ( int **ptr )
    {
        int b ;

        b = **ptr***ptr ;
        return ( b ) ;
    }



(6)  main( )
    {
        int i = 3 ;
        float f = 3.50, *prod ;
        float * multiply ( int, float ) ;

        prod = multiply ( i, f ) ;
        printf ( "\nprod = %u  value at address = %f", prod, *prod ) ;
    }

    float * multiply ( int ii, float ff )
    {
        float product ;

        product = ii * ff ;
        printf ( "\nproduct = %f  address of product = %u", product,
                                                        &product) ;
```

```
          return ( &product ) ;
      }

(7)   main( )
      {
          char *c = 4000 ;
          int *i = 4000 ;
          long *l = 4000 ;
          float *f = 4000 ;
          double *d = 4000 ;

          printf ( "\nc = %u, c + 1 = %u", c, c + 1 ) ;
          printf ( "\ni = %u, i + 1 = %u", i, i + 1 ) ;
          printf ( "\nl = %u, l + 1 = %u", l, l + 1 ) ;
          printf ( "\nf = %u, f + 1 = %u", f, f + 1 ) ;
          printf ( "\nd = %u, d + 1 = %u", d, d + 1 ) ;
      }

(8)   main( )
      {
          int i = 10, j = 20, diff ;

          diff = &j - &i ;
          printf ( "\naddress of i = %u  address of j = %u", &i, &j ) ;
          printf ( "\ndifference of addresses of i and j is %d", diff );
      }

(9)   main( )
      {
          int *i, *j ;
          j = i * 2 ;
          printf ( "\nj = %u", j ) ;
      }

(10)  main( )
      {
          int i = 10 ;
          printf ( "\nvalue of i = %d  address of i = %u", i, &i ) ;
```

```
        &i = 7200 ;
        printf ( "\nnew value of i = %d  new address of i = %u", i, &i ) ;
    }

(11) float a = 3.14 ;
     float **z ;
     float **y ;
     float ***x ;
     float ****v ;
     float ****w ;

     float ** fun1 ( float * ) ;
     float **** fun2 ( float *** ) ;

     main( )
     {
         clrscr( ) ;
         z = fun1 ( &a ) ;
         printf ( "%u %f", z, **z ) ;
     }

     float ** fun1 ( float *z )
     {
         y = &z ;
         v = fun2 ( &y ) ;
         return ( **v ) ;
     }

     float **** fun2 ( float ***x )
     {
         w = &x ;
         return ( w ) ;
     }
```

[B] State True or False:

(1) Multiplication of a pointer and an **unsigned** integer is allowed.

(2) Address of a **float** can be assigned to a **char** pointer.

(3) A **float** pointer always contains a whole number.

(4) A pointer **p** contains address of a pointer to a pointer to an integer pointer. To reach the integer value we should use ******p**.

No matter how much time you have spent with pointers you would always find some application of it that would leave you guessing.

2 *Pointers and Arrays*

The C language provides a capability called array that enables the user to design a set of similar data types. Array is a very popular data type with C programmers. This is because of the convenience with which arrays lend themselves to programming. Pointers and arrays are so closely related that discussing arrays without discussing pointers or vice versa would make the discussion incomplete and wanting. In fact all arrays make use of pointers internally. Hence it is all too relevant to study them together rather than as isolated topics.

What are Arrays

An Array is a collection of similar elements stored in adjacent memory locations. An ordinary variable is capable of storing only one value at a time. However, there are situations in which we would be wanting to store more than one value at a time in a single variable. Suppose we wish to store the percentage marks obtained by 100 students in memory. In such a case we have two options to store these marks in memory:

(a)   Construct 100 variables to store percentage marks obtained by 100 different students; i.e. each variable containing one student's marks.

(b)   Construct one variable (called a subscripted variable) capable of storing or holding all the hundred marks.

Obviously, the second alternative is better. A simple reason for this is, it would be much easier to handle one variable than handling 100 different variables. Moreover, there are certain logics that cannot be dealt with, without the use of a subscripted variable.

Now a formal definition of subscripted variables: A subscripted variable is a collective name given to a group of 'similar quantities'. These similar quantities could be percentage marks of 100 students, or salaries of 300 employees, or ages of 50 employees. What is important is that the quantities must be 'similar'. Each member in the group is referred to by its position in the group. For example, assume the following group of numbers that represent percentage marks obtained by five students.

per = { 48, 88, 34, 23, 96 }

If we want to refer to the second number of the group, the usual notation used is per_2. Similarly, the fourth number of the group is referred as per_4. However, in C, the fourth number is referred as **per[3]**. Note that, in C counting of elements begins with 0, and not

1. Thus, in this example **per[3]** refers to 23 and **per[4]** refers to 96. In general, the notation would be **per[i]**, where, **i** can take a value 0, 1, 2, 3, or 4, depending on the position of the element being referred. Here **per** is the subscripted variable, whereas, **i** is its subscript.

A subscripted variable is also called an 'array'. Thus, an array is a collection of similar elements. These similar elements could be all **int**s, or all **float**s, or all **char**s, etc. Usually, the array of **char**s is called a 'string', whereas an array of **int**s or **float**s is called simply an array. Remember that all elements of any given array must be of the same type i.e. we cannot have an array of 10 numbers, of which 5 are **int**s and 5 are **float**s.

To begin with, like other variables an array needs to be declared, so that the compiler will know what kind of an array and how large an array we want. For example,

int marks[30] ;

Here, **int** specifies the type of the variable, just as it does with ordinary variables and the word **marks** is the name of the variable. The number 30 tells how many elements of the type **int** will be in our array. This number is often known as 'dimension' of the array. The bracket ([ ]) tells the compiler that we are dealing with an array.

To fix our ideas, let us note down a few facts about arrays:

(a) An array is a collection of similar elements. It is also known as a subscripted variable.

(b) Before using an array its type and size must be declared. For example,

int arr[30] ;
float a[60] ;

```
char ch[25] ;
```

(c) The first element in the array is numbered 0, so the last element is 1 less than the size of the array.

(d) However big an array may be, its elements are always stored in contiguous memory locations. This is a very important point that we would discuss in more detail later on.

(e) If we so desire an array can be initialised at the same place where it is declared. For example,

```
int num[6] = { 2, 4, 12, 5, 45, 5 } ;
int n[ ] = { 2, 4, 12, 5, 45, 5 } ;
float press[ ] = { 12.3, 34.2, -23.4, -11.3 } ;
```

(f) If the array is initialised where it is defined, mentioning the dimension of array is optional as in second example above.

(g) If the array elements are not given any specific values, they are supposed to contain garbage values.

(h) In C there is no check to see if the subscript used for an array exceeds the size of the array. Data entered with a subscript exceeding the array size will simply be placed in memory outside the array; probably on top of other data or on the program itself. This will lead to unpredictable results, to say the least, and there will be no error message to warn you that you are going beyond the array size. In some cases the computer may just hang. Thus, the following program may turn out to be suicidal:

```
/* Program 11 */
main( )
{
    int num[40], i ;
    for ( i = 0 ; i <= 100 ; i++ )
```

```
            num[i] = i ;
      }
```

So do remember that, ensuring that we do not reach beyond the array size is entirely the programmer's botheration and not the compiler's.

Passing Array Elements to a Function

Array elements can be passed to a function by calling the function:

(a) by value, i.e. by passing values of array elements to the function.
(b) by reference, i.e. by passing addresses of array elements to the function.

Programs showing how these calls are made are given below.

```
/* Program 12 */
/* Demonstration of call by value */
main( )
{
      int i ;
      int marks[ ] = { 55, 65, 75, 56, 78, 78, 90 } ;

      for ( i = 0 ; i <= 6 ; i++ )
            display ( marks[i] ) ;
}

display ( int m )
{
      printf ( "\n%d", m ) ;
}
```

And here's the output...

```
55
65
75
```

56
78
78
90

Here, we are passing an individual array element at a time to the function **display( )** and getting it printed in the function **display( )**. Note that since at a time only one element is being passed, in the function it is collected in an ordinary integer variable **m**.

And now the call by reference.

```
/* Program 13 */
/* Demonstration of call by reference */
main( )
{
    int i ;
    int marks[ ] = { 55, 65, 75, 56, 78, 78, 90 } ;

    for ( i = 0 ; i <= 6 ; i++ )
        disp ( &marks[i] ) ;
}
disp ( int *n )
{
    printf ( "\n%d", *n ) ;
}
```

And here's the output...

55
65
75
56
78
78
90

Here, we are passing addresses of individual array elements to the function **display( )**. Hence, the variable in which this address is collected **(n)** must be a pointer variable. And since **n** contains the address of array element, to print out the array element we must use the 'value at address' operator **(*)**.

Read the following program carefully. The purpose of the function is to just display the array elements on the screen. The program is only partly complete. You are required to write the function **show( )** on your own. Try your hand at it.

```
/* Program 14 */
main( )
{
    int i ;
    int marks[ ] = { 55, 65, 75, 56, 78, 78, 90 } ;
    for ( i = 0 ; i <= 6 ; i++ )
        disp ( &marks[i] ) ;
}

disp ( int *n )
{
    show ( &n ) ;
}
```

Pointers and Arrays

To be able to see what pointers have got to do with arrays, let us first learn some pointer arithmetic. Consider the following example:

```
/* Program 15 */
main( )
{
    int i = 3, *x ;
    float j = 1.5, *y ;
    char k = 'c', *z ;
```

```
        printf (."\nValue of i = %d", i ) ;
        printf ( "\nValue of j = %f", j ) ;
        printf ( "\nValue of k = %c", k ) ;

        x = &i ;
        y = &j ;
        z = &k ;

        printf ( "\n\nOriginal value in x = %u", x ) ;
        printf ( "\nOriginal value in y = %u", y ) ;
        printf ( "\nOriginal value in z = %u", z ) ;

        x++ ;
        y++ ;
        z++ ;

        printf ( "\n\nNew value in x = %u", x ) ;
        printf ( "\nNew value in y = %u", y ) ;
        printf ( "\nNew value in z = %u", z ) ;
}
```

Suppose **i**, **j** and **k** are stored in memory at addresses 1002, 2004 and 5006, the output would be...

```
Value of i = 3
Value of j = 1.500000
Value of k = c

Original value in x = 1002
Original value in y = 2004
Original value in z = 5006

New value in x = 1004
New value in y = 2008
New value in z = 5007
```

Observe the last three lines of the output. 1004 is equal to original value in **x** plus 2, 2008 is equal to original value in **y** plus 4, and 5007 is equal to original value in **z** plus 1. This so happens because every time a pointer is incremented it points to the immediately next location of its type. That is why, when the integer pointer **x** is incremented, it points to an address two locations after the current location, since an **int** is always 2 bytes long. Similarly, **y** points to an address 4 locations after the current location and **z** points 1 location after the current location. This is a very important result and can be effectively used while passing the entire array to a function.

The way a pointer can be incremented, it can be decremented as well, to point to earlier locations. Thus, the following operations can be performed on a pointer:

(a) Addition of a number to a pointer. For example,

```
int i = 4, *j, *k ;
j = &i ;
j = j + 1 ;
j = j + 9 ;
k = j + 3 ;
```

(b) Subtraction of a number from a pointer. For example,

```
int i = 4, *j, *k ;
j = &i ;
j = j - 2 ;
j = j - 5 ;
k = j - 6 ;
```

A word of caution! Do not attempt the following operations on pointers... they would never work out.

(a) Addition of two pointers
(b) Multiplying a pointer with a number
(c) Dividing a pointer with a number

Now we will try to correlate the following two facts, which we have already learnt:

(a) Array elements are always stored in contiguous memory locations.

(b) A pointer when incremented always points to an immediately next location of its type.

Suppose we have an array,

int num[ ] = { 23, 34, 12, 44, 56, 17 } ;

The following figure shows how this array is located in memory.

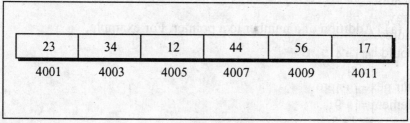

Figure 2.1

Here is a program that prints out the memory locations in which the elements of this array are stored.

```
/* Program 16 */
main( )
{
    int num[ ] = { 24, 34, 12, 44, 56, 17 } ;
    int i = 0 ;

    while ( i <= 5 )
    {
        printf ( "\nelement no. %d  ", i ) ;
```

```
        printf ( "address = %u" , &num[i] ) ;
        i++ ;
    }
}
```

The output of this program would be:

```
element no. 0   address = 4001
element no. 1   address = 4003
element no. 2   address = 4005
element no. 3   address = 4007
element no. 4   address = 4009
element no. 5   address = 4011
```

Note that the array elements are stored in contiguous memory locations, each element occupying two bytes, since it is an integer array. When you run this program, you may get different addresses, but what is promised is that each subsequent address would be 2 bytes greater than its immediate predecessor.

Our next two programs show two ways in which we can access the elements of this array. The first one uses the subscript notation.

```
/* Program 17 */
main( )
{
    int num[ ] = { 24, 34, 12, 44, 56, 17 } ;
    int i = 0 ;

    while ( i <= 5 )
    {
        printf ( "\naddress = %u   ", &num[i] ) ;
        printf ( "element = %d", num[i] ) ;
        i++ ;
    }
}
```

The output of this program would be:

```
address = 4001    element = 24
address = 4003    element = 34
address = 4005    element = 12
address = 4007    element = 44
address = 4009    element = 56
address = 4011    element = 17
```

The next method accesses the array elements using pointers.

```
/* Program 18 */
main( )
{
    int num[ ] = { 24, 34, 12, 44, 56, 17 } ;
    int i = 0, *j ;

    j = &num[0] ;  /* assign address of zeroth element */

    while ( i <= 5 )
    {
        printf ( "\naddress = %u    ", &num[i] ) ;
        printf ( "element = %d", *j ) ;

        i++ ;
        j++ ;  /* increment pointer to point to next location */
    }
}
```

The output of the program would look like this:

```
address = 4001    element = 24
address = 4003    element = 34
address = 4005    element = 12
address = 4007    element = 44
address = 4009    element = 56
address = 4011    element = 17
```

In this program, to begin with we have collected the base address of the array (address of 0th element) in the variable **j** using the statement,

```
j = &num[0] ; /* assigns address 4001 to j */
```

When we are inside the loop for the first time **j** contains the address 4001, and the value at this address is 24. These are printed using the statements,

```
printf ( "\naddress = %u    " , &num[i] ) ;
printf ( "element = %d", *j ) ;
```

On incrementing **j** it points to the next memory location of its type, that is location no. 4003. But location number 4003 contains the second element of the array, therefore when the **printf( )** statements are executed for the second time they print out the second element of the array and its address (i.e. 34 and 4003). This continues till the last element of the array has been printed.

Obviously, a question arises as to which of the above two methods should be used when? Accessing array elements using pointers is **always** faster than accessing them by subscripts. However, from the point of view of convenience in programming we should observe the following:

Array elements should be accessed using pointers, if the elements are to be accessed in a fixed order, say from beginning to end, or from end to beginning, or every alternate element or any such definite logic.

It would be easier to access the elements using a subscript if there is no fixed logic in accessing the elements. However, in this case also, accessing the elements by pointers would work faster than subscripts.

Passing an Entire Array to a Function

Earlier we saw two programs one in which we passed individual elements of an array to a function, and another in which we passed addresses of individual elements to a function. Let us now see how to pass the entire array to the function rather than individual elements. Consider the following example:

```
/* Program 19 */
main( )
{
    int num[ ] = { 24, 34, 12, 44, 56, 17 } ;
    display ( &num[0], 6 ) ;
}

display ( int *j, int n )
{
    int i = 1 ;
    while ( i <= n )
    {
        printf ( "\nelement = %d", *j ) ;
        i++ ;
        j++ ; /* increment pointer to point to next location */
    }
}
```

Here, the **display( )** function is used to print out the array elements. Note that address of the zeroth element is being passed to the **display( )** function. The **while** loop is same as the one used in the earlier program to access the array elements using pointers.

Thus, just passing the address of the zeroth element of the array to a function is as good as passing the entire array to the function. It is also necessary to pass the total number of elements in the array, otherwise the **display( )** function would not know when to terminate the **while** loop.

Note that the address of the zeroth element (often known as the base address) can also be passed by just passing the name of the array. Thus, the following two function calls are same:

```
display ( &num[0], 6 ) ;
display ( num, 6 ) ;
```

The Real Thing

If you have grasped the concept of storage of array elements in memory and the arithmetic of pointers, here is some real food for thought. Once again consider the following array.

23	34	12	44	56	17
4001	4003	4005	4007	4009	4011

Figure 2.2

This is how we would declare the above array in C,

```
int num[ ] = { 23, 34, 12, 44, 56, 17 } ;
```

We already know that on mentioning the name of the array we get its base address. Thus, by saying ***num** we would be able to refer to the zeroth element of the array, that is, 23. One can easily see that ***num** and ***(num + 0)** both refer to 23. Similarly, by saying ***(num + 1)** we can refer to first element of the array, that is, 34. In fact, this is what the C compiler internally does. When we say, **num[i]**, the C compiler internally converts it to ***(num + i)**. This means that all the following notations are same:

```
num[i]
*( num + i )
```

```
*( i + num )
i[num]
```

And here is a program to prove my point.

```
/* Program 20 */
/* Accessing array elements in different ways */
main( )
{
    int num[ ] = { 24, 34, 12, 44, 56, 17 } ;
    int i = 0 ;

    while ( i <= 5 )
    {
        printf ( "\naddress = %u    " , &num[i] ) ;
        printf ( "element = %d  ", num[i] ) ;
        printf ( "%d ", *( num + i ) ) ;
        printf ( "%d ", *( i + num ) ) ;
        printf ( "%d", i[num] ) ;
        i++ ;
    }
}
```

The output of the program would look like this:

```
address = 4001   element = 24  24  24  24
address = 4003   element = 34  34  34  34
address = 4005   element = 12  12  12  12
address = 4007   element = 44  44  44  44
address = 4009   element = 56  56  56  56
address = 4011   element = 17  17  17  17
```

More Than One Dimension

So far we have looked at arrays with only one dimension. It is also possible for arrays to have two or more dimensions. The two-dimensional array is also called a matrix. Here is a sample program that initialises a 2-D array and prints out its elements.

```
/* Program 21 */
main( )
{
    int stud[5][2] = {
                        { 1234, 56 },
                        { 1212, 33 },
                        { 1434, 80 },
                        { 1312, 78 },
                        { 1203, 75 }
                    };
    int i, j ;

    for ( i = 0 ; i <= 4 ; i++ )
    {
        printf ( "\n" ) ;
        for ( j = 0 ; j <= 1 ; j++ )
            printf ( "%d  ", stud[i][j] ) ;
    }
}
```

Look at the **printf( )** statement...

```
printf ( "%d  ", stud[i][j] ) ;
```

In **stud[i][j]** the first subscript is row number. The second subscript tells which of the two columns are we talking about... the zeroth column or the first column. Remember that counting of rows and columns begins with zero.

The complete array arrangement is shown below:

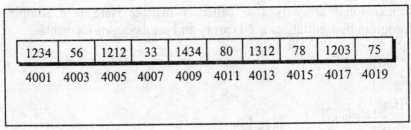

1234	56	1212	33	1434	80	1312	78	1203	75
4001	4003	4005	4007	4009	4011	4013	4015	4017	4019

Figure 2.3

Thus, 1234 is stored in **stud[0][0]**, 56 is stored in **stud[0][1]** and so on. The above arrangement highlights the fact that a two-dimensional array is nothing but a collection of a number of one-dimensional arrays placed one after another.

Remember that the arrangement of a 2-D array into row and columns is only conceptually true. This is because in memory there are no rows and columns. In memory whether it's a 1-D or a 2-D array the elements are stored in one continuous chain.

Pointers and Two Dimensional Arrays

Can we not refer elements of a 2-D array using pointer notation, the way we did in one-dimensional array? Answer is yes, only the procedure is slightly difficult to understand. Let us see how.

The C language embodies an unusual but powerful capability: it can treat parts of an array as arrays. More specifically, each row of a two-dimensional array can be thought as a one-dimensional array. This is a very important fact if we wish to access array elements of a two-dimensional array using pointers.

Thus, the declaration,

int stud[5][2] ;

can be thought of as setting up a one-dimensional array of 5 elements, each of which is a one-dimensional array 2 elements long. We refer to an element of a one-dimensional array using a single subscript. Similarly, if we can imagine **stud** to be a one-dimensional array then we can refer to its zeroth element as **stud[0]**, the next element as **stud[1]** and so on. More specifically, if we execute the statement,

```
printf ( "%u", stud[0] ) ;
```

we expect the 0th element to get printed and the 0th element is a 1-D array. We know that just mentioning a 1-D array gives its base address. Hence the **printf( )** would print base address of the 0th 1-D array. Similarly, **stud[1]** would give address of 1st 1-D array and so on.

This fact can be illustrated by the following program:

```
/* Program 22 */
/* Refer figure 2.3 given in the previous section */
main( )
{
    int stud[5][2] = {
                        { 1234, 56 },
                        { 1212, 33 },
                        { 1434, 80 },
                        { 1312, 78 },
                        { 1203, 75 }
                      };
    int i, j ;

    for ( i = 0 ; i <= 4 ; i++ )
        printf ( "\nAddress of %d th 1-D array = %u", i, stud[i] ) ;
}
```

And here is the output...

```
Address of 0 th 1-D array = 4001
```

Address of 1 th 1-D array = 4005
Address of 2 th 1-D array = 4009
Address of 3 th 1-D array = 4013
Address of 4 th 1-D array = 4017

Let's figure out how the program works. Once the 2-D array is declared, there onwards **stud** is treated as pointer to zeroth element of the 2-D array. Hence the expression (**stud + 0**) gives us the address of the 0th element of the 2-D array. Naturally, the expression *(**stud + 0**) should give us the 0th element. But the 0th element of the 2-D array is a 1-D array. And on mentioning 1-D array we get its base address. Hence *(**stud + 0**) gives the base address of the 0th 1-D array. Referring to Figure 2.3 this turns out to be 4001. Similarly, can you interpret the meaning of **stud[1]** (which is nothing but *(**stud + 1**))? **stud** gives address of the 0th element, hence **stud + 1** would give the address of the 1st element and *(**stud + 1**) would give the first element. Since the 1st element is nothing but a 1-D array, and on mentioning the 1-D array we get its base address, *(**stud + 1**) gives base address of 1st 1-D array. In general the expression **stud[i]** (or *(**stud + i**)) would give base address of ith 1-D array.

Now, we have been able to reach each individual row. What remains is to be able to refer to individual elements of a row. Suppose we want to refer to the element **stud[2][1]** using pointers. We know (from the above program) that **stud[2]** would give the address 4009, the address of the second one-dimensional array. Obviously (4009 + 1) would give the address 4011. Or **(stud[2]+1)** would give the address 4011. And the value at this address can be obtained by using the expression *(**stud[2] + 1**). But, we have already noted while learning 1-D arrays that **num[i]** is same as *(**num + i**). Similarly *(**stud[2] + 1**) is same as, *(*(**stud + 2**) + 1). Thus, all the following expressions refer to the same element,

stud[2][1]

```
* ( stud[2] + 1 )
* ( *( stud + 2 ) + 1 )
```

Using these concepts the following program prints out each element of a two-dimensional array using pointer notation.

```
/* Program 23 */
main( )
{
    int stud[5][2] = {
                    { 1234, 56 },
                    { 1212, 33 },
                    { 1434, 80 },
                    { 1312, 78 },
                    { 1203, 75 }
                };
    int i, j ;

    for ( i = 0 ; i <= 4 ; i++ )
    {
        printf ( "\n" ) ;
        for ( j = 0 ; j <= 1 ; j++ )
            printf ( "%d ", *( *( stud + i ) + j ) ) ;
    }
}
```

And here is the output...

```
1234  56
1212  33
1434  80
1312  78
1203  75
```

Pointer to an Array

The way we can have a pointer to an integer, or a pointer to a float, can we also have a pointer to an array? The answer is yes. Declaration of a pointer to an array, however, is a little clumsy. For example, the declaration **int (*q)[4]** means that **q** is a pointer to an array of 4 integers. Let us use this pointer to an array in a program. Here it is...

```
/* Program 24 */
main( )
{
    int a[ ][4] =   {
                        5, 7, 5, 9,
                        4, 6, 3, 1,
                        2, 9, 0, 6
                    } ;
    int *p ;
    int ( *q )[4] ;

    p = ( int * ) a ;
    q = a ;

    printf ( "\n%u %u", p, q ) ;
    p++ ;
    q++ ;
    printf ( "\n%u %u", p, q ) ;
}
```

And here is the output...

```
65500 65500
65502 65508
```

To begin with both **p** and **q** contain the same address 65500. However, **p** is an integer pointer, whereas **q** is a pointer to an array of 4 integers. Hence on incrementing **p** it points to the next integer, whereas, **q** starts pointing to the next 1-D array of 4 integers. Pointer to an array is very useful while passing a 2-D array to a function, as we would see in the next section.

Passing 2-D Array to a Function

There are three ways in which we can pass a 2-D array to a function. These are illustrated in the following program.

```
/* Program 25 */
/* Three ways of accessing a 2-D array */
#include <alloc.h>
main( )
{
    int a[3][4] =  {
                        1, 2, 3, 4,
                        5, 6, 7, 8,
                        9, 0, 1, 6
                    } ;

    clrscr( ) ;
    display ( a, 3, 4 ) ;
    show ( a, 3, 4 ) ;
    print ( a, 3, 4 ) ;
}

display ( int *q, int row, int col )
{
    int i, j ;

    for ( i = 0 ; i < row ; i++ )
    {
        for ( j = 0 ; j < col ; j++ )
            printf ( "%d ", * ( q + i * col + j ) ) ;

        printf ( "\n" ) ;
    }
```

```
        printf ("\n") ;
}

show ( int ( *q )[4], int row, int col )
{
    int i, j ;
    int *p ;

    for ( i = 0 ; i < row ; i++ )
    {
        p = q + i ;
        for ( j = 0 ; j < col ; j++ )
            printf ( "%d ", * ( p + j ) ) ,

        printf ( "\n" ) ;
    }
    printf ( "\n" ) ;
}

print ( int q[ ][4], int row, int col )
{
    int i, j ;

    for ( i = 0 ; i < row ; i++ )
    {
        for ( j = 0 ; j < col ; j++ )
            printf ( "%d ", q[i][j] ) ;

        printf ( "\n" ) ;
    }
    printf ( "\n" ) ;
}
```

And here is the output...

```
1 2 3 4
5 6 7 8
9 0 1 6
```

```
1 2 3 4
5 6 7 8
9 0 1 6

1 2 3 4
5 6 7 8
9 0 1 6
```

In the **display( )** function we have collected the base address of the 2-D array being passed to it in an ordinary **int** pointer. Then through the two **for** loops using the expression *** (q + i * col + j)** we have reached the appropriate element in the array. Suppose **i** is equal to 2 and **j** is equal to 3, then we wish to reach the element **a[2][3]**. Let us see whether the expression *** (q + i * col + j) does** give this element or not. Refer Figure 2.4 to understand this.

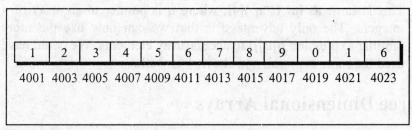

Figure 2.4

The expression *** (q + i * col + j)** becomes *** (4001 + 2 * 4 + 3)**. This turns out to be *** (4001 + 11)**. Since **4001** is address of an integer, *** (4001 + 11)** turns out to be *** (4023)**. Value at this address is 6. This is indeed same as **a[2][3]**. A more general formula for accessing each array element would be:

* (base address + row no. * no. of columns + column no.)

In the **show( )** function we have defined **q** to be a pointer to an array of 4 integers through the declaration:

```
int ( *q )[4] ;
```

To begin with, **q** holds the base address of the zeroth 1-D array, i.e. 4001 (refer Figure 2.4). This address is then assigned to **p**, an **int** pointer, and then using this pointer all elements of the zeroth 1-D array are accessed. Next time through the loop when **i** takes a value 1, the expression **q + i** fetches the address of the first 1-D array. This is because, **q** is a pointer to zeroth 1-D array and adding 1 to it would give us the address of the next 1-D array. This address is once again assigned to **p**, and using it all elements of the next 1-D array are accessed.

In the third function **print( )**, the declaration of **q** looks like this:

```
int q[ ][4] ;
```

This is same as **int (*q)[4]**, where **q** is pointer to an array of 4 integers. The only advantage is that we can now use the more familiar expression **q[i][j]** to access array elements. We could have used the same expression in **show( )** as well.

Three Dimensional Arrays

Consider the following array declaration:

```
int a[3][4][2] = {
                    {
                        { 2, 4 },
                        { 7, 8 },
                        { 3, 4 },
                        { 5, 6 }
                    },
                    {
                        { 7, 6 },
                        { 3, 4 },
                        { 5, 3 },
```

```
            { 2, 3 }
        },
        {
            { 8, 9 },
            { 7, 2 },
            { 3, 4 },
            { 5, 1 }
        }
    };
```

Here a is a 3-dimensional array. A 3-D array can be thought of as an array of arrays of arrays. The outer array has three elements, each of which is a two-dimensional array of four rows, each of which is a one-dimensional array of two elements. In other words, a one-dimensional array of two elements is constructed first. Then four such one-dimensional arrays are placed one below the other to give a two-dimensional array containing four rows. Then, three such two-dimensional arrays are placed one behind the other to yield a three-dimensional array containing three 2-dimensional arrays. In the array declaration note how the commas have been given. Following figure would possibly help you in visualising the situation better.

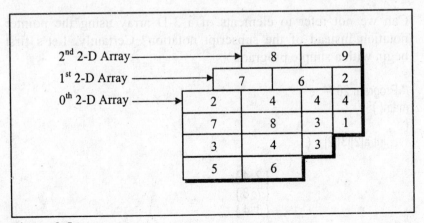

Figure 2.5

Again remember that the arrangement shown above is only conceptually true. In memory the same array elements are stored linearly as shown in the following figure.

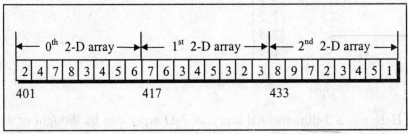

Figure 2.6

How would you refer to the array element 1 in the above array? The first subscript should be [2], since the element is in third two-dimensional array; the second subscript should be [3] since the element is in fourth row of the two-dimensional array; and the third subscript should be [1] since the element is in the second position in the one-dimensional array. We can therefore say that the element 1 can be referred as, **arr[2][3][1]**. It may be noted here that the counting of array elements even for a 3-D array begins with zero.

Can we not refer to elements of a 3-D array using the pointer notation instead of the subscript notation? Certainly. Let's first begin with a simple program.

```
/* Program 26 */
main( )
{
    int a[2][3][2] = {
                        {
                          { 2, 4 },
                          { 7, 8 },
                          { 3, 4 }
                        },
```

```
                    {
                      { 2, 2 },
                      { 2, 3 },
                      { 3, 4 }
                    }
                };
    printf ( "\n%u", a ) ;
    printf ( "\n%u", *a ) ;
    printf ( "\n%u", **a ) ;
    printf ( "\n%d", ***a ) ;
    printf ( "\n%u", a + 1 ) ;
    printf ( "\n%u", *a + 1 ) ;
    printf ( "\n%u", **a + 1 ) ;
    printf ( "\n%d", ***a + 1 ) ;
}
```

Figure 2.7 shows the arrangement of the 3-D array in memory.

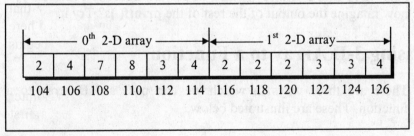

Figure 2.7

And here is the output of the program...

104
104
104
2
116
108
106

3

Referring Figure 2.7 it's not difficult to imagine why the first **printf( )** prints out 104. However, the output of second and third **printf( )** is a little surprising. Let's try to understand it.

Each element of a 3-D array is a 2-D array. Once the 3-D array is declared **a** is treated as pointer to zeroth element of the array. Hence ***a** gives the zeroth element which is a 2-D array. We know that on mentioning a 2-D array we get its base address hence the second **printf( )** outputs 104. What about the expression ****a**? ***a** gives pointer to zeroth element of the 2-D array, hence ****a** would give the zeroth element. But the zeroth element of the 2-D array is a 1-D array. And on mentioning 1-D array we get the address of its zeroth element. Hence ****a** also yields 104. Now you can guess that *****a** would give the element at address 104, i.e. 2. Let's now try to analyse the output of the next **printf( )** statement. **a** gives the address of zeroth 2-D array, therefore, **a + 1** would give the address of first 2-D array, which as per the figure is 116. Can you now imagine the output of the rest of the **printf( )**s? Try it.

Passing 3-D Array to a Function

There are three ways in which we can pass a 3-D array to a function. These are illustrated below.

```
/* Program 27 */
/* Three ways of passing a 3-D array to function */
main( )
{
    int i, j, k ;
    int a[2][3][4] = {
                        {
                            1, 2, 3, 4,
                            5, 6, 7, 8,
                            9, 3, 2, 1
```

```
                        },
                        {
                            2, 3, 5, 7,
                            4, 3, 9, 2,
                            1, 6, 3, 6
                        }
                    } ;

    clrscr( ) ;
    display ( a, 2, 3, 4 ) ;
    show ( a, 2, 3, 4 ) ;
    print ( a, 2, 3, 4 ) ;
    getch( ) ;
}

display ( int *q, int ii, int jj, int kk )
{
    int i, j, k ;
    for ( i = 0 ; i < ii ; i++ )
    {
        for ( j = 0 ; j < jj ; j++ )
        {
            for ( k = 0 ; k < kk ; k++ )
                printf ( "%d ", *( q + i * jj * kk + j * kk + k ) ) ;
            printf ( "\n" ) ;
        }
        printf ( "\n" ) ;
    }
    printf ( "\n" ) ;
}

show ( int ( *q )[3][4], int ii, int jj, int kk )
{
    int i, j, k ;
    int *p ;

    for ( i = 0 ; i < ii ; i++ )
    {
```

```
        for ( j = 0 ; j < jj ; j++ )
        {
            p = q[i][j] ;
            for ( k = 0 ; k < kk ; k++ )
                printf ( "%d ", *( p + k) ) ;
            printf ( "\n" ) ;
        }
        printf ( "\n" ) ;
    }
}

print ( int q[ ][3][4], int ii, int jj, int kk )
{
    int i, j, k ;
    for ( i = 0 ; i < ii ; i++ )
    {
        for ( j = 0 ; j < jj ; j++ )
        {
            for ( k = 0 ; k < kk ; k++ )
                printf ( "%d ", q[i][j][k] ) ;
            printf ( "\n" ) ;
        }
        printf ( "\n" ) ;
    }
}
```

And here is the output...

```
1 2 3 4
5 6 7 8
9 3 2 1

2 3 5 7
4 3 9 2
1 6 3 6

1 2 3 4
5 6 7 8
```

9 3 2 1

2 3 5 7
4 3 9 2
1 6 3 6

1 2 3 4
5 6 7 8
9 3 2 1

2 3 5 7
4 3 9 2
1 6 3 6

The working of this program is same as that of Program 25 discussed earlier. Hence all that I would do here is explain how **q** has been declared in each function.

Expression	Meaning
int *q	q is an integer pointer
int (*q)[3][4]	q is a pointer to a 2-D array of 3 rows and 4 columns
int q[ ][3][4]	q is a pointer to a 2-D array of 3 rows and 4 columns

Table 2.1

Returning Array from Function

Now that we know how to pass a 2-D or a 3-D array to a function, let us find out how to return an array from a function. There are again three methods to achieve this. Suppose we wish to return a 2-D array of integers from a function we can return the base address of the array as:

- A pointer to an integer
- A pointer to the zeroth 1-D array
- A pointer to the 2-D array

This is shown in the following program. The function **fun1( )** returns the base address as pointer to integer, the function **fun2( )** returns it as pointer to zeroth 1-D array, whereas **fun3( )** returns it as pointer to 2-D array of integers. Note the prototype declarations of the functions carefully.

```
/* Program 28 */
/* Three ways of returning a 2-D array from a function */
#define ROW 3
#define COL 4

main( )
{
    int i, j ;

    int *a ;
    int *fun1( ) ;

    int ( *b )[COL] ;
    int ( *fun2( ) )[COL] ;
    int *p ;

    int ( *c )[ROW][COL] ;
    int ( *fun3( ) )[ROW][COL] ;

    clrscr( ) ;
    a = fun1( ) ;

    printf ( "\nArray a[ ][ ] in main( ):\n" ) ;
    for ( i = 0 ; i < ROW ; i++ )
    {
        for ( j = 0 ; j < COL ; j++ )
            printf ( "%d ", * ( a + i * COL + j ) ) ;

        printf ( "\n" ) ;
    }
    getch( ) ;
```

```
        b = fun2( ) ;

        printf ( "\nArray b[ ][ ] in main( ):\n" ) ;
        for ( i = 0 ; i < ROW ; i++ )
        {
            p = b + i ;
            for (  j = 0 ; j < COL ; j++ )
            {
                printf ( "%d ", *p ) ;
                p++ ;
            }

            printf ( "\n" ) ;
        }
        getch( ) ;
        c = fun3( ) ;

        printf ( "\nArray c[ ][ ] in main( ):\n" ) ;
        for ( i = 0 ; i < ROW ; i++ )
        {
            for (  j = 0 ; j < COL ; j++ )
                printf ( "%d ", ( *c )[ i ][ j ] ) ;

            printf ( "\n" ) ;
        }
        getch( ) ;
}

int *fun1( )
{
    static int a[ROW][COL] =  {
                                1, 2, 3, 4,
                                5, 6, 7, 8,
                                9, 0, 1, 6
                              } ;
    int i, j ;
```

```c
    printf ( "\nArray a[ ][ ] in fun1( ):\n" ) ;
    for ( i = 0 ; i < ROW ; i++ )
    {
        for ( j = 0 ; j < COL ; j++ )
            printf ( "%d ", a[ i ][ j ] ) ;

        printf ( "\n" ) ;
    }
    return ( int * ) a ;
}

int ( *fun2( ) )[COL]
{
    static int b[ROW][COL] =  {
                                    9, 4, 6, 4,
                                    1, 3, 2, 1,
                                    7, 5, 1, 6
                                } ;
    int i, j ;

    printf ( "\nArray b[ ][ ] in fun2( ):\n" ) ;
    for ( i = 0 ; i < ROW ; i++ )
    {
        for ( j = 0 ; j < COL ; j++ )
            printf ( "%d ", b[ i ][ j ] ) ;

        printf ( "\n" ) ;
    }
    return b ;
}

int ( *fun3( ) )[ROW][COL]
{
    static int c[ROW][COL] =  {
                                    6, 3, 9, 1,
                                    2, 1, 5, 7,
                                    4, 1, 1, 6
                                } ;
```

```
    int i, j ;

    printf ( "\nArray c[ ][ ] in fun3( ):\n" ) ;
    for ( i = 0 ; i < ROW ; i++ )
    {
        for ( j = 0 ; j < COL ; j++ )
            printf ( "%d ", c[ i ][ j ] ) ;

        printf ( "\n" ) ;
    }
    return ( int ( * )[ROW][COL] ) c ;
}
```

And here is the output...

```
Array a[ ][ ] in fun1( ):
1 2 3 4
5 6 7 8
9 0 1 6

Array a[ ][ ] in main( ):
1 2 3 4
5 6 7 8
9 0 1 6

Array b[ ][ ] in fun2( ):
9 4 6 4
1 3 2 1
7 5 1 6

Array b[ ][ ] in main( ):
9 4 6 4
1 3 2 1
7 5 1 6

Array c[ ][ ] in fun3( ):
6 3 9 1
2 1 5 7
```

4 1 1 6

Array c[ ][ ] in main( ):
6 3 9 1
2 1 5 7
4 1 1 6

Returning 3-D Array from a Function

If you have understood how to return a 2-D array from a function, on similar lines we can return a 3-D array from a function. The four possible ways to do so would be to return the base address as:

- A pointer to an integer
- A pointer to the zeroth 1-D array
- A pointer to the zeroth 2-D array
- A pointer to the 3-D array

Given below is the program, which implements these four ways of returning a 3-D array.

```
/* Program 29 */
/* Four ways of returning a 3-D array from a function */
#define SET 2
#define ROW 3
#define COL 4

main( )
{
    int i, j, k ;

    int *a ;
    int *fun1( ) ;

    int ( *b )[COL] ;
    int ( *fun2( ) )[COL] ;
```

```
int ( *c )[ROW][COL] ;
int ( *fun3( ) )[ROW][COL] ;
int *p ;

int ( *d )[SET][ROW][COL] ;
int ( *fun4( ) )[SET][ROW][COL] ;

clrscr( ) ;
a = fun1( ) ;

printf ( "\nArray a[ ][ ][ ] in main( ):\n" ) ;
for ( i = 0 ; i < SET ; i++ )
{
    for ( j = 0 ; j < ROW ; j++ )
    {
        for ( k = 0 ; k < COL ; k++ )
            printf ( "%d ", * ( a + i * ROW * COL + j * COL + k ) ) ;

            printf ( "\n" ) ;
    }

    printf ( "\n" ) ;
}
getch( ) ;

b = fun2( ) ;

printf ( "\nArray b[ ][ ][ ] in main( ):\n" ) ;
for ( i = 0 ; i < SET ; i++ )
{
    p = ( int * ) ( b + i * ROW ) ;
    for ( j = 0 ; j < ROW ; j++ )
    {
        for ( k = 0 ; k < COL ; k++ )
        {
            printf ( "%d ", *p ) ;
            p++ ;
```

```
            }

                printf ( "\n" ) ;
            }

        printf ( "\n" ) ;
    }

    getch( ) ;

    c = fun3( ) ;

    printf ( "\nArray c[ ][ ][ ] in main( ):\n" ) ;
    for ( i = 0 ; i < SET ; i++ )
    {
        p = ( int * ) ( c + i ) ;
        for ( j = 0 ; j < ROW ; j++ )
        {
            for ( k = 0 ; k < COL ; k++ )
            {
                printf ( "%d ", *p ) ;
                p++ ;
            }

            printf ( "\n" ) ;
        }

        printf ( "\n" ) ;
    }
    getch( ) ;

    d = fun4( ) ;

    printf ( "\nArray d[ ][ ][ ] in main( ):\n" ) ;
    for ( i = 0 ; i < SET ; i++ )
    {
        for ( j = 0 ; j < ROW ; j++ )
        {
```

```
                for ( k = 0 ; k < COL ; k++ )
                    printf ( "%d ", ( *d )[ i ][ j ][ k ] ) ;

                printf ( "\n" ) ;
            }

            printf ( "\n" ) ;
        }
    getch( ) ;
}

int * fun1( )
{
    int i, j, k ;
    static int a[SET][ROW][COL] =       {
                                            {
                                                1, 2, 3, 4,
                                                5, 6, 7, 8,
                                                9, 3, 2, 1
                                            },
                                            {
                                                2, 3, 5, 7,
                                                4, 3, 9, 2,
                                                1, 6, 3, 6
                                            }
                                        } ;

    printf ( "\nArray a[ ][ ][ ] in fun1( ):\n" ) ;
    for ( i = 0 ; i < SET ; i++ )
    {
        for ( j = 0 ; j < ROW ; j++ )
        {
            for ( k = 0 ; k < COL ; k++ )
                printf ( "%d ", a[ i ][ j ][ k ] ) ;

            printf ( "\n" ) ;
        }
```

```
            printf ( "\n" ) ;
    }

    return ( int * ) a ;
}

int ( *fun2( ) )[COL]
{
    int i, j, k ;
    static int b[SET][ROW][COL] = {
                                    {
                                        9, 4, 6, 4,
                                        1, 3, 2, 1,
                                        7, 5, 1, 6
                                    },
                                    {
                                        6, 3, 9, 1,
                                        2, 1, 5, 7,
                                        4, 1, 1, 6
                                    }
                                  } ;

    printf ( "\nArray b[ ][ ][ ] in fun2( ):\n" ) ;
    for ( i = 0 ; i < SET ; i++ )
    {
        for ( j = 0 ; j < ROW ; j++ )
        {
            for ( k = 0 ; k < COL ; k++ )
                printf ( "%d ", b[ i ][ j ][ k ] ) ;
            printf ( "\n" ) ;
        }

        printf ( "\n" ) ;
    }

    return ( int (*)[COL] ) b ;
}
```

```
int ( *fun3( ) )[ROW][COL]
{
    int i, j, k ;
    static int c[SET][ROW][COL] =      {
                                        {
                                            9, 4, 6, 4,
                                            1, 3, 2, 1,
                                            7, 5, 1, 6
                                        },
                                        {
                                            6, 3, 9, 1,
                                            2, 1, 5, 7,
                                            4, 1, 1, 6
                                        }
                                    } ;

    printf ( "\nArray c[ ][ ][ ] in fun3( ):\n" ) ;
    for ( i = 0 ; i < SET ; i++ )
    {
        for ( j = 0 ; j < ROW ; j++ )
        {
            for ( k = 0 ; k < COL ; k++ )
                printf ( "%d ", c[ i ][ j ][ k ] ) ;

            printf ( "\n" ) ;
        }

        printf ( "\n" ) ;
    }

    return ( int (*)[ROW][COL] ) c ;
}

int ( *fun4( ) )[SET][ROW][COL]
{
    int i, j, k ;
    static int d[SET][ROW][COL] =      {
                                        {
```

```
                                        3, 1, 8, 5,
                                        9, 6, 5, 2,
                                        2, 0, 1, 6
                                    },
                                    {
                                        7, 3, 2, 7,
                                        1, 4, 2, 3,
                                        9, 1, 0, 6
                                    }
                                } ;

    printf ( "\nArray d[ ][ ][ ] in fun4( ):\n" ) ;
    for ( i = 0 ; i < SET ; i++ )
    {
        for ( j = 0 ; j < ROW ; j++ )
        {
            for ( k = 0 ; k < COL ; k++ )
                printf ( "%d ", d[ i ][ j ][ k ] ) ;

            printf ( "\n" ) ;
        }

        printf ( "\n" ) ;
    }

    return ( int ( * )[SET][ROW][COL] ) d ;
}
```

And here is the output...

```
Array a[ ][ ][ ] in fun1( ):
1 2 3 4
5 6 7 8
9 3 2 1

2 3 5 7
4 3 9 2
1 6 3 6
```

Array a[ ][ ][ ] in main( ):
1 2 3 4
5 6 7 8
9 3 2 1

2 3 5 7
4 3 9 2
1 6 3 6

Array b[ ][ ][ ] in fun2( ):
9 4 6 4
1 3 2 1
7 5 1 6

6 3 9 1
2 1 5 7
4 1 1 6

Array b[ ][ ][ ] in main( ):
9 4 6 4
1 3 2 1
7 5 1 6

6 3 9 1
2 1 5 7
4 1 1 6

Array c[ ][ ][ ] in fun3( ):
3 1 8 5
9 6 5 2
2 0 1 6

7 3 2 7
1 4 2 3
9 1 0 6

Array c[ ][ ][ ] in main( ):

```
3 1 8 5
9 6 5 2
2 0 1 6

7 3 2 7
1 4 2 3
9 1 0 6

Array d[ ][ ][ ] in fun4( ):
1 7 0 5
2 3 9 1
5 1 1 6

5 3 1 7
1 4 2 3
7 2 1 6

Array d[ ][ ][ ] in main( ):
1 7 0 5
2 3 9 1
5 1 1 6

5 3 1 7
1 4 2 3
7 2 1 6
```

Array of Pointers

The way there can be an array of **ints** or an array of **floats**, similarly there can be an array of pointers. Since a pointer variable always contains an address, an array of pointers would be nothing but a collection of addresses. The addresses present in the array of pointers can be addresses of isolated variables or addresses of array elements or any other addresses. All rules that apply to an ordinary array apply in toto to the array of pointers as well. I think a program would clarify the concept.

```
/* Program 30 */
main( )
{
    int *arr[4] ;  /* array of integer pointers */
    int i = 31, j = 5, k = 19, l = 71, m ;

    arr[0] = &i ;
    arr[1] = &j ;
    arr[2] = &k ;
    arr[3] = &l ;
    for ( m = 0 ; m <= 3 ; m++ )
        printf ( "\n%d", *( arr[m] ) ) ;
}
```

And here is the output...

```
31
5
19
71
0
```

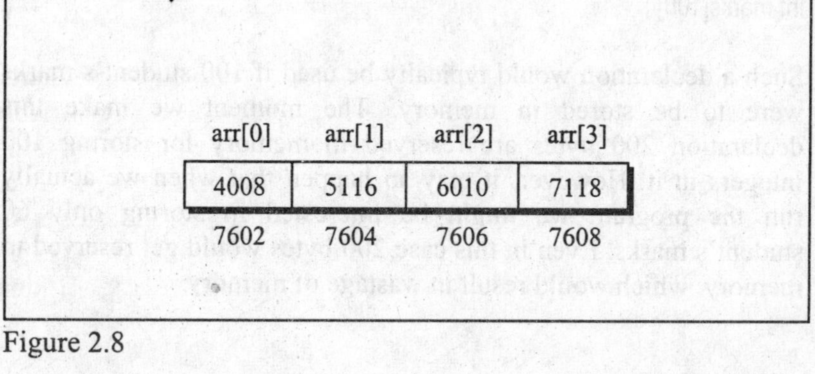

Figure 2.8

Figure 2.8 shows the contents and the arrangement of the array of pointers in memory. As you can observe, **arr** contains addresses of isolated **int** variables **i, j, k** and **l**. The **for** loop in the program picks up the addresses present in **arr** and prints the values present at these addresses.

An array of pointers can even contain the addresses of other arrays. The following program would justify this.

```
/* Program 31 */
main( )
{
    static int a[ ] = { 0, 1, 2, 3, 4 } ;
    static int *p[ ] = { a, a + 1, a + 2, a + 3, a + 4 } ;

    printf ( "\n%u %u %d", p, *p, *( *p ) ) ;
}
```

I would leave it for you to figure out the output of this program. An array of pointers is very popularly used for storing several strings in memory, as you would see in the next chapter.

Dynamic Memory Allocation

Consider the array declaration,

int marks[100] ;

Such a declaration would typically be used if 100 student's marks were to be stored in memory. The moment we make this declaration 200 bytes are reserved in memory for storing 100 integers in it. However, it may so happen that when we actually run the program we might be interested in storing only 60 student's marks. Even in this case 200 bytes would get reserved in memory, which would result in wastage of memory.

Other way round there always exists a possibility that when you run the program you need to store more than 100 student's marks. In this case the array would fall short in size. Moreover, there is no way to increase or decrease the array size during execution of the program. In other words, when we use arrays static memory allocation takes place. What if we want to allocate memory only at the time of execution? This is done using standard library functions **malloc( )** and **calloc( )**. Since these functions allocate memory on the fly (during execution) they are often known as 'Dynamic memory allocation functions'. Let us now see a program, which uses the concept of dynamic memory allocation.

```
/* Program 32 */
#incude "alloc.h"
main( )
{
    int n, avg, i, *p, sum = 0 ;

    printf ( "\nEnter the number of students " ) ;
    scanf ( "%d", &n ) ,

    p = ( int * ) malloc ( n * 2 ) ;
    if ( p == NULL )
    {
        printf ( "\nMemory allocation unsuccessful" ) ;
        exit( ) ;
    }

    for ( i = 0 ; i < n ; i++ )
        scanf ( "%d", ( p + i ) ) ;

    for ( i = 0 ; i < n ; i++ )
        sum = sum + *( p + i ) ;

    avg = sum / n ;
    printf ( "Average marks = %d", avg ) ;
}
```

Here, we have first asked for the number of students whose marks are to be entered and then allocated only as much memory as is really required to store these marks. Not a byte more, not a byte less. The allocation job is done using the standard library function **malloc( )**. **malloc( )** returns a NULL if memory allocation is unsuccessful. If successful it returns the address of the memory chunk that is allocated. We have collected this address in an integer pointer **p**. Since **malloc( )** returns a **void** pointer we have typecasted it into an integer pointer. In the first **for** loop using simple pointer arithmetic we have stored the marks entered from keyboard into the memory that has been allocated. In the second **for** loop we have accessed the same values to find the average marks.

The **calloc( )** functions works exactly similar to **malloc( )** except for the fact that it needs two arguments. For example,

```
int *p ,
p = ( int * ) calloc ( 10, 2 ) ;
```

Here 2 indicates that we wish to allocate memory for storing integers, (since an integer is a 2-byte entity) and 10 indicates that we want to reserve space for storing 10 integers. Another minor difference between **malloc( )** and **calloc( )** is that, by default, the memory allocated by **malloc( )** contains garbage values, whereas that allocated by **calloc( )** contains all zeros. While using these functions it is necessary to include the file "alloc.h" at the beginning of the program.

Solved Problems

[A] What will be the output of the following programs:

(1)
```
main( )
{
    int a[ ] = { 10, 20, 30, 40, 50 } ;
    int j ;
    for ( j = 0 ; j < 5 ; j++ )
    {
        printf ( "\n%d", *a ) ;
        a++ ;
    }
}
```

Output

Error message: Lvalue required in function main

Explanation

Whenever we mention the name of the array, we get its base address. Therefore, first time through the loop, the **printf( )** should print the value at this base address. There is no problem up to this. The problem lies in the next statement, **a++**. Since C doesn't perform bounds checking on an array, the only thing that it remembers about an array once declared is its base address. And **a++** attempts to change this base address, which C won't allow because if it does so, it would be unable to remember the beginning of the array. Anything, which can change is called lvalue in compiler's language. Since value of **a** cannot be changed through **++**, it flashes the error saying 'Lvalue required' so that **++** operator can change it.

(2) main( )
```
{
    float a[ ] = { 13.24, 1.5, 1.5, 5.4, 3.5 } ;
    float *j, *k ;
    j = a ;
    k = a + 4 ;
    j = j * 2 ;
    k = k / 2 ;
    printf ( "\n%f %f", *j, *k ) ;
}
```

Output

Error message: Illegal use of pointer in function main

Explanation

j and **k** have been declared as pointer variables, which would contain the addresses of **float**s. In other words, **j** and **k** are **float** pointers. To begin with, the base address of the array **a[ ]** is stored in **j**. The next statement is perfectly acceptable; the address of the 4th **float** from the base address is stored in **k**. The next two statements are erroneous. This is because the only operations that can be performed on pointers are addition and subtraction. Multiplication or division of a pointer is not allowed. Hence the error message.

(3) main( )
```
{
    int n[25] ;
    n[0] = 100 ;
    n[24] = 200 ;
    printf ( "\n%d %d", *n, *( n + 24 ) + *( n + 0 ) ) ;
}
```

Output

100 300

Explanation

n[ ] has been declared as an array capable of holding 25 elements numbered from 0 to 24. Then 100 and 200 are assigned to **n[0]** and **n[24]** respectively. Then comes the most important part—the **printf( )** statement. Whenever we mention the name of the array, we get its base address (i.e. address of the zeroth element of the array). Thus, ***n** would give the value at this base address, which in this case is 100. This is then printed out. Look at the next expression,

*(n + 24) + *(n + 0)

n gives the address of the zeroth element, **n + 1** gives the address of the next element of the array, and so on. Thus, **n + 24** would give the address of the last element of the array, and therefore ***(n + 24)** would give the value at this address, which is 200 in our case. Similarly, ***(n + 0)** would give 100 and the addition of the two would result into 300, which is outputted next.

(4)   main( )
```
{
    int b[ ] = { 10, 20, 30, 40, 50 } ;
    int i, *k ;
    k = &b[4] - 4 ;
    for ( i = 0 ; i <= 4 ; i++ )
    {
        printf ( "%d ", *k ) ;
        k++ ;
    }
}
```

Output

10 20 30 40 50

Explanation

First look at Figure 2.9. The array elements are stored in contiguous memory locations and each element is an integer, hence is occupying 2 locations.

b[0]	b[1]	b[2]	b[3]	b[4]
10	20	30	40	50
4002	4004	4006	4008	4010

Figure 2.9

The expression **&b[4]** gives the address of **b[4]** (4010 in this case). From this address if we subtract 4, we get 4002. Or did you expect to get 4006? Remember that by subtracting 4 from 4010 what we mean is get the address of an integer, which is 4 integers to the left of the integer whose address is 4010. Now, address of the integer, which is 4 integers to the left of the integer whose address is 4010, is the address 4002. This address, 4002, is stored in **k**, which has been declared as a variable capable of holding an integer's address. First time through the **for** loop *k would result into 10, i.e. value at the address contained in **k**. k++ then increments **k** such that it contains the address of the next integer, i.e. 4004. Next time through the **for** loop *k would yield the value at address contained in **k**, i.e. value at the address 4004, which is 20. Similarly, the loop prints out the rest of the elements of the array.

(5) main( )
```
{
    char a[ ] = "Visual C++" ;
    char *b = "Visual C++" ;
    printf ( "\n%d %d", sizeof ( a ), sizeof ( b ) ) ;
    printf ( "\n%d %d", sizeof ( *a ), sizeof ( *b ) ) ;
}
```

Output

11 2
1 1

Explanation

sizeof reports the number of bytes occupied by an entity in memory. The array **a** is reported to be of 11 bytes because there is a '\0' sitting at the end. **b** is a pointer hence its size is 2 bytes. ***a** and ***b** both yield a character 'V', whose size is one byte.

(6) main( )
```
{
    /* Assume array begins at address 1200 */
    int arr[ ] = { 2, 3, 4, 1, 6 } ;
    printf ( "%u %d", arr, sizeof ( arr ) ) ;
}
```

Output

1200 10

Explanation

Mentioning the name of an array yields its base address. Hence, **arr** would give 1200. Since the array contains five elements, each of 2 bytes, size of the array is reported as 10 bytes. Note that except when used with **sizeof( )**, name of the array yields its base address.

(7) main( )
```
{
    /* Assume array begins at address 65486 */
    int arr[ ] = { 12, 14, 15, 23, 45 } ;
    printf ( "%u %u", arr, &arr ) ;
    printf ( "%u %u", arr + 1, &arr + 1 ) ;
}
```

Output

```
65486  65486
65488  65496
```

Explanation

Both **arr** and **&arr** yield the base address of the array. However, **arr+1** gives 65488, i.e. the address of the next integer. However, **&arr + 1** gives 65496, i.e. the address of the next array of 5 integers.

(8) main( )
```
{
    /* Assume array begins at address 65472 */
    int a[3][4] = {
                    1, 2, 3, 4,
                    4, 3, 2, 1,
                    7, 8, 9, 0
                  } ;
    printf ( "\n%u %u", a + 1, &a + 1 ) ;
}
```

Output

65480 65496

Explanation

Name of a 2-D array always acts as pointer to the zeroth element of the array. Since the zeroth element of our 2-D array is 1-D array of 4 integers, **a** acts as pointer to this zeroth 1-D array. Hence **a+1** gives us the address of the next 1-D array, i.e. 65480.

The expression **&a + 1** yields 65496, i.e. the address of the next 2-D array of 3 rows and 4 columns.

(9)
```
main( )
{
    /* Assume array begins at location 1002 */
    int a[3][4] = {
                    1, 2, 3, 4,
                    5, 6, 7, 8,
                    9, 10, 11, 12
                  } ;

    printf ( "\n%u %u %u", a[0] + 1, * ( a[0] + 1 ), * ( * ( a + 0 ) + 1 ) ) ;
}
```

Output

1004 2 2

Explanation

A 2-D array is a collection of several 1-D arrays. Name of a 2-D array always acts as pointer to zeroth element of the array. Hence, **a** acts as pointer to the zeroth 1-D array.

The expression **a[0] + 1** is interpreted by the compiler as *(**a + 0**) + 1. This is same as *a +1. The expression *a gives 1002. Therefore, *a +1 would give the address of the next integer, i.e. 1004. Since **a[0] + 1** yields 1004, *(**a[0] + 1**) would yield the value at address 1004, i.e. *(**a[0] + 1**) can be expanded as *(*(**a + 0**) + **1**). Hence, both the expressions would yield the same result, i.e. 2.

(10) main( )

```
{
    int a[3][4] = {
                    1, 2, 3, 4,
                    4, 3, 2, 8,
                    7, 8, 9, 0
                  } ;
    int *ptr ;
    ptr = &a[0][0] ;
    fun ( &ptr ) ;
}

fun ( int **p )
{
    printf ( "\n%d", **p ) ;
}
```

Output

1

Explanation

Here, in **ptr** we have stored address of 1. Then we have passed address of **ptr** to **fun( )** and collected it in a pointer to an **int** pointer. Dereferencing this pointer yields 1.

(11) main( )
```
{
    /* Assume array begins at location 1002 */
    int a[2][3][4] = {
                        {
                            1, 2, 3, 4,
                            5, 6, 7, 8,
                            9, 1, 1, 2
                        },
                        {
                            2, 1, 4, 7,
                            6, 7, 8, 9,
                            0, 0, 0, 0
                        }
                     };
    printf ( "\n%u %u %u %d", a, *a, **a, ***a ) ;
}
```

Output

1002 1002 1002 1

Explanation

The expressions **a, *a, **a,** would give the base address, i.e. 1002, whereas the expression ***a would give the value at address 1002, i.e. 1. Note that the expression **a[0][0][0]** is expanded into *(*(*(a + 0) + 0) + 0). This is same as ***a.

(12) main( )

```
{
    int a[ ] = { 2, 4, 6, 8, 10 } ;
    int i ;
    for ( i = 0 ; i <= 4 ; i++ )
    {
        *( a + i ) = a[i] + i[a] ;
        printf ( "%d ", *( i + a ) ) ;
    }
}
```

Output

4 8 12 16 20

Explanation

Imbibe the following three facts and the program becomes very simple to understand:

— Mentioning the name of the array gives the base address of the array.
— Array elements are stored in contiguous memory locations.
— On adding 1 to the address of an integer, we get the address of the next integer.

With those facts clearly laid out, let us now try to understand the program. Remember that internally C always accesses array elements using pointers. Thus, when we say **a[i]**, internally C converts it to ***(a + i)**, which means value of ith integer from the base address. Now, if the expression **a[i]** is same as ***(a + i)** then ***(i + a)** must be same as **i[a]**. But ***(a + i)** is same as ***(i + a)**. Therefore **a[i]** must be same as **i[a]**.

Thus **a[i]**, ***(a + i)**, ***(i + a)** and **i[a]** refer to the same element— the ith element from the base address.

Therefore, the expression used in the **for** loop, ***(a + i) = a[i] + i[a]** is nothing but **a[i] = a[i] + a[i]**. Thus all that is done in the **for** loop is, each array element is doubled and then printed out through **printf( )**.

(13) main( )
```
{
    int a[5] = { 2, 4, 6, 8, 10 } ;
    int i, b = 5 ;

    for ( i = 0 ; i < 5 ; i++ )
    {
        f ( a[i], &b ) ;
        printf ( "\n%d %d", a[i], b ) ;
    }
}

f ( int x, int *y )
{
    x = *( y ) += 2 ;
}
```

Output

```
2 7
4 9
6 11
8 13
10 15
```

Explanation

After initialising the array when the control enters the **for** loop, the function f( ) gets called with value of **a[i]** and address of **b**. In **f( )** these are collected in variables **x** and **y**. Then comes the expression x = *(y) += 2. Here *(y) += 2 is evaluated first and then the result of this expression is assigned to **x**. The first time through the **for** loop ***(y)** gives 5, to which 2 is added and the result is stored at ***(y)**. It means 7 is assigned to **b**. Finally, the = operator assigns 7 to **x**. However, on assigning a new value to **x**, the array element **a[0]** in **main( )** remains unchanged. Thus, during every call to **f( )**, **b**'s value keeps getting updated, whereas there is no change in the values of the array elements.

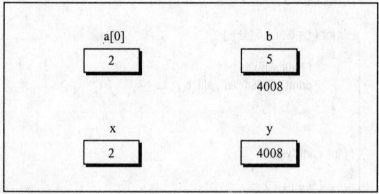

Figure 2.10

```
(14)  main( )
      {
          int a[5] = { 2, 3, 4, 5, 6 } ;
          int i ;

          change ( a ) ;
          for ( i = 4 ; i >= 0 ; i-- )
              printf ( "%d ", a[i] ) ;
      }

      change ( int *b )
      {
          int i ;
          for ( i = 0 ; i <= 4 ; i++ )
          {
```

```
        *b = *b + 1 ;
        b++ ;
    }
}
```

Output

7 6 5 4 3

Explanation

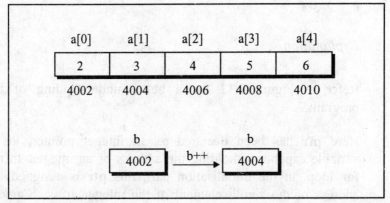

Figure 2.11

While calling **change( )** we are passing the base address of the array, which as per Figure 2.11 is 4002. This address is collected in **b** in the function **change( )**. Then the control enters the **for** loop, where we meet the expression ***b = *b + 1**. This means replace the value at the address contained in **b**, with value at the address contained in **b** plus 1. Every time **b++** is executed, the address of the next integer gets stored in **b**. Thus, using the address stored in b, we get an access to array elements that are now changed to 3, 4, 5, 6 and 7. Once the control comes back from **change( )**, the current array contents are then printed out from end to beginning through the **for** loop.

```
(15)  main( )
      {
          int arr[ ] = { 0, 1, 2, 3, 4 } ;
          int *ptr ;
          for ( ptr = &arr[0] ; ptr <= &arr[4] ; ptr++ )
              printf ( "%d ", *ptr ) ;
      }
```

Output

0 1 2 3 4

Explanation

Refer to Figure 2.12 for a better understanding of the program.

Here **ptr** has been declared as an integer pointer, i.e. a variable capable of holding the address of an integer. In the **for** loop, in the initialisation part, this **ptr** is assigned the address of the zeroth element of the integer array. Suppose this address turns out to be 6004. Then address of the first element of the array would be 6006, address of the second element would be 6008, and so on. In the condition part of the **for** loop, the address stored in **ptr** is compared with the address of the fourth array element, i.e. 6012. Since for the first time the condition is satisfied (since 6004 is less than 6012), the control reaches **printf( )** where the value at address 6004, i.e. 0 gets printed. After executing **printf( )** the control reaches **ptr++**, where **ptr** is incremented such that it contains the address of the next integer. Since the next integer is stored at 6006, **ptr** now contains 6006. Once again the condition is tested. Since 6006 is also smaller than 6012, the condition is satisfied hence the **printf( )** prints out the value at 6006, i.e. 1. And then **ptr++** is executed again so that it contains the address of the next integer, i.e. 6008. This process continues till all the array elements have been printed.

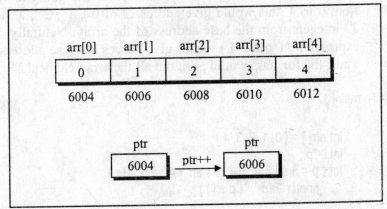

Figure 2.12

```
(16)  main( )
      {
          int arr[ ] = { 0, 1, 2, 3, 4 } ;
          int i, *ptr ;
          for ( ptr = &arr[0], i = 0 ; i <= 4 ; i++ )
              printf ( "%d ", ptr[i] ) ;
      }
```

Output

0 1 2 3 4

Explanation

In the initialisation part of the **for** loop, multiple initialisations are being done. Firstly, **ptr** is set up with the base address of the array and then **i** is set to 0. Since 0 is less than 4, the condition is satisfied for the first time and the control reaches **printf( )**. Here the value of the expression **ptr[i]** gets printed.

Now **ptr[i]** is nothing but ***(ptr + i)**. Since **ptr** contains the base address of the array, (**ptr + i**) would give the address of the ith integer from the base address. Since **i** is going to vary from 0 to 4, this would give addresses of 0th, 1st, 2nd, 3rd and 4th integers from the base address of the array. Naturally, the expression ***(ptr + i)** would give values at these addresses. Thus, the **for** loop would print out all the array elements.

(17)
```
main( )
{
    int arr[ ] = { 0, 1, 2, 3, 4 } ;
    int i, *p ;
    for ( p = arr, i = 0 ; p + i <= arr + 4 ; p++, i++ )
        printf ( "%d ", *( p + i ) ) ;
}
```

Output

0 2 4

Explanation

The following figure would help in understanding the program.

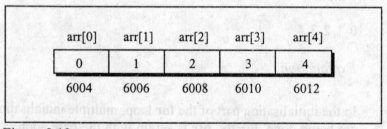

Figure 2.13

In the **for** loop there are multiple initialisations and multiple increments, each separated by the comma operator. In the initialisation part, **p** is initialised to the base address of the array, whereas **i** is initialised to 0. After these initialisations the control reaches the condition. The condition is a little complicated so let us isolate it for a clearer understanding.

p + i <= arr + 4

Here + enjoys a higher priority than <=. Therefore, first **p + i** and **arr+4** are performed and then the <= goes to work. **p+i** yields 6004, whereas **arr+4** evaluates to 6012. Since 6004 is less than 6012, the condition is satisfied and the control reaches **printf( )**, where value at (**p+i**), i.e. 0 gets printed. Then the control reaches the incrementation part of the **for** loop, where **p++** increments **p** to 6006, and **i++** increments **i** to 1. Next, once again the condition is tested. This time **p+i** gives 6008 (since **p** is 6006 and **i** is 1) and **arr+4** gives 6012. Since the condition once again gets satisfied, the **printf( )** prints out the value at (p+i), i.e. 2. Similarly, next time around 4 gets printed and then the condition fails therefore the execution is terminated.

(18) main( )
```
{
    int arr[ ] = { 0, 1, 2, 3, 4 } ;
    int *ptr ;
    for ( ptr = arr + 4 , ptr >= arr ; ptr-- )
        printf ( "%d ", arr [ ptr - arr ] ) ;
}
```

Output

4 3 2 1 0

Explanation

The following figure would lead to a better understanding of the program.

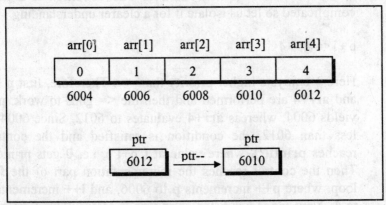

Figure 2.14

In the initialisation part, **ptr** is assigned the address of the last element in the array. This is because **arr+4** gives the address of the fourth integer from the base address. First time through the loop the condition evaluates to true, since the address of the fourth element (6012) would certainly be bigger than the base address (6004) of the array. Next, the control reaches **printf( )**, which prints out the value at address contained in **ptr**, i.e. value at address 6012. Next, the statement **ptr--** gets executed which reduces **ptr** to 6010. Since 6010 is also bigger than 6004, the condition is satisfied once again, and the value at 6010 gets printed through the **printf( )**. This process is repeated for all the array elements.

(19) main( )
```
{
    int arr[ ] = { 0, 1, 2, 3, 4 } ;
    int i, *ptr ;
    for ( ptr = arr + 4, i = 0 ; i <= 4 ; i++ )
        printf ( "%d ", ptr[-i] ) ;
}
```

Output

4 3 2 1 0

Explanation

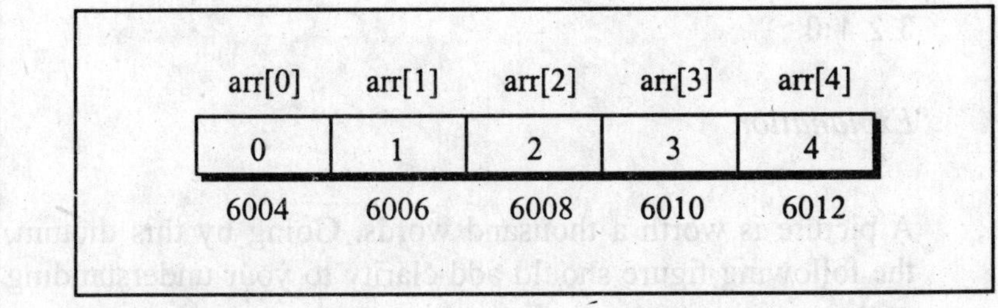

	arr[0]	arr[1]	arr[2]	arr[3]	arr[4]
	0	1	2	3	4
	6004	6006	6008	6010	6012

Figure 2.15

The above figure shows the arrangement of the array elements in memory.

In the initialisation part of the **for** loop, **ptr** is assigned a value 6012, since **arr+4** gives the address of the fourth integer from the base address of the array. Here, the variable **i** is also initialised to 0. Since the condition is satisfied for the first time (**i** being 0), the **printf( )** prints out the value of **ptr[-i]**. But what is **ptr[-i]**? Nothing but *(**ptr - i**). And since **i** is 0, *(**ptr - i**) evaluates to *(6012 - 0), i.e. 4. Then the control reaches **i++** where **i** is incremented to 1. Next, the condition is checked and since it evaluates to true, the **printf( )** prints out the value of **ptr[-i]**. Since this time **i** is 1, **ptr[-i] becomes** *(**ptr - 1**), i.e. *(6012 - 1), i.e. * (6010). Thus the value 3 gets printed. Likewise, 2, 1 and 0 also get printed subsequent times through the **for** loop.

(20) main( )
    {
        int arr[ ] = { 0, 1, 2, 3, 4 } ;
        int *ptr ;

```
    for ( ptr = arr + 4 , ptr >= arr ; ptr-- )
        printf ( "%d ", arr [ ptr - arr ] ) ;
}
```

Output

3 2 1 0

Explanation

A picture is worth a thousand words. Going by this dictum, the following figure should add clarity to your understanding of the program.

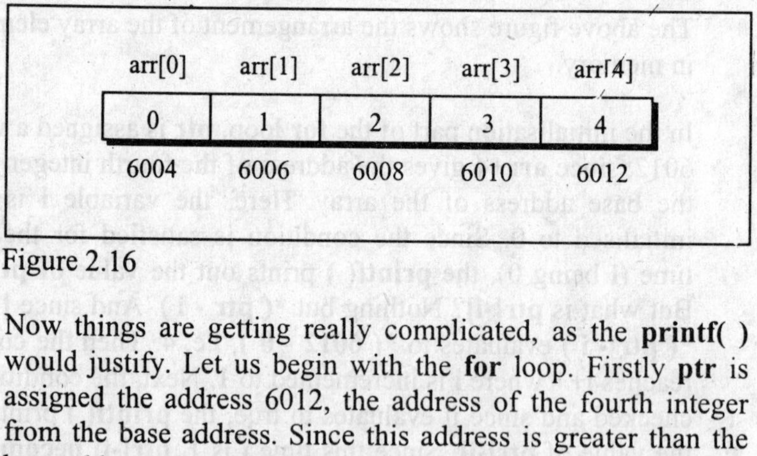

Figure 2.16

Now things are getting really complicated, as the **printf( )** would justify. Let us begin with the **for** loop. Firstly **ptr** is assigned the address 6012, the address of the fourth integer from the base address. Since this address is greater than the base address, the condition is satisfied and the control reaches **printf( )**. What does **arr [ptr - arr]** evaluate to? **ptr - arr** means 6012 - 6004, which yields 4, and hence **arr[4]** prints out the fourth element of the array. Then **ptr--** reduces **ptr** to 6010. Since 6010 is greater than the base address 6004, the condition is satisfied and once again the control reaches the **printf( )**. This time **ptr - arr** becomes 6010 - 6004, i.e. 3. Thus **arr[3]** prints out 3. This process is repeated till all the integers in the array have been printed out.

Possibly an easier way of understanding the expression **ptr - arr** would be as follows. Suppose **ptr** contains 6012 and **arr** contains 6004. We can then view the subtraction as (**arr + 4 - arr**), since **ptr** is nothing but **arr + 4.** Now I suppose its quite logical to expect the result of the subtraction as 4.

(21) main( )

```
{
    static int a[ ] = { 0, 1, 2, 3, 4 } ;
    static int *p[ ] = { a, a + 1, a + 2, a + 3, a + 4 } ;
    int **ptr = p ;
    printf ( "\n%u %d", a, *a ) ;
    printf ( "%u %u %d", p, *p, **p ) ;
    printf ( "\n%u %u %d", ptr, *ptr, **ptr ) ;
}
```

Output

```
6004  0
9016  6004  0
9016  6004  0
```

Explanation

Look at the initialisation of the array **p[ ]**. During initialisation, the addresses of various elements of the array **a[ ]** are stored in the array **p[ ]**. Since the array **p[ ]** contains addresses of integers, it has been declared as an array of pointers to integers. Figure 2.17 shows the contents of arrays **a[ ]** and **p[ ]**. In the variable **ptr**, the base address of the array **p[ ]**, i.e. 9016 is stored. Since this address is the address of **p[0]**, which itself is a pointer, **ptr** has been declared as pointer to an integer pointer.

Let us understand the first **printf( )** now.

printf ("\n%u %d", a, *a) ;

It prints out the base address of the array **a[ ]** and the value at this base address.

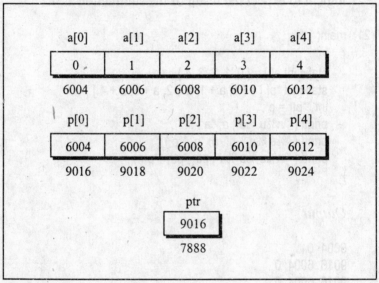

Figure 2.17

Looking at the figure, this would turn out to be 6004 and 0. When you execute the program, the address may turn out to be something other than 6004, but the value at the address would be surely 0.

Now look at the second **printf( ).**

printf ("\n%u %u %d", p, *p, **p) ;

Here **p** would give the base address of the array **p[ ]**, i.e. 9016; ***p** would give the value at this address, i.e. 6004; ****p** would give the value at the address given by ***p**, i.e. value at address 6004, which is 0.

Now onto the last **printf( )**.

printf ("\n%u %u %d", ptr, *ptr, **ptr) ;

Here **ptr** contains the base address of the array **p[ ]**, i.e. 9016; ***ptr** would give the value at this address, i.e. 6004; ****ptr** would give the value at the address given by ***ptr**, i.e. value at address 6004, which is 0.

(22) main( )
{
    static int a[ ] = { 0, 1, 2, 3, 4 } ;
    static int *p[ ] = { a, a + 1, a + 2, a + 3, a + 4 } ;

    int **ptr = p ;

    ptr++ ;
    printf ("\n%d %d %d", ptr - p, *ptr - a, **ptr) ;

    *ptr++ ;
    printf ("\n%d %d %d", ptr - p, *ptr - a, **ptr) ;

    *++ptr ;
    printf ("\n%d %d %d", ptr - p, *ptr - a,**ptr) ;

    ++*ptr ;
    printf ("\n%d %d %d", ptr - p, *ptr - a, **ptr) ;
}

Output

1 1 1
2 2 2
3 3 3
3 4 4

Explanation

Figure 2.18 would go a long way in helping us to understand this program.

Here **ptr** has been declared as a pointer to an integer pointer and assigned the base address of the array **p[ ]**, which has been declared as an array of integer pointers. What happens when **ptr++** gets executed? **ptr** points to the next integer pointer in the array **p[ ]**. In other words, now **ptr** contains the address 9018. Now let us analyse the meaning of **ptr - p**, ***ptr - a** and ****ptr**.

ptr - p

Since **ptr** is containing the address 9018, we can as well say that **ptr** is containing the address given by **p + 1**. Then **ptr - p** is reduced to **(p + 1 - p)**, which yields 1.

*ptr – a

*ptr means value at the address contained in **ptr**. Since **ptr** contains 9018, the value at this address would be 6006. Now 6006 can be imagined as **(a + 1)**. Thus the expression becomes **(a + 1 - a)**, which is nothing but 1.

**ptr

ptr contains 9018, so ***ptr** yields 6006, and hence ****ptr** becomes ***(6006)**, which yields 1.

Thus the output of the first **printf( )** becomes 1 1 1.

Take a deep breath and then begin with the analysis of ***ptr++**. Here * and ++ both are unary operators. Since ++ occurs after the variable, ++ would be done later. Firstly ***(9018)** is performed, but since this value is not being assigned to any variable it gets ignored. Next, ++ goes to work and increments value in **ptr** to 9020. Now with **ptr** containing 9020, let us once again analyse the expressions **ptr - p**, ***ptr - a** and ****ptr**.

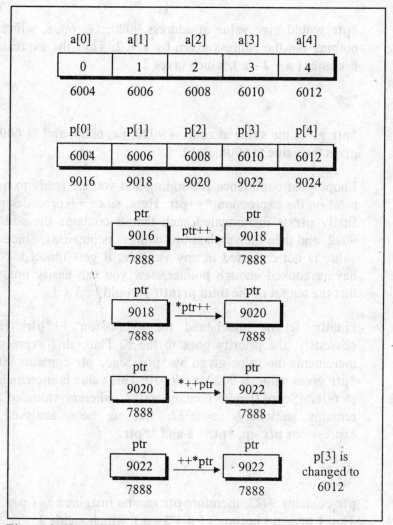

Figure 2.18

ptr - p

Since **ptr** contains 9020, it can be visualised as (**p + 2**). Thus **ptr - p** would become (**p + 2 - p**), which gives 2.

*ptr – a

*ptr would give value at address 9020, i.e. 6008, which is nothing but the address given by **a + 2**. Thus the expression becomes (**a + 2 - a**), which gives 2.

**ptr

*ptr gives the value at address 9020, i.e. 6008, and ***(6008)** gives the value at 6008, i.e. 2.

I hope your confidence is building and you are ready to meet head on the expression ***++ptr**. Here, since **++** precedes **ptr**, firstly **ptr** is incremented such that it contains the address 9022, and then the value at this address is obtained. Since the value is not collected in any variable, it gets ignored. Now having cooked enough pointer stew you can easily imagine that the output of the third **printf( )** would be 3 3 3.

Finally, let us understand the expression **++*ptr**. Here obviously, the priority goes to the *****. Thus, this expression increments the value given by ***ptr**. Since **ptr** contains 9022, ***ptr** gives value at 9022, i.e. 6010. This value is incremented to 6012. So **p[3]** now contains 6012, whereas value of **ptr** remains stationary at 9022. Let us now analyse the expressions **ptr - p**, ***ptr - a** and ****ptr.**

ptr - p

ptr contains 9022, therefore **ptr** can be imagined as (**p + 3**). Thus (**ptr - p**) becomes (**p + 3 - p**), which yields 3.

*ptr - a

*ptr yields 6012 which can be thought of as (**a + 4**). Thus the expression is reduced to (**a + 4 - a**), which yields 4.

**ptr

*ptr yields 6012, therefore ****ptr** would yield the value at ***ptr**, or the value at 6012, which is 4.

(23)
```
main( )
{
    static int a[ ] = { 0, 1, 2, 3, 4 };
    static int *p[ ] = { a, a + 1, a + 2, a + 3, a + 4 };

    int **ptr ;

    ptr = p ;
    **ptr++ ;
    printf ( "\n%d %d %d", ptr - p, *ptr - a, **ptr ) ;
    *++*ptr ;
    printf ( "\n%d %d %d", ptr - p, *ptr - a, **ptr ) ;
    ++**ptr ;
    printf ( "\n%d %d %d", ptr - p, *ptr - a, **ptr ) ;
}
```

Output

```
1 1 1
1 2 2
1 2 3
```

Explanation

To begin with, the array **a[ ]** is initialised and the array **p[ ]** is set such that it contains the addresses of elements of array **a[ ]**. Thus array **p[ ]** becomes an array of pointers. The base address of this array of pointers is then assigned to **ptr**, which is rightly called a pointer to a pointer. The possible arrangement of the array elements in memory is shown in the following figure.

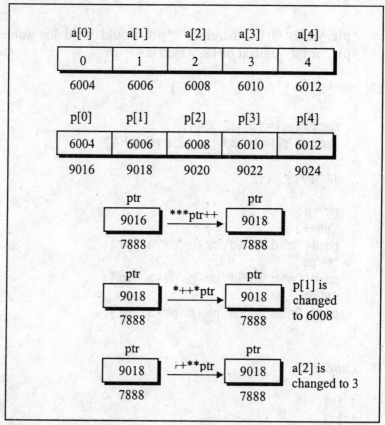

Figure 2.19

Let us now analyse the expression ****ptr++**. **ptr** contains the address 9016, therefore ***ptr** would yield the address 6004. ****ptr** would give the value at this address. This value turns out to be 0. However, this value is not assigned to any variable. Lastly **ptr++** goes to work. This increments the value stored in **ptr** to 9018. Once you are sure that **ptr** contains 9018, let us now proceed to find out what the output of **printf( )** is. Let us take one expression at a time and analyse it step by careful step.

ptr - p

Since **ptr** is containing the address 9018, we can as well say that **ptr** is containing the address given by **p + 1**. Thus **ptr - p** is reduced to (**p + 1 - p**), which yields 1.

*ptr - a

***ptr** means value at the address contained in **ptr**. Since **ptr** contains 9018, the value at this address would be 6006. Now 6006 can be imagined as (**a + 1**). Thus the expression becomes (**a + 1 - a**), which is nothing but 1.

**ptr

ptr contains 9018, so *ptr would yield 6006, and hence ****ptr** becomes *(**6006**), which would yield 1.

Thus the output of the first **printf( )** turns out to be 1 1 1.

The next statement needs a closer look. In *++*ptr, the order of evaluation would be *(++(*ptr)). Since **ptr** contains 9018, *(ptr) would yield the value at 9018, i.e. 6006. Then ++ goes to work on 6006 and increments it such that it is now 6008. Thus **p[1]** would now contain 6008. And finally *(**6008**) would give 2, which is ignored since it is not assigned to any variable.

Now, with **ptr** containing 9018, let us once again analyse the expressions **ptr - p**, ***ptr - a** and ****ptr**.

ptr - p

Since **ptr** contains 9018, it can be visualised as (**p + 1**), thus **ptr - p** would become (**p + 1 - p**), which would be 1.

*ptr - a

*ptr would give value at address 9018, i.e. 6008, which is nothing but the address given by **a + 2**. Thus the expression becomes (**a + 2 - a**), which gives 2.

**ptr

*ptr gives the value at address 9018, i.e. 6008, and ***(6008)** gives the value at 6008, i.e. 2.

Thus the output of the second **printf( )** would be 1 2 2.

Finally, we reach the third expression **++**ptr**. As the unary operators are evaluated from right to left, the order of evaluation of the above expression becomes: (**++(*(*ptr)**)). Since **ptr** contains 9018, ***ptr** yields 6008. ***(6008)** results into 2. This value at the address 6008 is then incremented from 2 to 3.

ptr - p

Since **ptr** contains 9018, it can be visualised as (**p + 1**), thus **ptr - p** would become (**p + 1 - p**), which would be 1.

*ptr - a

*ptr would give value at address 9018, i.e. 6008, which is nothing but the address given by **a + 2**. Thus the expression becomes (**a + 2 - a**), which gives 2.

**ptr

*ptr gives the value at address 9018, i.e. 6008, and ***(6008)** gives the value at 6008, i.e. 3.

Thus the output of the third **printf( )** is 1 2 3.

```
(24)  main( )
      {
          int n[3][3] =  {
                               2, 4, 3,
                               6, 8, 5,
                               3, 5, 1
                         } ;

          /* Assume that array begins at address 404 */
          printf ( "\n%u %u %d", n, n[2], n[2][2] ) ;
      }
```

Output

404 416 1

Explanation

n[ ][ ], to begin with, is declared as a two-dimensional array. Whenever we mention the name of the array, we get its base address. Therefore in **printf( )**, the first output would be the base address of the array. In our case it turned out to be 404. The array elements are arranged in memory as shown in Figure 2.20. Remember that there are no rows and columns in memory.

A two-dimensional array is nothing but an array of several one-dimensional arrays. The 2-D array contains addresses of these 1-D arrays. Thus **n[0]**, **n[1]** and **n[2]** contain the addresses 404, 410 and 416 respectively. Hence the second output of **printf( )**. The third output is quite straightforward.

n[2][2] prints out the element in the second row and second column of the array.

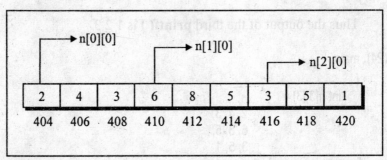

Figure 2.20

(25) main( )
```
{
    int n[3][3] = {
                    2, 4, 3,
                    6, 8, 5,
                    3, 5, 1
                } ;
    int *ptr ;
    ptr = n ;
    printf ( "\n%u ", n[2] ) ;
    printf ( "%d ", ptr[2] ) ;
    printf ( "%d", *( ptr + 2 ) ) ;
}
```

Output

416 3 3

Explanation

ptr has been declared as an integer pointer, and to begin with is assigned the base address of the array, i.e. 404.

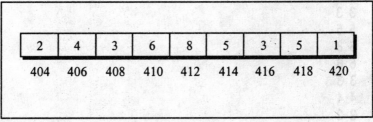

Figure 2.21

n[2] gives the base address of the second one-dimensional array, that is 416. Next comes the expression **ptr[2]**. Can we use such an expression? Yes, because ultimately **ptr[2]** is nothing but *(**ptr + 2**). Thus, even though **ptr** has not been declared as an array, we are perfectly justified in using the expression **ptr[2]**. **ptr** stores the address 404, so *(**ptr + 2**) gives the value of the second integer from 404, which in this program happens to be 3.

(26) main( )

```
{
    int n[3][3] = {
                        2, 4, 3,
                        6, 8, 5,
                        3, 5, 1
                } ;
    int i, j ;
    for ( i = 2 ; i >= 0 ; i-- )
    {
        for ( j = 2 ; j >= 0 ; j-- )
            printf ( "\n%d %d", n[i][j], *( *( n + i ) + j ) ) ;
    }
}
```

Output

1 1

```
5 5
3 3
5 5
8 8
6 6
3 3
4 4
2 2
```

Explanation

The output of **n[i][j]** is as per the expectations, I believe. All that is done is, using the **for** loops, rows and columns are varied, **i** controlling the row and **j** controlling the column. What is definitely difficult to comprehend is the second expression in **printf( )**, **(*(n + i) + j)*. Let us try to understand it. The following figure should prove helpful in doing so.

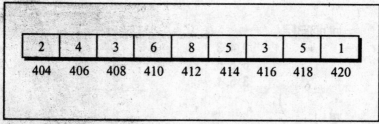

Figure 2.22

Imagine a 2-D array as a collection of several 1-D arrays. The only thing that the compiler needs to remember about a 1-D array is its base address. Thus, if three 1-D arrays are to be remembered, the compiler should store somewhere the base addresses of these arrays. These base addresses are stored in **n[0]**, **n[1]** and **n[2]**. Now if **n[1]** gives the base address of the first array, then **n[1] + 2** would give the address of the second integer from this base address. In this case it turns out to be

414. The value at this address, that is 5, can be obtained through the expression *(n[1] + 2). We know all too well that **n[1]** can also be expressed as *(**n + 1**). Thus, the expression *(n[1] + 2) is same as *(*(n + 1) + 2), which is same as **n[1][2]**. Therefore in general, we can say that **n[i][j]** is same as *(*(n + i) + j). With that I suppose the output of the above program is quite simple.

(27) main( )

```
    {
        static int a[3][3] = {
                                1, 2, 3,
                                4, 5, 6,
                                7, 8, 9
                            };
        static int *ptr[3] = { a[0], a[1], a[2] } ;
        int **ptr1 = ptr ;
        int i ;

        printf ( "\n" ) ;
        for ( i = 0 ; i <= 2 ; i++ )
            printf ( "%d ", *ptr[i] ) ;

        printf ( "\n" ) ;
        for ( i = 0 ; i <= 2 ; i++ )
            printf ( "%d ", *a[i] ) ;

        printf ( "\n" ) ;
        for ( i = 0 ; i <= 2 ; i++ )
        {
            printf ( "%d ", **ptr1 ) ;
            ptr1++ ;
        }
    }
```

Output

```
1 4 7
1 4 7
1 4 7
```

Explanation

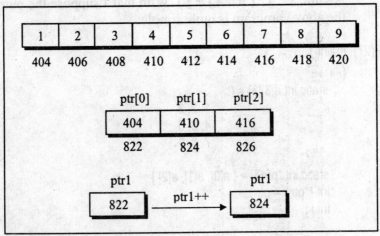

Figure 2.23

ptr[ ] has been declared as an array of pointers containing the base addresses of the three 1-D arrays as shown in Figure 2.23. Once past the declarations, the control reaches the first **for** loop. In this loop the **printf( )** prints the values at addresses stored in **ptr[0]**, **ptr[1]** and **ptr[2]**, which turn out to be 1, 4 and 7.

In the next **for** loop, the values at base addresses stored in the array **a[ ]** are printed, which once again turn out to be 1, 4 and 7. The third **for** loop is also simple.

Since **ptr1** has been initialised to the base address of the array **ptr[ ]**, it contains the address 822. Therefore ***ptr1** would give the value at address 822, i.e. 404, and ****ptr1** would give the value at address given by ***ptr1**, i.e. value at 404, which is

1. On incrementing **ptr1** it points to the next location after 822, i.e. 824. Therefore, next time through the **for** loop, ****ptr1** gives value at 410 (which is obtained through ***ptr1**), i.e. 4. Similarly, last time through the loop, the value 7 gets printed.

(28) main( )

```
    {
        int t[3][2][4] = {
                            {
                                2, 4, 3, 6,
                                1, 6, 7, 9
                            },
                            {
                                8, 2, 1, 1,
                                2, 3, 7, 3
                            },
                            {
                                1, 6, 2, 4,
                                0, 7, 9, 5
                            }
                          };
        printf ( "\n%d %d", t[2][1][3], *( *( *( t + 2 ) + 1 ) + 3 ) );
    }
```

Output

5 5

Explanation

In memory the 3-D array elements are arranged as shown in Figure 2.24.

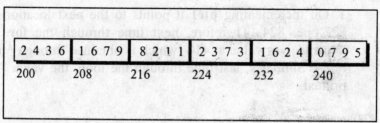

Figure 2.24

Here **t[ ][ ][ ]** has been declared as a three-dimensional array. A 3-D array can be considered as a collection of a number of 2-D arrays. Thus, the first expression in the **printf( )**, **t[2][1][3]** refers to the element in 1st row, 3rd column of the 2nd 2-D array. This turns out to be 5, which is printed through **printf( )**.

The next expression in **printf( )** is a little complicated. Since the only thing that the compiler needs to remember about the three 2-D arrays is their base addresses, these addresses are stored in **t[0]**, **t[1]** and **t[2]**. Therefore, the expression **t[2][1]** would give the address of the first row of the second 2-D array. Referring to the figure, this address turns out to be 240. To this address if we add 3, we would get the address of the third integer from this address. This address would be 246. Naturally, the value at this address (i.e. 5) can be obtained through the expression ***(t[2][1] + 3)**. But **t[2][1]** itself can be expressed as ***(t[2] + 1)**. And in this expression **t[2]** can be expressed as ***(t + 2)**. Thus the expression ***(t[2][1] + 3)** can be expressed as ***(*(*(t + 2) + 1) + 3)**.

[B] Answer the following:

(1) For the following statements would **arr[3]** and **ptr[3]** fetch the same character? <Yes/No>:

```
char arr[ ] = "Surprised" ,
char *ptr = "Surprised" ;
```

Explanation

Yes

(2) For the statements in (1) does the compiler fetch the character **arr[3]** and **ptr[3]** in the same manner?

Explanation

No. For **arr[3]** the compiler generates code to start at location **arr**, move three past it, and fetch the character there. When it sees the expression **ptr[3]** it generates the code to start at location stored in **ptr**, add three to the pointer, and finally fetch the character pointed to.

In other words, **arr[3]** is three places past the start of the object named **arr**, whereas **ptr[3]** is three places past the object pointed to by **ptr**.

(3) Can you combine the following two statements into one?

```
char *p ;
p = malloc ( 100 ) ;
```

Explanation

```
char *p = malloc ( 100 )
```

(4) Does mentioning the array name gives the base address in all the contexts?

Explanation

No. Whenever mentioning the array name gives its base address it is said that the array has decayed into a pointer. This decaying doesn't take place in two situations:

- When array name is used with **sizeof** operator.
- When the array name is an operand of the **&** operator.

(5) Are the expressions **arr** and **&arr** same for an array of 10 integers?

Explanation

No. Even though both may give the same addresses they mean two different things. **arr** gives the address of the first **int**, whereas **&arr** gives the address of array of **int**s. Since these addresses happen to be same the results of the expressions are same.

(6) When **char a[ ]** and **char *a** are treated as same by the compiler?

Explanation

When using them as formal parameters while defining a function.

(7) Would the following program compile successfully?

```
main( )
{
    char a[ ] = "Sunstroke" ;
    char *p = "Coldwave" ;
    a = "Coldwave" ;
    p = "Sunstroke" ;
    printf ( "\n%s %s", a, p ) ;
}
```

Explanation

No, because we may assign a new string to a pointer but not to an array.

(8) A pointer to a block of memory is effectively same as an array. <True/False>

Explanation

True

(9) What does the following declaration mean:

int (*ptr)[10] ;

Explanation

ptr is a pointer to an array of 10 integers.

(10) If we pass the name of a 1-D **int** array to a function it decays into a pointer to an **int**. If we pass the name of a 2-D array of integers to a function what would it decay into?

Explanation

It decays into a pointer to an array and not a pointer to a pointer.

(11) Are the three declarations **char **apple, char *orange[ ],** and **char cherry[ ][ ]** same? <Yes/No>

Explanation

No

(12) What would be the equivalent pointer expression for referring the element **a[i][j][k][l]**?

Explanation

* (* (* (* (a + i) + j) + k) + l)

(13) In the following program how would you print 50 using **p**?

```
main( )
{
    int a[ ] = { 10, 20, 30, 40, 50 } ;
    char *p ;
    p = ( char * ) a ;
}
```

Explanation

printf ("\n%d", * ((int *) p + 4)) ;

(14) How would you define the function **f( )** in the following program?

```
int arr[MAXROW][MAXCOL] ;
fun ( arr ) ;
```

Explanation

```
fun ( int a[ ][MAXCOL] )
{
}
```
or

```
fun ( int ( *ptr )[.MAXCOL] )  /* ptr is pointer to an array */
{
}
```

Exercise

[A] What will be the output of the following programs:

```
(1)   main( )
      {
          int arr[3][3][3] ;

          /* Assume base address of arr to be 1000 */
          printf ( "\n%u %u %u", arr, arr + 1, arr + 2 ) ;
          printf ( "\n%u %u %u", arr[0], arr[0] + 1, arr[1] ) ;
          printf ( "\n%u %u %u", arr[1][1], arr[1][0] + 1, arr[0][1] ) ;
      }

(2)   main( )
      {
          static int a[3][3][3] = {
                                   {
                                       1, 2, 3,
                                       4, 5, 6,
                                       7, 8, 9
                                   },
                                   {
                                       2, 4, 6,
                                       8, 10, 12,
                                       14, 16, 18
                                   },
                                   {
                                       3, 6, 9,
                                       12, 15, 18,
                                       21, 24, 27
                                   }
                                  } ;
          static int *ptr[ ] = {
                                   a[0][0], a[0][1], a[0][2],
                                   a[1][0], a[1][1], a[1][2],
                                   a[2][0], a[2][1], a[2][2]
```

```
                                  } ;
        int *ptr1[ ] = { a[0], a[1], a[2] } ;
        int **ptr2 = ptr, i ;

        printf ( "\n" ) ;
        for ( i = 0 ; i <= 8 ; i++ )
        {
            printf ( "%d ", *ptr2 ) ;
            ptr2++ ;
        }

        printf ( "\n" ) ;
        for ( i = 0 ; i <= 2 ; i++ )
            printf ( "%d ", *( ptr1[i] ) ) ;

        printf ( "\n" ) ;
        for ( i = 0 ; i <= 8 ; i++ )
            printf ( "%d ", *ptr[i] ) ;
    }

(3)  main( )
    {
        static int arr[ ] = { 97, 98, 99, 100, 101, 102, 103, 104 } ;
        int *ptr = arr + 1 ;

        print ( ++ptr, ptr--, ptr, ptr++, ++ptr ) ;
    }

    print ( int *a, int *b, int *c, int *d, int *e )
    {
        printf ( "\n%d %d %d %d %d", *a, *b, *c, *d, *e ) ;
    }

(4)  main( )
    {
        int a[3][3][2] = {
                            {
                                1, 2,
```

```
                              3, 4,
                              5, 6
                         },
                         {
                              3, 4,
                              1, 2,
                              5, 6
                         },
                         {
                              5, 6,
                              3, 4,
                              1, 2
                         }
                    } ;

     printf ( "\n%d %d %d ", * ( * ( a[0] + 2 ) + 1 ),
               * ( * ( * ( a + 2 ) + 1 ) + 1 ), * ( a[1][2] + 1 ) ) ;
}
```

(5)   main( )
```
     {
          static int a[ ] = { 0, 1, 2, 3, 4 } ;
          static int *p[ ] = { a, a + 2, a + 1, a + 4, a + 3 } ;
          int **ptr ;

          ptr = p ;
          **++ptr ;

          printf ( "\n%d %d %d ", **ptr, ptr - p, *ptr - a ) ;
     }
```

3

Pointers and Strings

In the last chapter you learnt how to define arrays of differing sizes and dimensions, how to initialise them, how to pass them to a functions, etc. With this knowledge under your belt, you should be ready to handle strings, which are, simply put, a special kind of array. Strings, the ways to manipulate them, and how pointers are related to strings are going to be the topics of discussion in this chapter.

What are Strings

The way a group of integers can be stored in an integer array, similarly a group of characters can be stored in a character array. Character arrays are many a time also known as 'strings'. Most languages (like Basic, Fortran etc.) internally treat strings as character arrays, but somehow conceal this fact from the programmer. Character arrays or strings are the data types used by programming languages to manipulate text such as words and sentences.

A string constant is a one-dimensional array of characters terminated by a null ('\0'). For example,

char name[ ] = { 'H', 'A', 'E', 'S', 'L', 'E', 'R', '\0' } ;

Each character in the array occupies one byte of memory and the last character is always '\0'. What character is this? It looks like two characters, but it is actually an escape sequence like '\n'. It is called 'null character'. Note that '\0' and '0' are not same. ASCII value of '\0' is 0, whereas ASCII value of '0' is 48. The character array in memory would look like this:

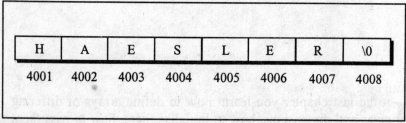

Figure 3.1

Note that the array elements are stored in contiguous memory locations.

The terminating null ('\0') is important, because it is the only way the functions that work with string can know where a string ends. In fact, a string not terminated by a '\0' is not really a string, but merely a collection of characters.

C concedes the fact that you would use strings very often and hence provides a shortcut for initialising strings. For example, the string initialised above can also be initialised as,

```
char name[ ] = "HAESLER" ;
```

Note that, in this declaration '\0' is not necessary. C inserts the null automatically. The '\0' comes very handy in printing strings. This is illustrated in the following program.

```
/* Program 33 */
main( )
{
    char name[ ] = "Klinsman" ;
    int i ;

    i = 0 ;
    while ( name[i] )
    {
        printf ( "\n%c %c %c %c", name[i], * ( name + i ),
                                    * ( i + name ), i[name] ) ;
        i++ ;
    }
}
```

And here is the output...

```
KKKK
llll
iiii
nnnn
ssss
mmmm
aaaa
nnnn
```

This program doesn't rely on the length of the string (number of characters in string) to print out its contents and hence is definitely more general. Here is another version of the same program; this one uses pointers to access the array elements.

```
/* Program 34 */
/* Program to print string elements using pointer notation */
main( )
{
    char name[ ] = "Klinsman" ;
    char *ptr ;

    ptr = name ;  /* store base address of string */

    while ( *ptr != '\0' )
    {
        printf ( "%c", *ptr ) ;
        ptr++ ;
    }
}
```

As with the integer array, by mentioning the name of the array we get the base address (address of the zeroth element) of the array. This base address is stored in the variable **ptr** using,

```
ptr = name ;
```

Once the base address is obtained in **ptr**, ***ptr** would yield the value at this address, which gets printed promptly through,

```
printf ( "%c", *ptr ) ;
```

Then, **ptr** is incremented to point to the next character in the string. This derives from two facts: array elements are stored in contiguous memory locations and on incrementing a pointer it points to the immediately next location of its type. This process is carried out till **ptr** doesn't point to the last character in the string, that is, '\0'

Even though there are so many ways (as shown above) to refer to the elements of character array, rarely is any one of them used to print out an array. This is because, **printf( )** function has got a sweet and simple way of doing it, as shown below. Note that **printf( )** doesn't print the '\0'.

```
/* Program 35 */
main( )
{
    char name[ ] = "Klinsman" ;
    printf ( "\n%s", name ) ;
}
```

The **%s** is a format specification for printing out a string. The same specification can be used to receive a string from the keyboard, as shown below.

```
/* Program 36 */
main( )
{
    char name[25] ;

    printf ( "\nEnter your name: " ) ;
    scanf ( "%s", name ) ;
    printf ( "Hello %s!", name ) ;
}
```

And here is the output...

```
Enter your name: Debashish
Hello Debashish!
```

Note that the declaration **char name[25]** sets aside 25 characters under the array **name[ ]**, whereas the **scanf( )** function fills in the characters typed at keyboard into this array until the enter key is hit. Naturally, we should pass the base address of the array to the **scanf( )** function.

Standard Library String Functions

C has a large set of useful string handling library functions. Here, we would illustrate the usage of most commonly used functions (**strlen( ), strcpy( ), strcat( )** and **strcmp( )**) through a program.

```
/* Program 37 */
#include <string.h>
main( )
{
    char str1[20] = "Bamboozled" ;
    char str2[ ] = "Chap" ;
    char str3[20] ;
    int l, k ;

    l = strlen ( str1 ) ;
    printf ( "\nlength of string = %d", l ) ;

    strcpy ( str3, str1 ) ;
    printf ( "\nafter copying, string str3 = %s", str3 ) ;

    k = strcmp ( str1, str2 ) ;
    printf ( "\non comparing str1 and str2, k = %d", k ) ;

    k = strcmp ( str3, str1 ) ;
    printf ( "\non comparing str3 and str1, k = %d", k ) ;

    strcat ( str1, str2 ) ;
    printf ( "\non concatenation str1 = %s", str1 ) ;
}
```

The output would be...

```
length of string = 10
after copying, string str3 = Bamboozled
on comparing str1 and str2, k = -1
on comparing str3 and str1, k = 0
```

on concatenation str1 = BamboozledChap

Note that in the call to the function **strlen( )**, we are passing the base address of the string, and the function in turn returns the length of the string. While calculating the length it doesn't count '\0'. Can we not write a function **xstrlen( )** which imitates the standard library function **strlen( )**? Let us give it a try...

```
/* Program 38 */
main( )
{
    char arr[ ] = "Bamboozled" ;
    int len1, len2 ;

    len1 = xstrlen ( arr ) ;
    len2 = xstrlen ( "HumptyDumpty" ) ;
    printf ( "\nstring = %s length = %d", arr, len1 ) ;
    printf ( "\nstring = %s length = %d", "HumptyDumpty", len2 ) ;
}

xstrlen ( char *s )
{
    int length = 0 ;
    while ( *s != '\0' )
    {
        length++ ;
        s++ ;
    }

    return ( length ) ;
}
```

The output would be...

```
string = Bamboozled length = 10
string = HumptyDumpty length = 12
```

The function **xstrlen( )** is fairly simple. All that it does is it keeps counting the characters till the end of string is not met. Or in other words keeps counting characters till the pointer **s** doesn't point to '\0'.

Another function that we have used in Program 37 is **strcpy( )**. This function copies the contents of one string into another. The base addresses of the source and target strings should be supplied to this function. On supplying the base addresses, **strcpy( )** goes on copying the source string into the target string till it doesn't encounter the end of source string. It is our responsibility to see to it that target string's dimension is big enough to hold the string being copied into it. Thus, a string gets copied into another, piece-meal, character by character. There is no shortcut for this. Let us now attempt to mimic **strcpy( )** via our own string copy function, which we would call **xstrcpy( )**.

```
xstrcpy ( char *t, char *s )
{
    while ( *s != '\0' )
    {
        *t = *s ;
        s++ ;
        t++ ;
    }
    *t = '\0' ;
}
```

Note that having copied the entire source string into the target string, it is necessary to place a '\0' into the target string to mark its end.

The **strcat( )** function concatenates the source string at the end of the target string. For example, "Bamboozled" and "Chap" on concatenation would result into a string "BamboozledChap". Note that the target string **str1[ ]** has been made big enough to hold the final string. I leave it to you to develop your own **xstrcat( )** on lines of **xstrlen( )** and **xstrcpy( )**.

Another useful string function is **strcmp( )** which compares two strings to find out whether they are same or different. The two strings are compared letter by letter until there is a mismatch or end of one of the strings is reached, whichever occurs first. If the two strings are identical, **strcmp( )** returns a value zero. If they're not, it returns the numeric difference between the ASCII values of the first non-matching pair of characters.

The exact value of mismatch will rarely concern us. All we usually want to know is whether or not the first string is alphabetically above the second string. If it is, a negative value is returned; if it isn't, a positive value is returned. Any non-zero value means there is a mismatch. Let us try to implement this procedure into a function **xstrcmp( )**, which works similar to the **strcmp( )** function.

```
xstrcmp ( char *s1, char *s2 )
{
    while ( *s1 == *s2 )
    {
        if ( *s1 == '\0' )
            return ( 0 ) ;

        s1++ ;
        s2++ ;
    }

    return ( *s1 - *s2 ) ;
}
```

Pointers and Strings

Suppose we wish to store "Hello". We may either store it in a string or we may ask the C compiler to store it at some location in memory and assign the address of the string in a **char** pointer. This is shown below:

```
char str[ ] = "Hello" ;
char *p = "Hello" ;
```

There is a subtle difference in usage of these two forms. For example, we cannot assign a string to another, whereas, we can assign a **char** pointer to another **char** pointer. This is shown in the following program.

```
/* Program 39 */
main( )
{
    char str1[ ] = "Hello" ;
    char str2[10] ;

    char *s = "Good Morning" ;
    char *q ;

    str2 = str1 ; /* error */
    q = s ; /* works */
}
```

Also, once a string has been defined it cannot be initialised to another set of characters. Unlike strings, such an operation is perfectly valid with **char** pointers.

```
/* Program 40 */
main( )
{
    char str1[ ] = "Hello" ;
    char *p = "Hello" ;
```

```
        str1 = "Bye" ; /* error */
        p = "Bye" ; /* works */
}
```

The *const* Qualifier

The keyword **const** (for constant), if present, precedes the data type of a variable. It specifies that the value of the variable will not change throughout the program. Any attempt to alter the value of the variable defined with this qualifier will result into an error message from compiler. **const** is usually used to replace **#defined** constants.

const qualifier ensures that your program does not inadvertently alter a variable that you intended to be a constant. It also reminds anybody reading the program listing that the variable is not intended to change. Variables with this qualifier are often named in all uppercase, as a reminder that they are constants. The following program shows the usage of **const**.

```
/* Program 41 */
main( )
{
    float r, a ;
    const float PI = 3.14 ;

    printf ( "\nEnter radius: " ) ;
    scanf ( "%f", &r ) ;

    a = PI * r * r ;
    printf ( "Area of circle = %f", a ) ;
}
```

const is a better idea as compared to **#define** because its scope of operation can be controlled by placing it appropriately either inside a function or outside all functions. If a **const** is placed inside a function its effect would be localised to that function, whereas, if it is placed outside all functions then its effect would be global. We cannot exercise such finer control while using a **#define**.

const **Pointers**

Look at the following program:

```
/* Program 42 */
main( )
{
    char str1[ ] = "Nagpur" ;
    char str2[10] ;

    xstrcpy ( str2, str1 ) ;
    printf ( "\n%s", str2 ) ;
}

xstrcpy ( char *t, char *s )
{
    while ( *t != '\0' )
    {
        *t = *s ;
        t++ ;
        s++ ;
    }
    *t = '\0' ;
}
```

This program simply copies the contents of **str1[ ]** into **str2[ ]** using the function **xstrcpy( )**. What would happen if we add the following lines beyond the last statement of **xstrcpy( )**?

s = s – 6 ;

```
*s = 'K' ;
```

This would change the source string to "Kagpur". Can we not ensure that the source string doesn't change even accidentally in **xstrcpy( )**? We can, by changing the prototype of the function to

```
void xstrcpy ( char*, const char* ) ;
```

Correspondingly the definition would change to:

```
void xstrcpy ( char *t, const char *s )
{
    /* code */
}
```

The following code fragment would help you to fix your ideas about **const** further.

```
char *p = "Hello" ; /* pointer is variable, so is string */
*p = 'M' ; /* works */
p = "Bye" ; /* works */

const char *q = "Hello" ; /* string is constant pointer is not */
*q = 'M' ; /* error */
q = "Bye" ; /* works */

char const *s = "Hello" ; /* string is constant pointer is not */
*s = 'M' ; /* error */
s = "Bye" ; /* works */

char * const t = "Hello" ; /* pointer is constant string is not */
*t = 'M' ; /* works */
t = "Bye" ; /* error */

const char * const u = "Hello" ; /* string is constant, so is pointer */
*u = 'M' ; /* error */
u = "Bye" ; /* error */
```

Returning *const* Values

A function can return a pointer to a constant string as shown below.

```
/* Program 43 */
main( )
{
    const char *fun( ) ;
    const char *p ;

    p = fun( ) ;
    *p = 'A' ; /* error */
    printf ( "\n%s", p ) ;
}

const char * fun( )
{
    return "Rain" ;
}
```

Here since the function **fun( )** is returning a constant string, we cannot use the pointer **p** to modify it. Not only this, the following operations too would be invalid:

(a) **main( )** cannot assign the return value to a pointer to a non-**const** string.

(b) **main( )** cannot pass the return value to a function that is expecting a pointer to a non-**const** string.

Two Dimensional Array of Characters

In the previous chapter we saw several examples of 2-D numeric arrays. Let's now look at a similar phenomenon, but one dealing with characters. The best way to understand this concept is through a program. Our example program asks you to type your name. When you do so, it checks your name against a master list to see if you are worthy of entry to the palace. Here's the program...

```c
/* Program 44 */
#include <string.h>
#define FOUND 1
#define NOTFOUND 0
main( )
{
    char masterlist[6][10] = {
                                "akshay",
                                "parag",
                                "raman",
                                "srinivas",
                                "gopal",
                                "rajesh"
                            } ;
    int i, flag, a ;
    char yourname[10] ;

    printf ( "\nEnter your name: " ) ;
    scanf ( "%s", yourname ) ;

    flag = NOTFOUND ;
    for ( i = 0 ; i <= 5 ; i++ )
    {
        a = strcmp ( &masterlist[i][0], yourname ) ;
        if ( a == 0 )
        {
            printf ( "Welcome, you can enter the palace" ) ;
            flag = FOUND ;
            break ;
        }
    }

    if ( flag == NOTFOUND )
        printf ( "Sorry, you are a trespasser" ) ;
```

}

And here is the output for two sample runs of this program...

Enter your name: dinesh
Sorry, you are a trespasser

Enter your name: raman
Welcome, you can enter the palace

Notice how the two-dimensional character array has been initialised. The order of the subscripts in the array declaration is important. The first subscript gives the number of names in the array, while the second subscript gives the length of each item in the array.

Instead of initialising names, had these names been supplied from the keyboard, the program segment would look like this...

```
for ( i = 0 ; i <= 5 ; i++ )
    scanf ( "%s", &masterlist[i][0] ) ;
```

While comparing the strings through **strcmp( )**, note that the addresses of the strings are being passed to **strcmp( )**. As seen in the last section, if the two strings match, **strcmp( )** would return a value 0, otherwise it would return a non-zero value.

The variable **flag** is used to keep a record of whether the control did reach inside the **if** or not. To begin with, we set this **flag** to NOTFOUND. Later through the loop if the names match this flag is set to FOUND. When the control reaches beyond the **for** loop, if **flag** is still set to NOTFOUND, it means none of the names in the **masterlist[ ][ ]** matched with the one supplied from the keyboard.

The names would be stored in memory as shown in Figure 3.2. Note that each string ends with a '\0'. The arrangement as you can appreciate is similar to that of a two-dimensional numeric array.

akshay\0	parag\0	raman\0	srinivas\0	gopal\0	rajesh\0
1001	1011	1021	1031	1041	1051

Figure 3.2

Here, 1001, 1011, 1021, etc. are the base addresses of successive names. As seen from the above figure, some of the names do not occupy all the bytes reserved for them. For example, even though 10 bytes are reserved for storing the name "akshay", it occupies only 7 bytes. Thus, 3 bytes go waste. Similarly, for each name there is some amount of wastage. In fact, more the number of names, more would be the wastage. Can this not be avoided? Yes, it can be... by using a data type called an array of pointers to strings, which is our next topic of discussion.

Array of Pointers to Strings

As we know, a pointer variable always contains an address. Therefore, if we construct an array of pointers it would contain a number of addresses. Let us see how the names in the earlier example can be stored in the array of pointers.

```
char *names[ ] = {
                "akshay",
                "parag",
                "raman",
                "srinivas",
                "gopal",
                "rajesh"
            };
```

In this declaration **names[ ]** is an array of pointers. It contains base addresses of respective names. That is, base addresses of "akshay" is stored in **names[0]**, base addresses of "parag" is stored in **names[1]** and so on. This is depicted in the following figure.

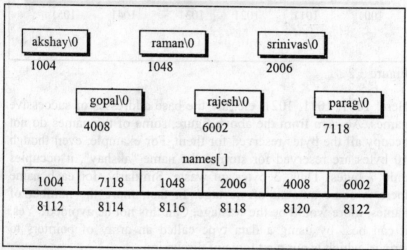

Figure 3.3

In the two-dimensional array of characters, the strings were occupying a total of 60 bytes. As against this by using the array of pointers to strings the same strings can now be stored using only 53 bytes, 41 bytes for the actual strings and 12 for the array of pointers. A substantial saving that goes on increasing with the number of names being stored.

Thus, one reason to store strings in an array of pointers is to make more efficient use of available memory.

Another reason to use array of pointers to store strings is to obtain greater ease in the manipulation of the strings. The following program shows this. The purpose of the program is very simple. We want to exchange the positions of the names "raman" and "srinivas".

```
/* Program 45 */
main( )
{
    char *names[ ] = {
                        "akshay",
                        "parag",
                        "raman",
                        "srinivas",
                        "gopal",
                        "rajesh"
                     };
    char *temp ;

    printf ( "\nOriginal: %s %s", names[2], names[3] ) ;
    temp = names[2] ;
    names[2] = names[3] ;
    names[3] = temp ;

    printf ( "\nNew: %s %s", names[2], names[3] ) ;
}
```

And here is the output...

```
Original: raman  srinivas
New: srinivas  ramam
```

In this program all that we are required to do is exchange the addresses of the names stored in the array of pointers, rather than the names themselves. Thus, by effecting just one exchange we are able to interchange names. This makes managing strings very convenient.

Thus, from the point of view of efficient memory usage and ease of programming, an array of pointers to strings definitely scores over a two-dimensional character array. That is why, even though in principle strings can be stored and handled through a two-dimensional array of characters, in actual practice it is the array of pointers to strings which is more commonly used.

In Program 45 instead of exchanging the names within **main( )** suppose we decide to carry out this exchange through a function **swap( )**. To this function suppose we would pass the addresses given by (**names + 2**) and (**names + 3**). These addresses would be collected in two variables, which are pointers to pointers (why?). Using these pointers then the names can be exchanged. This is how the **swap( )** function would look like...

```
swap ( char **s1, char **s2 )
{
    char *t ;

    t = *s1 ;
    *s1 = *s2 ;
    *s2 = t ;
}
```

Limitation of Array of Pointers to Strings

When we are using a two-dimensional array of characters we are at liberty to either initialise the strings where we are declaring the array, or receive the strings using **scanf( )** function. However, when we are using an array of pointers to strings we can initialise the strings at the place where we are declaring the array, but we cannot receive the strings from keyboard using **scanf( )**. Thus, the following program would never work out.

```
/* Program 46 */
main( )
{
    char *names[6] ;
    int i ;
```

```
    for ( i = 0 ; i <= 5 ; i++ )
    {
        printf ( "\nEnter name: " ) ;
        scanf ( "%s", names[i] ) ;
    }
}
```

The program doesn't work because when we are declaring the array it is containing garbage values. And it would be definitely wrong to send these garbage values to **scanf( )** as the addresses where it should keep the strings received from the keyboard.

As a compromise solution we may first allocate space for each name using **malloc( )** and then store the address returned by **malloc( )** in the array of pointers to strings. This is shown in the following program.

```
/* Program 47 */
/* Program to overcome limitation of array of pointers to strings */
#include <alloc.h>
#include <string.h>
main( )
{
    char *name[5] ;
    char str[20] ;
    int i ;

    for ( i = 0 ; i < 5 ; i++ )
    {
        printf ( "Enter a String: " ) ;
        gets ( str ) ;
        name[i] = ( char * ) malloc ( strlen ( str ) ) ;
        strcpy ( name[i], str ) ;

    for ( i = 0 ; i < 5 ; i++ )
        printf ( "\n%s", name[i] ) ;
}
```

Solved Problems

[A] What will be the output of the following programs:

(1)
```
#include <string.h>
main( )
{
    char s[ ] = "Rendezvous !" ;
    printf ( "\n%d", * ( s + strlen ( s ) ) ) ;
}
```

Output

0

Explanation

No 'Rendezvous !', but a zero is printed out. Mentioning the name of the string gives the base address of the string. The function **strlen(s)** returns the length of the string **s[ ]**, which in this case is 12. In **printf( )**, using the 'value at address' operator (often called 'contents of' operator), we are trying to print out the contents of the 12th address from the base address of the string. At this address there is a '\0', which is automatically stored to mark the end of the string. The ASCII value of '\0' is 0, which is what is being printed by the **printf( )**.

(2)
```
main( )
{
    printf ( 5 + "Fascimile" ) ;
}
```

Output

mile

Explanation

When we pass a string to a function, what gets passed is the base address of the string. In this case what is being passed to **printf( )** is the base address plus 5, i.e. address of 'm' in "facsimile". **printf( )** prints a string starting from the address it receives, up to the end of the string. Hence, in this case 'mile' gets printed.

(3)   main( )
```
{
    char ch[20] ;
    int i ;
    for ( i = 0 ; i < 19 ; i++ )
        *( ch + i ) = 67 ;
    *( ch + i ) = '\0' ;
    printf ( "\n%s", ch ) ;
}
```

Output

CCCCCCCCCCCCCCCCCCC

Explanation

Mentioning the name of the array always gives its base address. Therefore (**ch + i**) would give the address of the ith element from the base address, and *(**ch + i**) would give the value at this address, i.e. the value of the ith element. Through the **for** loop we store 67, which is the ASCII value of upper case 'C', in all the locations of the string. Once the control reaches outside the **for** loop the value of i would be 19, and in the 19th location from the base address we store a '\0' to mark the end of the string. This is essential, as the compiler has no other way of knowing where the string is terminated. In the **printf( )** that follows, **%s** is the format specification for printing a string, and **ch** gives the base address of the string. Hence starting from the first element, the complete string is printed out.

(4)
```
main( )
{
    char str[ ] = { 48, 48, 48, 48, 48, 48, 48, 48, 48, 48 } ;
    char *s ;
    int i ;
    s = str ;
    for ( i = 0 ; i <= 9 ; i++ )
    {
        if ( *s )
            printf ( "%c ", *s ) ;
        s++ ;
    }
}
```

Output

0 0 0 0 0 0 0 0 0 0

Explanation

In all 10 elements of **str[ ]**, an integer, 48 is stored. Wondering whether a **char** string can hold **int**s? The answer is yes, as 48 does not get stored literally in the elements. 48 is interpreted as the ASCII value of the character to be stored in the string. The character corresponding to ASCII 48 happens to be 0, which is assigned to all the locations of the string.

s, a character pointer, is assigned the base address of the string **str[ ]**. Next, in the **if** condition, the value at address contained in **s** is checked for truth/falsity. As 0 represents ASCII 48, the condition evaluates to true every time. Irrespective of whether the condition is satisfied or not, **s** is incremented so that each time it points to the subsequent array element. This entire logic is repeated in the **for** loop, printing out 10 zeros in the process.

(5)
```
main( )
{
    char str1[ ] = "Hello" ;
    char str2[ ] = "Hello" ;
    if ( str1 == str2 )
        printf ( "\nEqual" ) ;
    else
        printf ( "\nUnequal" ) ;
}
```

Output

Unequal

Explanation

When we mention the name of the array we get its base address. Since **str1** and **str2** are two different arrays, their base addresses would always be different. Hence, the condition in **if** is never going to get satisfied. If we are to compare the contents of two **char** arrays, we should compare them on a character by character basis or use **strcmp( )**.

(6)
```
main( )
{
    char str[10] = { 0, 0, 0, 0, 0, 0, 0, 0, 0, 0 } ;
    char *s ;
    int i ;
    s = str ;
    for ( i = 0 ; i <= 9 ; i++ )
```

```
    {
        if ( *s )
            printf ( "%c", *s ) ;
        s++ ;
    }
}
```

Output

No output

Explanation

Though you may not have expected zeroes to be outputted this time, you surely did expect some output! We stored the character corresponding to ASCII 0 in all 10 elements of the string. Next, we assign **s**, a **char** pointer, the base address of the string. Through the **for** loop, we are attempting to print out all elements one by one, but not before imposing the **if** condition.

The **if** is made to test the value at address contained in **s** before the execution of **printf( )**. First time through the loop, ***s** yields ASCII 0. Therefore the **if** statement reduces to **if (0`)**, and as 0 stands for falsity, the condition fails. Hence, **s** is incremented and control loops back to **for** without executing the **printf( )**. The same thing happens the next time around, and the next, and so on, till the **for** loop ends, resulting in no output at all.

(7) ```
     main( )
     {
         printf ("%c", "abcdefgh"[4]) ;
     }
     ```

*Output*
     ```

e

Explanation

We know that expression **a[4]** gets converted to ***(a + 4)**, where **a** gives the base address of the array. On similar lines **"abcdefgh"[4]** becomes ***("abcdefgh" + 4)**. This is same as ***(base address + 4)**. **(base address + 4)** yields address of 'e'. Thus, what gets passed to **printf( )** is the character 'e', which is promptly printed out.

(8) main( )
```
{
    char str[7] = "Strings" ;
    printf ( "%s", str ) ;
}
```

Output

Cannot predict.

Explanation

Here **str[ ]** has been declared as a 7 character array and into it a 8 character string has been stored. This would result into overwriting of the byte beyond the seventh byte reserved for the array with a '\0'. There is always a possibility that something important gets overwritten, which would be unsafe.

(9) main( )
```
{
    char *str[ ] = { "Frogs", "Do", "Not", "Die.", "They", "Croak!" } ;
    printf ( "%d %d", sizeof ( str ), sizeof ( str[0] ) ) ;
}
```

Output

12 2

Explanation

Mentioning the name of the array gives its base address. However, when used with **sizeof( )** it yields the number of bytes occupied by the array in memory. Since **str** is holding six addresses, of 2 bytes each, **sizeof (str)** gives 12.

str[0] yields address of "Frogs". This address is reported as 2 bytes big.

(10) main( )
```
    {
        char s[ ] = "C smart!" ;
        int i ;
        for ( i = 0 ; s[i] ; i++ )
            printf ( "\n%c %c %c %c", s[i], *( s + i ) , i[s], *( i + s ) ) ;
    }
```

Output

```
C C C C
s s s s
m m m m
a a a a
r r r r
t t t t
! ! ! !
```

Explanation

The above program rubs in the point that **s[i]**, **i[s]**, ***(s + i)** and ***(i + s)** are various ways of referring to the same element, that is the ith element of the string **s**. Each element of the string is printed out four times, till the end of the string is encountered. Note that in the **for** loop there is an expression **s[i]** in the condition part. This means the loop would continue to get executed till **s[i]** is not equal to zero. We can afford to say this because a string always ends with a '\0', whose ASCII value is 0. Thus the **for** loop will be terminated when the expression **s[i]** yields a '\0'.

(11)
```
main( )
{
    char s[ ] = "Oinks Grunts and Guffaws" ;
    printf ( "\n%c", *( &s[2] ) ) ;
    printf ( "\n%s", s + 5 ) ;
    printf ( "\n%s", s ) ;
    printf ( "\n%c", *( s + 2 ) ) ;
    printf ( "\n%u", s ) ;
}
```

Output

```
n
Grunts and Guffaws
Oinks Grunts and Guffaws
n
404
```

Explanation

In the first **printf( )** the 'address of' operator, **&**, gives the address of the second element of the string. Value at this address is 'n', which is printed out by the **printf( )** using **%c**.

Since **s** gives the base address of the array, (**s + 5**) would give the address of the fifth element from the base address.

This address is passed to the second **printf( )**. Using the format specification **%s**, the contents of the string are printed out the 5th element onwards.

The third **printf( )** prints the entire string, as the base address of the string is being passed to it.

The fourth **printf( )** is made to print the second character of the string, as ***(s + 2)** is nothing but s[2]. Thus 'n' gets printed.

Does the output of the final **printf( )** surprise you by printing out a number, 404? Note that the format specification **%u** is used with **s**, which gives the base address of the string. It happened to be 404 when we executed the program, which got printed out. On executing the same yourself, you may get any other address, depending on what address is allotted to the string by the compiler.

```
(12)  main( )
      {
          char arr[ ] = "Pickpocketing my peace of mind.."
          int i ;
          printf ( "\n%c", *arr ) ;
          arr++ ;
          printf ( "\n%c", *arr ) ;
      }
```

Output

Error message: Lvalue required in function main

Explanation

Though everything seems to be in order at first glance, there lies a fundamental error in our program. When we say **arr**, we are referring to the base address of the string. This is the only information that helps the C compiler keep track of the string **arr[ ]**. If this information is lost, there is no way the compiler can access the string. So, this particular address is given a favoured status, that of a constant. The statement **arr++** is essentially wrong because a constant can't be incremented and hence the compiler asks for an Lvalue, which is a value that can be changed.

```
(13)  main( )
      {
          char str[ ] = "Limericks" ;
          char *s ;
          s = &str[6] - 6 ;
          while ( *s )
              printf ( "%c", *s++ ) ;
      }
```

Output

Limericks

Explanation

The following figure would help in analyzing this program.

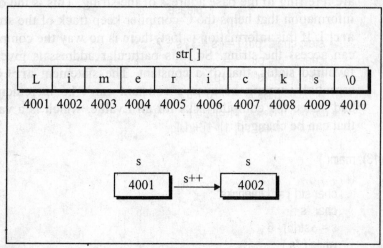

Figure 3.4

s has been declared as a pointer to a **char**, whereas **str[ ]** has been declared as a character string. Let us now evaluate the expression **&str[6] - 6**. Here **&str[6]** gives the address of the sixth element of the string. This address can also be obtained by the expression **str + 6**. On subtracting 6 from this, we end up with good old **str**, the address of the zeroth element, which is assigned to **s**.

In the **printf( )**, the value at address contained in **s** is printed, and then **s** gets incremented so that it points to the next character in the string. The **while** loop continues till **s** doesn't point to '\0', which marks the end of the string. When **s** points to '\0', the value of ***s** would be 0, a falsity. Hence the **while** loop will be terminated.

```
(14)  main( )
      {
          static char *s[ ] = {
                              "ice",
                              "green",
                              "cone",
```

```
                    "please"
                } ;
    staic char **ptr[ ] = { s + 3 , s + 2 , s + 1 , s } ;
    char ***p = ptr ;
    printf ( "\n%s" , **++p ) ;
    printf ( "\n%s" , *--*++p + 3 ) ;
    printf ( "\n%s" , *p[-2] + 3 ) ;
    printf ( "\n%s" , p[-1][-1] + 1 ) ;
}
```

Output

cone

ase
reen

Explanation

This time we seem to be faced with a galaxy of stars! We would do well to take the help of a figure in crossing them one by one. At the outset, **s[ ]** has been declared and initialised as an array of pointers. Simply saying **s** gives us the base address of this array, 4006 as can be seen from Figure 3.5. **ptr[ ]** stores the addresses of the locations where the base addresses of strings comprising **s[ ]** have been stored, starting with the last string. To put it more clearly, **ptr[0]** stores the address 4012, which is the address at which base address of the string "please" is stored. Similarly, **ptr[1]** stores the address 4010, which is where the base address of the string "cone" is stored, and so on. Since **ptr[ ]** essentially stores addresses of addresses, each element of it is a pointer to a pointer, and has been declared as such using ******.

Finally, the base address of **ptr[ ]** is assigned to a pointer to a pointer to a pointer, **p**. Reeling?! Going through the figure would decidedly aid you to get disentangled. Thus, **p** is assigned the address 6020.

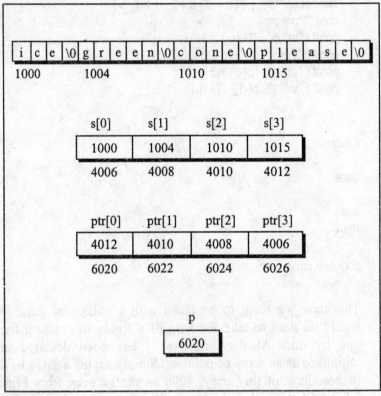

Figure 3.5

Having sorted out what is present where, we now proceed to the **printf( )**s. Let us tackle the expressions one by one.

**++p

The first one prints out the string starting from the address ****++p**. The ++ goes to work first and increments **p** not to 6021, but to 6022. The C compiler has been made to understand that on incrementing a pointer variable, it is to point to the next location of its type. The words 'of its type' hold significance here, A pointer to a **char** on incrementing goes one byte further, since a **char** is a 1-byte entity. A pointer to an **int** points 2 bytes further, as an **int** is a 2-byte entity. Also, a pointer by itself is always a 2-byte entity, so incrementing a pointer to a pointer would advance you by 2 bytes.

Having convinced ourselves that **p** now stores 6022, we go on to evaluate the expression further. ***p** signifies contents of 6022, i.e. 4010. ****p** means value at this address, i.e. value at 4010, which is the address 1010. The **printf( )** prints the string at this address, which is "cone".

--++p + 3

p, presently contains 6022, which on incrementing becomes 6024. Value at this address is the address 4008, or in terms of **s, s + 1**. On this the decrement operator -- works to give 4006, i.e. **s**. Value at 4006, or ***(s)** is 1000. Thus the expression is now reduced to (1000 + 3), and what finally gets passed to ̞rintf( ) is the address 1003. Value at this address is a '\0', as at the end of every string a '\0' is inserted automatically. This '\0' is printed out as a blank by **printf( )**.

*p[-2] + 3

The current address in **p** is 6024. ***p[-2]** can be thought of as ***(*(p - 2))**, as **num[i]** is same as ***(num + i)**. This in turn evaluates as ***(*(6024 - 2))**, i.e. ***(*(6020))**, as **p** is a pointer to a pointer. This is equal to ***(4012)**, as at 6020 the address 4012 is present. Value at 4012 is 1015, i.e. the base address of the fourth string, "please". Having reached the address of letter 'p', 3 is added, which yields the address 1018. The string starting from 1018 is printed out, which comprises of the last three letters of "please", i.e. 'ase'.

p[-1][-1] + 1

The above expression can be thought of as ***(p[-1] - 1) + 1**, as **num[i]** and ***(num + i)** amounts to the same thing. Further, **p[-1]** can itself be simplified to ***(p - 1)**. Hence we can interpret the given expression as ***(*(p - 1) - 1) + 1**. Now let us evaluate this expression.

After the execution of the third **printf( )**, **p** still holds the address 6024. ***(6024 - 1)** gives ***(6022)**, i.e. address 4010. Therefore the expression now becomes ***(4010 - 1) + 1**. Looking at the figure you would agree that 4010 can be expressed as **s + 2**. So now the expression becomes ***(s + 2 - 1) + 1** or ***(s + 1) + 1**. Once again the figure would confirm that ***(s + 1)** evaluates to ***(4008)** and ***(4008)** yields 1004, which is the base address of the second string "green". To this, 1 is added to yield the address of the first element, 'r'. With this as the starting address, **printf( )** prints out what is remaining of the string "green".

(15) main( )
```
{
    char str[ ] = "For your eyes only" ;
    int i ;
    char *p ;
    for ( p = str, i = 0 ; p + i <= str + strlen ( str ) ; p++, i++ )
        printf ( "%c", *( p + i ) ) ;
}
```

Output

Fryu ysol<space>

Explanation

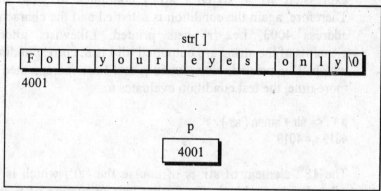

Figure 3.6

The **for** loop here hosts two initialisations and two increments, which is perfectly acceptable. However, there must always be a unique test condition.

In the initialisation part, **p** is assigned the base address of the string, and **i** is set to 0. Next the condition is tested. Let us isolate this condition for closer examination.

p + i <= str + strlen (str)

Since length of **str[ ]** is 18, **str + strlen (str)** would give the address of '\0' present at the end of the string. If we assume that the base address of the string is 4001, then the address of '\0' would be 4019. Since **p** has been assigned the base address of the string, in the first go, **p + 0** would yield 4001. Since this is less than 4019, the condition holds good, and the character present at the address (**p + 0**), i.e. 'F', is printed out. This can be understood better with the aid of the Figure 3.6.

After this, both **p** and **i** are incremented, so that **p** contains 4002 and **i** contains 1, and once again the condition in the **for** loop is tested. This time (**p + i**) yields 4003, whereas the expression **str + strlen (str)** continues to yield 4019. Therefore, again the condition is satisfied and the character at address 4003, i.e. 'r' gets printed. Likewise, alternate elements of the string are outputted till **i** is 8, corresponding to which 'l' is printed. Now, when **p** and **i** are incremented one more time, the test condition evaluates to:

```
p + i <= str + strlen ( str )
4019 <= 4019
```

The 18th element of **str** is of course the '\0', which is also printed out as a blank. On further incrementation of **p** and **i**, control snaps out of the **for** and the program execution is terminated.

```
(16) main( )
     {
         char str[ ] = "MalayalaM" ;
         char *s ;
         s = str + 8 ;
         while ( s >= str )
         {
             printf ( "%c", *s ) ;
             s-- ;
         }
     }
```

Output

MalayalaM

Explanation

s, a pointer to a **char**, is assigned an address 8 locations ahead of the base address of the string. That means **s** is currently pointing to the last element 'M' of the string. If we assume the base address to be 4001, then **s** would contain the address 4009. Since this address is greater than the base address, first time through the loop the condition is satisfied. Next the value of the expression ***s** is printed. Since **s** contains the address 4009, the value at this address, i.e. 'M', gets printed. Then **s** is decremented to point to the preceding element, i.e. the element at address 4008.

This way one by one, the elements of the string are printed out in the reverse order, till **s** equals **str**, the address of the zeroth element. That the output is indeed the reverse of the original string can be verified if you read "MalayalaM" backwards. You have been presented with a string that reads the same from either end. Such strings, incidentally, go by the name 'Palindrome'.

(17) main( )
```
{
    char a[ ] = "Able was I ere I saw elbA" ;
    char *t, *s, *b ;
    s = a ;
    b = a + strlen ( a ) - 1 ;
    t = b ;
    while ( s != t )
    {
        printf ( "%c", *s ) ;
        s++ ;
        printf ( "%c", *t ) ;
        t-- ;
    }
}
```

Output

AAbbllee wwaass ll ee

Explanation

The **char** pointer **s** is assigned the base address of string **a[ ]**. The **char** pointer **b** is assigned the address 24 elements ahead of the base address. Why 24? Because the function **strlen(a)** yields the length of the string **a[ ]**, which in this case turns out to be 25. Thus **b** points to 'A' present at the end of the string. Another character pointer, **t**, is also initialised to the same value as **b**. Assuming the base address of the string to be 5001, **s** would be assigned 5001 and **b** and **t** would be assigned the address 5025.

Naturally, first time through the **while** loop since **s** and **t** are not equal, the condition is satisfied. Hence the **printf( )** prints out the character at which **s** is pointing. Thus the character 'A' gets printed. Now **s** is incremented, so that it points to the character 'b'. The next **printf( )** prints the value at the address contained in **t**. Therefore another 'A' appears on the screen. After printing, **t** is decremented so that it starts pointing to 'b'. This goes on till **s** and **t** meet each other, whence the **while** ends. At this instance, **s** and **t** both are pointing to 'r', the middle character of the entire string.

```
(18)  main( )
      {
          char s[ ] = "C is a philosophy of life" ;
          char t[40] ;
          char *ss, *tt ;
          ss = s ;
          tt = t ;
          while ( *ss )
              *tt++ = *ss++ ;
          *tt = '\0' ;
          printf ( "\n%s", t ) ;
      }
```

Output

C is a philosophy of life

Explanation

To begin with, **ss** and **tt** are assigned the base addresses of the two strings s[ ] and t[ ]. In the **while**, the value at address contained in **ss** is tested for operating the loop. The first time through the loop **ss** contains the base address of the string. Hence ***ss** gives 'C', whose ASCII value is 67. As any non-zero value is a truth value, the condition evaluates to true, and this value is stored at the address contained in **tt**, i.e. at the base address of the string t[ ]. Note that the **++** operator occurs after the variables, so after 'C' has been stored in the first location of the string t[ ], both **ss** and **tt** are incremented, so that both now point to the first elements of s[ ] and t[ ] respectively. In the second go, value at the address contained in **ss** is tested in the **while**, and this time a blank is encountered, whose ASCII value is 32. The condition again holds good, therefore the blank is stored in string t[ ], and **ss** and **tt** are incremented. This goes on till the end of the string is encountered. At the end of any string, a '\0' is stored. ASCII value of '\0' is 0, which when tested in the **while**, evaluates to falsity, and the control comes out of the loop.

Note that the '\0' has not been stored into string t[ ], hence the compiler does not know where the string ends. We do so by inserting a '\0' on leaving the **while**. Finally, the contents of the string t[ ] are printed out.

(19) main( )
```
{
    char s[ ]= "Lumps, bumps, swollen veins, new pains";
    char t[40] ;
    char *ss, *tt ;
    tt = t ;
    ss = s ;
```

```
    while ( *tt++ = *ss++ ) ;
    printf ( "\n%s", t ) ;
}
```

Output

Lumps, bumps, swollen veins, new pains

Explanation

The program begins by assigning the base addresses of strings
s[ ] and **t[ ]** to the character pointers **ss** and **tt**. The **while** loop
that follows next may raise a few eyebrows. We have made it
compact by combining the assignment, test condition and the
incrementation in the **while** loop itself. In effect, the **while** has
been reduced to:

```
while ( *tt++ = *ss++ )
    ;
```

Here the null statement is executed so long as the condition
remains true. How the condition is evaluated is like this...

In the **while** the value at the address stored in **ss** replaces the
value at the address stored in **tt**. After assignment the test is
carried out to decide whether the **while** loop should continue
or not. This is done by testing the expression ***tt** for
truth/falsity. Since currently **tt** is pointing to 'l' of 'lumps', ***tt**
gives 'l' which is a truth-value. Following this **ss** and **tt** both
are incremented, so that they have the addresses of the first
elements of strings **s[ ]** and **t[ ]** respectively. Since the
condition has been satisfied the null statement is executed.
This goes on till the end of the string **s[ ]** is encountered,
which is marked by the presence of a '\0', having ASCII
value 0. When this character is stored in **t[ ]**, ***tt** would give
'\0'. This time when the condition is tested, it evaluates to

false since ***tt** yields a 0 (ASCII value of '\0'). Thus, all elements of the first string are faithfully copied into the second one, including the '\0'. On printing out string **t[ ]**, we get the entire string as it was in **s[ ]**.

(20)
```
main( )
{
    int arr[12] ;
    printf ( "\n%d", sizeof ( arr ) ) ;
}
```

Output

24

Explanation

The **sizeof( )** operator gives the size of its argument. As **arr[ ]** is an integer array of 12 elements, saying **sizeof (arr)** gives us the size of this array. Each integer is 2 bytes long, hence the array **arr[ ]** engages twice the number of elements, i.e. 24 bytes.

(21)
```
main( )
{
    char *mess[ ] = {
                        "Some love one",
                        "Some love two",
                        "I love one",
                        "That is you"
                    } ;
    printf ( "\n%d %d", sizeof ( mess ), sizeof ( mess [1] ) ) ;
}
```

Output

8 2

Explanation

mess[ ] has been declared as an array of pointers to strings.
This signifies that the array **mess[ ]** stores the starting
addresses of the four strings initialised in the program.
mess[0] has the starting address of the string "Some love
one", **mess[1]** the starting address of the second string "Some
love two" and so on. As each address is 2 bytes long, four
base addresses need 8 bytes, hence the array **mess[ ]** is 8 bytes
long.

The **sizeof( )** operator gives the size of the datatype that is
supplied as its argument. Therefore, **sizeof (mess)** is reported
as 8.

mess[1], the first element of the array of pointers stores an
address, which is invariably 2 bytes long. Therefore **printf( )**
reports **sizeof (mess[1])** as 2.

(22) main( )

```
main( )
{
    char names[3][20] ;
    int i ;
    for ( i = 0 ; i <= 2 ; i++ )
    {
        printf ( "\nENTER NAME: " ) ;
        scanf ( "%s", names[i] ) ;
        printf ( "You entered %s", names[i] ) ;
    }
}
```

Output

ENTER NAME: Parag
You entered Parag

ENTER NAME: Veenu
You entered Veenu
ENTER NAME: Jaina
You entered Jaina

Explanation

names[3][20] has been declared as a two-dimensional array of characters. We can think of it as an array of 3 elements, each element itself being an array of 20 characters.

Let the base address of the 2-D array, i.e. names be 4001. In the **scanf( )** and **printf( )** statements, **names[i]** refers to the address of the **i**[th] string in the array. **names[0]** refers to the zeroth element of the 2-D array, or the base address of the string of characters starting from 4001. **names[1]** denotes the address of the first element of the 2-D array, which is 20 bytes ahead, i.e. 4021, and so on.

Assured that **names[i]** stands for the base address of the **i**[th] string, we proceed to see what actually is going on in this program.

The first time through the **for** loop, when you are prompted "ENTER NAME:", say you entered 'Parag'. The **scanf( )** accepts this name and stores it at the address given by **names[0]**. The **printf( )** immediately reads from the same address **name[0]**, and prints the name starting at this address on to the screen. This is repeated by incrementing the value of **i** each time through the loop. When **i** is incremented for the third time, the process is terminated.

```
(23)  main( )
      {
          char names[5][20] = {
                                  "Roshni",
```

```
                              "Manish",
                              "Mona",
                              "Baiju",
                              "Ritu"
                     } ;
    int i ;
    char *t ;
    t = names[3] ;
    names[3] = names[4] ;
    names[4] = t ;
    for ( i = 0 ; i <= 4 ; i++ )
        printf ( "\n%s", names[i] ) ;
}
```

Output

Error message: Lvalue required in function main

Explanation

Apparently, what the program attempts to do is interchange the addresses stored in **names[3]** and **names[4]** using an auxiliary variable **t**. Sounds straight forward, but is essentially against the very concept of how the C compiler deals with strings. The compiler keeps track of any string by remembering only the base address of the string. So it has its reservations when it comes to changing this information, as it anticipates that there would be no one to blame but itself once this information is waylaid and we demand an access to the string later. And this is what is being attempted in the statement **names[3] = names[4]**. Here we are trying to change the base address stored in **names[3]**. As said earlier, this will not be allowed. Thus the starting address of a string is an indelible entity, in no way an Lvalue, which is a value that can change. Hence the error message.

```
(24)  main( )
      {
          char mess[8][30] = {
                                  "Don't walk in front of me ...",
                                  "I may not follow ;",
                                  "Don't walk behind me ...",
                                  "I may not lead ;",
                                  "Just walk beside me ...",
                                  "And be my friend."
                              };
          printf ( "\n%c %c", *( mess[2] + 9 ), *( *( mess + 2 ) + 9 ) );
      }
```

Output

k k

Explanation

The two-dimensional array comprises of one-dimensional arrays, each of which is 30 characters long. We know, **mess[2][9]** refers to the 9th element of the 2nd 1-D array.

Recall that **mess[2]** would give the base address of the second string. If this address turns out to be 4001, then the expression **mess[2] + 9** would become (4001 + 9), which would give the address of the ninth character from the address 4001. This address happens to be the address of the letter 'k' in the string "Don't walk behind me". Hence this letter 'k' can be accessed by the expression *(mess[2] + 9). But we already know that whenever we use the notation **mess[2]**, it is internally converted to *(mess + 2) by the compiler. Therefore *(mess[2] + 9) can also be expressed as *(*(mess + 2) + 9).

Thus, **mess[2][9]**, *(mess[2] + 9) and *(*(mess + 2) + 9) are one and the same, i.e. the 9th element of the 2nd string in the array. The same array element can thus be accessed in any of these three ways. The **printf( )** on execution outputs the letter 'k' twice.

[B] Answer the following:

(1) Is the following program correct? <Yes/No>

```
main( )
{
    char *str1 = "United" ;
    char *str2 = "Front" ;
    char *str3 ;
    str3 = strcat ( str1, str2 ) ;
    printf ( "\n%s", str3 ) ;
}
```

Explanation

No, since what is present in memory beyond "United" is not known and we are attaching "Front" at the end of "United", thereby overwriting something, which is an unsafe thing to do.

(2) How would you improve the code in (2) above?

Explanation

```
main( )
{
    char str1[15] = "United" ;
    char *str2 = "Front" ;
    char *str3 ;
    str3 = strcat ( str1, str2 ) ;
    printf ( "\n%s", str3 ) ;
}
```

(3) In the following code which function would get called, the user-defined **strcpy( )** or the one in the standard library?

```
#include <string.h>
main( )
{
    char str1[ ] = "Keep India Beautiful...  emigrate!" ;
    char str2[40] ;
    strcpy ( str2, str1 ) ;
    printf ( "\n%s", str2 ) ;
}

strcpy ( char *t, char *s )
{
    while ( *s )
    {
        *t = *s ;
        t++ ;
        s++ ;
    }
    *t = '\0' ;
}
```

Explanation

User-defined **strcpy( )**

(4) Can you compact the code of **strcpy( )** given in (3) above into one line?

Explanation

```
strcpy ( char *t, char *s )
{
    while ( *t++ = *s++ ) ;
```

}

(5) How would you find the length of each string in the program [A](9) above?

Explanation

```
main( )
{
    char *str[ ] = { "Frogs", "Do", "Not", "Die.", "They", "Croak!" } ;
    int i :

    for ( i = 0 ; i <= 5 ; i++ )
        printf ( "\n%s %d", str[i], strlen ( str[i] ) ) ;
}
```

(6) Would the following code compile successfully?

```
main( )
{
    printf ( "%c"  7[ "Sundaram" ] ) ;
}
```

Explanation

Yes. It would print 'm' of "Sundaram".

(7) What is the difference in the following declarations?

```
char *p = "Samuel" ;
char a[ ] = "Samuel" ;
```

Explanation

Here **a** is an array big enough to hold the message and the '\0' following the message. Individual characters within the array can be changed but the address of the array would remain same.

On the other hand, **p** is a pointer, initialized to point to a string constant. The pointer **p** may be modified to point to another string, but if you attempt to modify the string at which **p** is pointing the result is undefined.

(8) While handling a string do we always have to process it character by character or there exists a method to process the entire string as one unit.

Explanation

A string can be processed only on a character by character basis.

Exercise

[A] Attempt the following:

(1) Write a function **xstrchr( )** which scans a string from beginning to end in search of a character. If the character is found it should return a pointer to the first occurrence of the given character in the string. If the given character is not found in the string, the function should return a NULL. The prototype of the function would be:

char * xstrchr (char *string, char ch) ;

(2) Write a function **xstrstr( )** that will scan a string for the occurrence of a given sub-string. The prototype of the function would be:

char * xstrstr (char *string1, char *string2) ;

The function should return a pointer to the element in **string1** where **string2** begins. If **string2** doesn't occur in **string1** then **xstrstr( )** should return a NULL.

For example, if **string1** is "somewhere over the rainbow", and **string2** is "over" then **xstrstr( )** should return address of 'o' in **string1**.

(3) Suppose 7 names are stored in an array of pointers **names[ ]** as shown below:

char *names[ ] = {

        "Santosh",
        "Amol",
        "Santosh Jain",
        "Kishore",
        "Rahul",
        "Amolkumar",
        "Hemant"

    } ;

Write a program to arrange these names in alphabetical order.

(4) Write a program to compress any given string such that the multiple blanks present in it are eliminated. Store the compressed message in another string. Also write a decompressant program to get back the original string with all its spaces restored.

The uncompressed string can be:

"Imperial Palace. Rome. Attention Julius Caesar. Dear Caesar, we have the clarification you   requested. Details to follow by courier. Meanwhile   stay clear of   Brutus."

(5) Write a program to encode any given string such that it gets converted into an unrecognizable form. Also write a decode function to get back the original string. Try to make the encryption scheme as difficult to break as possible.

[B] What will be the output of the following programs:

(1)
```
main( )
{
    char string[ ] = "OddLengthString" ;
    char *ptr1 = string, *ptr2 = string + sizeof ( string ) - 1;
    int i ;

    for ( i = 0 ; ptr1 != ptr2 ; i++ )
    {
        ++ptr1 ;
        --ptr2 ;
    }
    printf ( "%d", i ) ;
}
```

(2)
```
main( )
{
    static char str1[ ] = "Good" ;
```

```
            static char str2[20] ;
            static char str3[20] = "Day" ;
            int l ;

            l = strcmp ( strcat ( str3, strcpy ( str2, str1 ) ), strcat (
                                str3, "good" ) ) ;
            printf ( "%d", l ) ;
        }

(3)    main( )
        {
            char str [ ] = "Way of trouble is out through it" ;
            int i ;

            for ( i = 0 ; i <= 3 ; i++ )
                printf ( "%c", *( str + i ) ) ;
            for ( i = 0 ; i <= 3 ; i++ )
                printf ( "%c", *( str + 18 + i ) ) ;
            for ( i = 0 ; i <= 13 ; i++ )
                printf ( "%c", *( str + 4 + i ) ) ;
            for ( i = 0 ; i <= 9 ; i++ )
                printf ( "%c", *( str + 22 + i ) ) ;
        }

(4)    main( )
        {
            char s[ ] = "C a of " ;
            char t[ ] = "is philosophy life" ;
            char u[40] ;
            char *ss = s, *tt = t, *uu = u ;

            while ( *ss || *tt )
            {
                while ( *ss )
                {
                    if ( ( *uu++ = *ss++ ) == ' ' )
                        break ;
                }
```

```
            while ( *tt )
            {
                if ( ( *uu++ = *tt++ ) == ' ' )
                    break ;
            }
        }
        *uu = '\0' ;
        puts ( u ) ;
    }

(5)  main( )
    {
        char a[2][2][25] = {
                                {
                                    "Jack and Jill",
                                    "Went up the hill"
                                },
                                {
                                    "Jack fell down",
                                    "And broke his crown"
                                }
                            };
        printf ( "\n%s %s %s %s", &a[0][0][9], &a[0][1][12],
                                &a[1][0][10], &a[1][1][14] ) ;
    }
```

An expert C Programmer is one who avoids all errors except those related with pointers.

4 *Pointers and Structures*

hile handling real world data, we usually deal with a collection of **int**s, **char**s and **float**s rather than isolated entities. For example, an entity we call a 'book' is a collection of things like a title, an author, a call number, a publisher, number of pages, date of publication, price, etc. As you can see, all this data is dissimilar; author is a string, price is a **float**, whereas number of pages is an **int**. For dealing with such collections, C provides a data type called 'structure'. A structure gathers together different atoms of information that form a given entity.

Look at the following program that combines dissimilar data types into an entity called structure.

```
/* Program 48 */
main( )
{
    struct account
```

```
{
    int no ;
    char acc_name[15] ;
    float bal ;
} ;
struct account a1, a2, a3 ;

printf ( "\nEnter account nos., names, and balances\n" ) ;
scanf ( "%d %s %f", &a1.no, a1.acc_name, &a1.bal ) ;
scanf ( "%d %s %f", &a2.no, a2.acc_name, &a2.bal ) ;
scanf ( "%d %s %f", &a3.no, a3.acc_name, &a3.bal ) ;

printf ( "\n%d %s %f", a1.no, a1.acc_name, a1.bal ) ;
printf ( "\n%d %s %f", a2.no, a2.acc_name, a2.bal ) ;
printf ( "\n%d %s %f", a3.no, a3.acc_name, a3.bal ) ;
}
```

Now a few tips about the program:

(a) The declaration at the beginning of the program combines dissimilar data types into a single entity called **struct account**. Here **struct** is a keyword, **account** is the structure name, and the dissimilar data types are structure elements.

(b) **a1, a2** and **a3** are structure variables of the type **struct account**.

(c) The structure elements are accessed using a '.' operator. So to refer **no** we use **a1.no** and to refer to **acc_name** we use **a1.acc_name**. Before the dot there must always be a structure variable and after the dot there must always be a structure element.

(d) Since **a1.acc_name** is a string, its base address can be obtained just by mentioning **a1.acc_name**. Hence the 'address of' operator **&** has been dropped while receiving the account name in **scanf( )**.

(e) The structure elements are always arranged in contiguous memory locations. This arrangement is shown in the following figure.

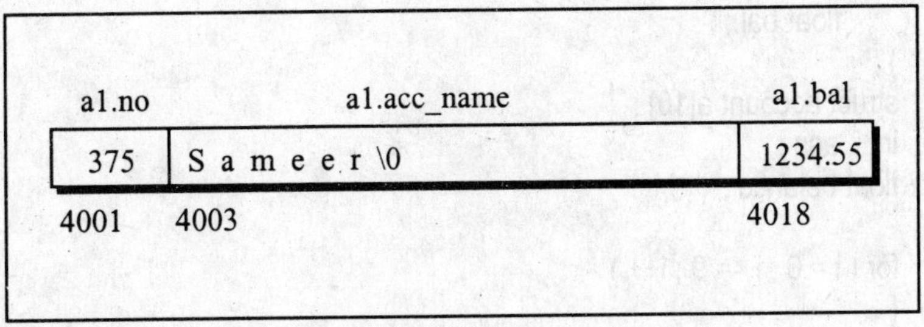

a1.no	a1.acc_name	a1.bal
375	S a m e e r \0	1234.55
4001	4003	4018

Figure 4.1 Structure elements in memory

An Array of Structures

In the above example if we were to store data of 100 accounts, we would be required to use 100 different structure variables from **a1** to **a100**, which is definitely not very convenient. A better approach would be to use an array of structures. The arrangement of the array of structures in memory is shown in the following figure.

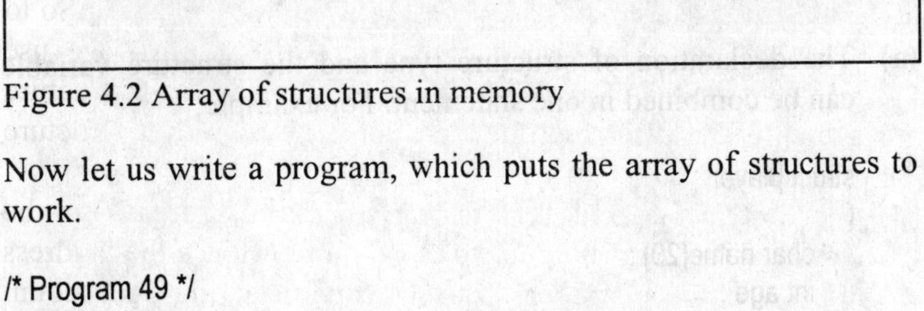

a[0].no	a[0].bal	a[1].no	a[1].bal		a[9].no	a[9].bal.
007	2000.55	134	4892.30	......	122	6432.90
4000	4002	4006	4008		4054	4056

Figure 4.2 Array of structures in memory

Now let us write a program, which puts the array of structures to work.

```
/* Program 49 */
main( )
{
    struct account
    {
```

```
        int no ;
        float bal ;
    } ;
    struct account a[10] ;
    int i, acc ;
    float balance ;

    for ( i = 0 ; i <= 9 ; i++ )
    {
        printf ( "\nEnter account no. and balance: " ) ;
        scanf ( "%d %f", &acc, &balance ) ;
        a[i].no = acc ;   a[i].bal = balance ;
        printf ( "%d %f", a[i].no, a[i].bal ) ;
    }
}
```

As you can see the structure elements are still accessed using the
'.' operator, and the array elements using the usual subscript
notation.

More about Structures

Let us now explore the intricacies of structures with a view of
programming convenience.

(a) The declaration of structure type and the structure variable
    can be combined in one statement. For example,

```
    struct player
    {
        char name[20] ;
        int age ;
    } ;
    struct player p1 = { "Nick Yates", 30 } ;
```

    is same as...

```
struct player
{
    char name[20] ;
    int age ;
} p1 = { "Nick Yates", 30 } ;
```

or even...

```
struct
{
    char name[20] ;
    int age ;
} p1 = { "Nick Yates", 30 } ;
```

(b) The value of one structure variable can be assigned to another structure variable of the same type using the assignment operator. It is not necessary to copy the structure elements piece-meal. For example,

```
struct player
{
    char name[20] ;
    int age ;
} ;
struct player p2, p1 = { "Nick Yates", 30 } ;
p2 = p1 ;
```

(c) One structure can be nested within another structure as shown below.

```
struct part
{
    char type ;
    int qty ;
} ;
struct vehicle
{
    char maruti[20] ;
```

```
        struct part bolt ;
} ;
struct vehicle v ;
v.bolt.qty = 300 ;
```

(d) Like an ordinary variable, a structure variable can also be passed to a function. We may either pass individual structure elements or the entire structure at one go. If need be we can also pass addresses of structure elements or address of a structure variable as shown below.

```
struct player
{
    char nam[20] ;
    int age ;
} ;
struct player p1 = { "Nick Yates", 30 } ;
display ( p1.nam, p1.age ) ;  /* passing individual elements */
show ( p1 ) ;  /* passing structure variable */
d ( p1.nam, &p1.age ) ;  /* passing addresses of structure elements */
print ( &p1 ) ;  /* passing address of structure variable */
```

Structure Pointers

The way we can have a pointer pointing to an **int**, or a pointer pointing to a **char**, similarly we can have a pointer pointing to a **struct**. Such pointers are known as 'structure pointers'. Let us look at a program, which demonstrates the usage of these pointers.

```
/* Program 50 */
main( )
{
    struct book
    {
        char name[25] ;
        char author[25] ;
        int callno ;
```

```
};
struct book b1 = { "Let us C", "YPK", 101 };
struct book *ptr ;

ptr = &b1 ;
printf ( "%s %s %d\n", b1.name, b1.author, b1.callno ) ;
printf ( "%s %s %d\n", ptr -> name, ptr -> author, ptr -> callno ) ;
}
```

The first **printf( )** is as usual. The second **printf( )** however is peculiar. We can't use **ptr.name** or **ptr.callno** because **ptr** is not a structure variable but a pointer to a structure, and the dot operator requires a structure variable on its left. In such cases C provides an operator **->**, called an arrow operator to refer to the structure elements. Remember that on the left hand side of the '.' structure operator, there must always be a structure variable, whereas on the left hand side of the **->** operator there must always be a pointer to a structure. The arrangement of the structure variable and pointer to structure in memory is shown in the figure given below.

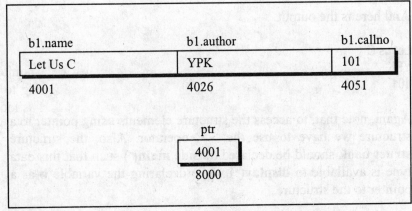

Figure 4.3

Can we not pass the address of a structure variable to a function? We can. The following program demonstrates this.

```
/* Program 51 */
/* Passing address of a structure variable */
struct book
{
    char name[25] ;
    char author[25] ;
    int callno ;
} ;

main( )
{
    void display ( struct book * ) ;
    struct book b1 = { "Let us C", "YPK", 101 } ;
    display ( &b1 ) ;
}

void display ( struct book *b )  /* b is a pointer to a structure */
{
    printf ( "\n%s\n%s\n%d", b->name, b->author, b->callno ) ;
}
```

And here is the output...

```
Let us C
YPK
101
```

Again, note that, to access the structure elements using pointer to a structure we have to use the '->' operator. Also, the structure **struct book** should be declared outside **main( )** such that this data type is available to **display( )** while declaring the variable **b** as a pointer to the structure.

Offsets of Structure Elements

Consider the following structure:

```
struct a
{
    struct b
    {
        int i ;
        float f ;
        char ch ;
    } x ;
    struct c
    {
        int j ;
        float g ;
        char ch ;
    } y ;
} z ;
```

Suppose we make a call to a function as shown below:

```
fun ( &z.y ) ;
```

In the function **fun( )** can we access the elements of structure **b** through the address of **z.y**? We can. For this we need to first find out the offset of **j**. Using this offset we can find out address where **x** begins in memory. Once we get this address we can have an access to elements **i, f** and **ch**. This is shown in the following program.

```
/* Program 52 */
struct a
{
    struct b
    {
        int i ;
        float f ;
        char ch ;
    } x ;
```

```
        struct c
        {
            int j ;
            float g ;
            char ch ;
        } y ;
} ;

main( )
{
    int *p ;
    struct a z ;

    clrscr( ) ;
    fun ( &z.y ) ;
    printf ( "\n%d %f %c", z.x.i, z.x.f, z.x.ch ) ;
    getch( ) ;
}

fun ( struct c * p )
{
    int offset ;
    struct b * address ;

    offset = ( char * ) & ( ( struct c * ) ( & ( ( struct a * ) 0 ) -> y ) -> j )
                                - ( char * ) ( ( struct a * ) 0 ) ;
    address = ( struct b * )( ( char * ) & ( p -> j ) - offset ) ;
    address -> i = 400 ;
    address -> f = 3.14 ;
    address -> ch = 'c' ;
}
```

In the above program structures **b** and **c** having members **i, f, ch** and **j, g, ch** are nested within the structure **a** with structure variables **x** and **y** of structure **b** and **c** respectively. Next we have called the function **fun( )** with the base address of the structure variable **y**. Now from **fun( )**, we wish to access the members of

structure variable **x**. But, since **fun( )** has been passed a pointer to structure **c**, we do not have direct access to elements of **x**. The solution is to calculate the offset of the first member of **y**, in our case, **j**. This has been achieved through the statement:

offset = (char *) & ((struct c *) (& ((struct a *) 0) -> y) -> j) (char *) ((struct a *) 0) ;

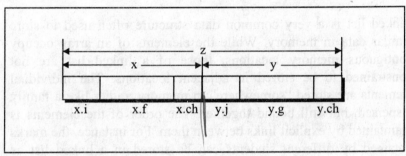

Figure 4.4

Let us understand this statement part by part.

In the expression **((struct a *) 0)**, 0 is being typecasted into pointer to **struct a**. This expression is pretending that there is a variable of type **struct a** at address 0. The expression **& (((struct a *) 0) -> y)** gives the address of structure variable **y**. But this is not the base address of the structure **c**. Hence we have typecasted it using **struct c ***. Using this address we can access the member **j** of the structure variable **y**. Finally, after taking the address of member **j**, we have typecasted it using **char *** to make the subtraction possible. The statement to the right of the '-' operator is straightforward. On subtraction, we get the offset of member **j** of structure variable **y**. Now using offset the base address is calculated through the following statement:

address = (struct b *) ((char *) & (p -> j) - offset) ;

In the above statement **& (p -> j)** gives the address of member **j** of structure variable **y**. Subtracting offset from this yields the address of structure variable **x**. Using this address, we have stored the values in the member variables **i, f** and **ch**. Back into **main( )**, we have printed these values using **printf( )**.

Linked Lists

Linked list is a very common data structure often used to store similar data in memory. While the elements of an array occupy contiguous memory locations, those of a linked list are not constrained to be stored in adjacent locations. The individual elements are stored "somewhere" in memory, rather like a family dispersed, but still bound together. The order of the elements is maintained by explicit links between them. For instance, the marks obtained by different students can be stored in a linked list as shown in Figure 4.5.

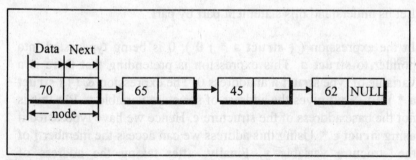

Figure 4.5

Observe that the linked list is a collection of elements called nodes, each of which stores two items of information—an element of the list and a link. A link is a pointer or an address that indicates explicitly the location of the node containing the successor of the list element. In Figure 4.5, the arrows represent the links. The **Data** part of each node consists of the marks obtained by a student and the **Next** part is a pointer to the next node. The NULL in the last node indicates that this is the last node in the list.

There are several operations that we can think of performing on linked lists. The following program shows how to build a linked list by adding new nodes at the beginning, at the end or in the middle of the linked list. It also contains a function **display( )** which displays all the nodes present in the linked list and a function **delete( )** which can delete any node in the linked list. Go through the program carefully, a step at a time.

```
/* Program 53 */
/* Program to maintain a linked list */
#include "alloc.h"

/* structure containing a data part and link part */
struct node
{
    int data ;
    struct node *link ;
};
main( )
{
    struct node *p ;
    p = NULL ;  /* empty linked list */

    printf ( "\nNo. of elements in the Linked List = %d", count ( p ) ) ;
    append ( &p, 1 ) ;
    append ( &p, 2 ) ;
    append ( &p, 3 ) ;
    append ( &p, 4 ) ;
    append ( &p, 17 ) ;

    clrscr( ) ;
    display ( p ) ;

    addatbeg ( &p, 999 ) ;
```

```
    addatbeg ( &p, 888 ) ;
    addatbeg ( &p, 777 ) ;

    display ( p ) ;

    addafter ( p, 7, 0 ) ;
    addafter ( p, 2, 1 ) ;
    addafter ( p, 1, 99 ) ;

    display ( p ) ;
    printf ( "\nNo. of elements in the Linked List = %d", count ( p ) ) ;

    delete ( &p, 888 ) ;
    delete ( &p, 1 ) ;
    delete ( &p, 10 ) ;

    display ( p ) ;
    printf ( "\nNo. of elements in the linked list = %d", count ( p ) ) ;
}

/* adds a node at the end of a linked list */
append ( struct node **q, int num )
{
    struct node *temp, *r ;
    temp = *q ;

    if ( *q == NULL ) /* if the list is empty, create first node */
    {
        temp = malloc ( sizeof ( struct node ) ) ;
        temp -> data = num ;
        temp -> link = NULL ;
        *q = temp ;
    }
    else
    {
        temp = *q ;

        /* go to last node */
```

```
            while ( temp -> link != NULL )
                temp = temp -> link ;

            /* add node at the end */
            r = malloc ( sizeof ( struct node ) ) ;
            r -> data = num ;
            r -> link = NULL ;
            temp -> link = r ;
    }
}

/* adds a new node at the beginning of the linked list */
addatbeg ( struct node **q, int num )
{
        struct node *temp ;

        /* add new node */
        temp = malloc ( sizeof ( struct node ) ) ;

        temp -> data = num ;
        temp -> link = *q ;
        *q = temp ;
}

/* adds a new node after the specified number of nodes */
addafter ( struct node *q, int loc, int num )
{
        struct node *temp, *r ;
        int i ;

        temp = q ;
        /* skip to desired portion */
        for ( i = 0 ; i < loc ; i++ )
        {
            temp = temp -> link ;

            /* if end of linked list is encountered */
            if ( temp == NULL )
```

```
            {
                printf ( "\nThere are less than %d elements in list", loc ) ;
                return ;
            }
    }

    /* insert new node */
    r = malloc ( sizeof ( struct node ) ) ;
    r -> data = num ;
    r -> link = temp -> link ;
    temp -> link = r ;
}

/* displays the contents of the linked list */
display ( struct node *q )
{
    printf ( "\n" ) ;

    /* traverse the entire linked list */
    while ( q != NULL )
    {
        printf ( "%d ", q -> data ) ;
        q = q -> link ;
    }
}

/* counts the number of nodes present in the linked list */
count ( struct node * q )
{
    int c = 0 ;

    /* traverse the entire linked list */
    while ( q != NULL )
    {
        q = q -> link ;
        c++ ;
    }
```

```
        return c ;
}

/* deletes the specified node from the linked list */
delete ( struct node **q, int num )
{
        struct node *old, *temp ;

        temp = *q ;

        while ( temp != NULL )
        {
                if ( temp -> data == num )
                {
                        /* if node to be deleted is the first node in the linked list */
                        if ( temp == *q )
                        {
                                *q = temp -> link ;
                                /* free the memory occupied by the node */
                                free ( temp ) ;
                                return ;
                        }

                        /* deletes the intermediate nodes in the linked list */
                        else
                        {
                                old -> link = temp -> link ;
                                free ( temp ) ;
                                return ;
                        }
                }

                /* traverse the linked list till the last node is reached */
                else
                {
                        old = temp ;  /* old points to the previous node */
                        temp = temp -> link ;  /* go to the next node */
                }
```

```
    }

    printf ( "\nElement %d not found", num ) ;
}
```

To begin with we have defined a structure for a node. It contains a data part and a link part. The variable **p** has been declared as pointer to a node. We have used this pointer as pointer to the first node in the linked list. No matter how many nodes get added to the linked list, **p** would continue to pointer to the first node in the list. When no node has been added to the list, **p** has been set to NULL to indicate that the list is empty.

The **append( )** function has to deal with two situations:

(a)   The node is being added to an empty list.
(b)   The node is being added at the end of an existing list.

In the first case, the condition

```
if ( *q == NULL )
```

gets satisfied. Hence, space is allocated for the node using **malloc( )**. Data and the link part of this node are set up using the statements:

```
temp -> data = num ;
temp -> link = NULL ;
```

Lastly **p** is made to point to this node, since the first node has been added to the list and **p** must always point to the first node. Note that ***q** is nothing but equal to **p**.

In the other case, when the linked list is not empty, the condition

```
if ( *q == NULL )
```

would fail, since ***q** (i.e. **p** is non-NULL). Now **temp** is made to point to the first node in the list through the statement

temp = *q ;

Then using **temp** we have traversed through the entire linked list using the statements:

while (temp -> link != NULL)
    temp = temp -> link ;

The position of the pointers before and after traversing the linked list is shown in Figure 4.6

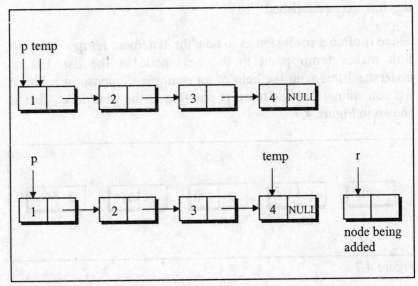

Figure 4.6

Each time through the loop the statement **temp = temp -> link** makes **temp** point to the next node in the list. When **temp** reaches the last node the condition **temp -> link != NULL** would fail. Once outside the loop we allocate space for the new node through the statement r = malloc (sizeof (struct node)) ;

Once the space has been allocated for the new node its **data** part is stuffed with **num** and the link part with NULL. Note that this node is now going to be the last Node in the list.

All that now remains to be done is connecting the previous last node with the new last node. The previous last node is being pointed to by **temp** and the new last node is being pointed to by **r**. They are connected through the statement

temp -> link = r ;

this link gets established

There is often a confusion as to how the statement **temp = temp -> link** makes **temp** point to the next node in the list. Let us understand this with the help of an example. Suppose in a linked list containing 4 nodes **temp** is pointing at the first node. This is shown in Figure 4.7.

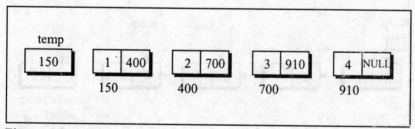

Figure 4.7

Instead of showing the links to the next node I have shown the addresses of the next node in the link part of each node.

When we execute the statement

temp = temp -> link ;

the right hand side yields 400. This address is now stored in **temp**. As a result, **temp** starts pointing to the node present at address 400. In effect the statement has shifted **temp** so that it has started pointing to the next node in the list.

Let us now understand the **addatbeg( )** function. Suppose there are already 5 nodes in the list and we wish to add a new node at the beginning of this existing linked list. This situation is shown in Figure 4.8.

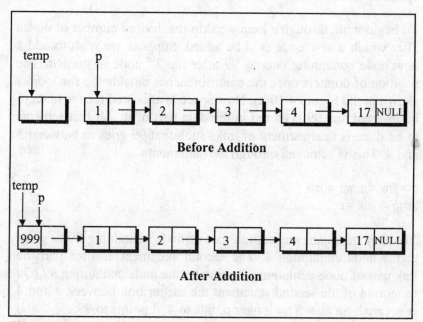

Figure 4.8

For adding a new node at the beginning, firstly space is allocated for this node and data is stored in it through the statement

temp -> data = num ;

Now we need to make the **link** part of this node point to the existing first node. This has been achieved through the statement temp -> link = *q ;

Lastly, this new node must be made the first node in the list. This has been attained through the statement

*q = temp ;

The **addafter( )** function permits us to add a new node after a specified number of node in the linked list.

To begin with, through a loop we skip the desired number of nodes after which a new node is to be added. Suppose we wish to add a new node containing data as 99 after the 3rd node in the list. The position of pointers once the control reaches outside the **for** loop is shown in the Figure 4.10(a). Now space is allocated for the node to be inserted and 99 is stored in the data part of it. All that remains to be done is readjustment of links such that 99 goes in between 3 and 4. This is achieved through the statements

r -> link = temp -> link ;
temp -> link = r ;

The first statement makes link part of node containing 99 to point to the node containing 4. The second statement ensures that the link part of node containing 3 points to the node containing 99. On execution of the second statement the earlier link between 3 and 4 is severed. So now 3 no longer points to 4, it points to 99.

The **display( )** and **count( )** functions are straight forward. I leave them for you to understand.

That brings us to the last function in the program i.e. **delete( )**. In this function through the **while** loop, we have traversed through the entire linked list, checking at each node, whether it is the node to be deleted. If so, we have checked if the node being deleted is the first node in the linked list. If it is so, we have simply shifted **p** (which is same as ***q**) to the next node and then deleted the earlier node.

If the node to be deleted is an intermediate node, then the position of various pointers and links before and after the deletion is shown in Figure 4.9.

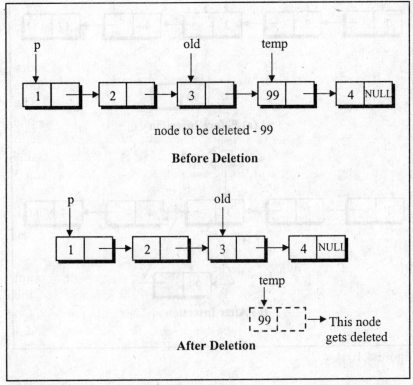

Figure 4.9

The **addafter( )** function permits us to add a new node after a specified number of node in the linked list.

To begin with, through a loop we skip the desired number of nodes after which a new node is to be added. Suppose we wish to add a new node containing data as 99 after the 3rd node in the list. The position of pointers once the control reaches outside the **for** loop is shown in the Figure 4.10(a).

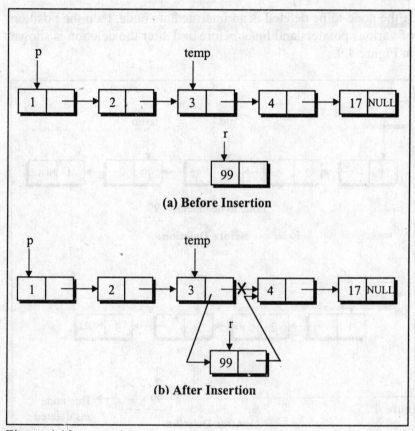

(a) Before Insertion

(b) After Insertion

Figure 4.10

A common and a wrong impression that beginners carry is that a linked list is used only for storing integers. However, a linked list can virtually be used for storing any similar data. For example, there can exist a linked list of floats, a linked list of names, or even a linked list of records, where each record contains name, age and salary of an employee. These linked lists are shown in the following figure.

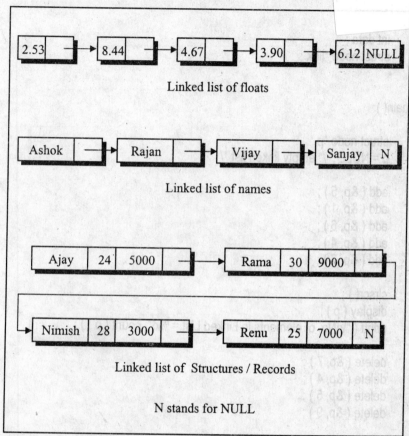

Linked list of floats

Linked list of names

Linked list of Structures / Records

N stands for NULL

Figure 4.11

Now that we have understood how a linked list can be maintained how about ensuring that every element added to the linked list gets inserted at such a place that the linked list is always maintained in ascending order? Here it is...

```
/* Program 54 */
/* Program for adding and deleting nodes from an ascending order
   linked list */
#include "alloc.h"
```

```
struct node
{
    int data ;
    struct node *link ;
} ;

main( )
{
    struct node *p ;
    p = NULL ;  /* empty linked list */

    add ( &p, 5 ) ;
    add ( &p, 1 ) ;
    add ( &p, 6 ) ;
    add ( &p, 4 ) ;
    add ( &p, 7 ) ;

    clrscr( ) ;
    display ( p ) ;
    printf ( "\nNo. of elements in Linked List = %d", count ( p ) ) ;

    delete ( &p, 7 ) ;
    delete ( &p, 4 ) ;
    delete ( &p, 5 ) ;
    delete ( &p, 9 ) ;

    display ( p ) ;
    printf ( "\nNo. of elements in Linked List = %d", count ( p ) ) ;
}

/* adds node to an ascending order linked list */
add ( struct node **q, int num )
{
    struct node *r, *temp = *q ;

    r = malloc ( sizeof ( struct node ) ) ;
    r -> data = num ;
```

```
/* if list is empty or if new node is to be inserted before
the first node */
if ( *q == NULL || ( *q ) -> data > num )
{
    *q = r ;
    ( *q ) -> link = temp ;
}
else
{
    /* traverse the entire linked list to search the position to insert
       the new node */
    while ( temp != NULL )
    {
        if ( temp -> data <= num && ( temp -> link -> data > num ||
                                      temp -> link == NULL ))
        {
            r -> link = temp -> link ;
            temp -> link = r ;
            return ;
        }
        temp = temp -> link ;  /* go to the next node */
    }
}
}

/* displays the contents of the linked list */
display ( struct node *q )
{
    printf ( "\n" ) ;

    /* traverse the entire linked list */
    while ( q != NULL )
    {
        printf ( "%d ", q -> data ) ;
        q = q -> link ;
    }
}
```

```
/* counts the number of nodes present in the linked list */
count ( struct node *q )
{
    int c = 0 ;

    /* traverse the entire linked list */
    while ( q != NULL )
    {
        q = q -> link ;
        c++ ;
    }

    return c ;
}

/* deletes the specified node from the linked list */
delete ( struct node **q, int num )
{
    struct node *old, *temp ;

    temp = *q ;

    while ( temp != NULL )
    {
        if ( temp -> data == num )
        {
            /* if node to be deleted is the first node in the linked list */
            if ( temp == *q )
            {
                *q = temp -> link ;
                /* free the memory occupied by the node */
                free ( temp ) ;
                return ;
            }
            /* deletes the intermediate node in the linked list */
            else
            {
                old -> link = temp -> link ;
```

```
                      free ( temp ) ;
                      return ;
               }
       }
       /* traverse the linked list till the last node is reached */
       else
       {
               old = temp ;  /* old points to the previous node */
               temp = temp -> link ;  /* go to the next node */
       }
    }

    printf ( "\nElement %d not found", num ) ;
}
```

Having had a feel of linked list let us explore what further operations can be performed on a linked list. How about reversing the links in the existing linked list such that the last node becomes the first node and the first becomes the last? Here is a program that shows how this reversal of links can be achieved.

```
/* Program 55 */
/* Program to reverse a linked list */
#include "alloc.h"

/* structure containing a data part and link part */
struct node
{
    int data ;
    struct node *link ;
} ;

reverse ( struct node ** ) ;

main( )
{
    struct node *p ;
```

```
p = NULL ;  /* empty linked list */

addatbeg ( &p, 1 ) ;
addatbeg ( &p, 2 ) ;
addatbeg ( &p, 3 ) ;
addatbeg ( &p, 4 ) ;
addatbeg ( &p, 5 ) ;
addatbeg ( &p, 6 ) ;

clrscr( ) ;
display ( p ) ;
printf ( "\nNo. of elements in the linked list = %d", count ( p ) ) ;

reverse ( &p ) ;
display ( p ) ;
printf ( "\nNo. of elements in the linked list = %d", count ( p ) ) ;
}
/* adds a new node at the beginning of the linked list */
addatbeg ( struct node **q, int num )
{
    struct node *temp ;

    /* add new node */
    temp = malloc ( sizeof ( struct node ) ) ;
    temp -> data = num ;
    temp -> link = *q ;
    *q = temp ;
}

reverse ( struct node **x )
{
    struct node *q, *r, *s ;

    q = *x ;
    r = NULL ;

    /* traverse the entire linked list */
```

```
    while ( q != NULL )
    {
        s = r ;
        r = q ;
        q = q -> link ;
        r -> link = s ;
    }

    *x = r ;
}

/* displays the contents of the linked list */
display ( struct node *q )
{
    printf ( "\n" ) ;

    /* traverse the entire linked list */
    while ( q != NULL )
    {
        printf ( "%d ", q -> data ) ;
        q = q -> link ;
    }
}

/* counts the number of nodes present in the linked list */
count ( struct node * q )
{
    int c = 0 ;

    /* traverse the entire linked list */
    while ( q != NULL )
    {
        q = q -> link ;
        c++ ;
    }
    return c ;
}
```

Stacks and Queues

Stacks and queues are two very common and popular data structures. These data structures are often implemented using arrays since most programming languages provide array as a predefined data type, and such an implementation is therefore quite easy. However, when implemented as an array these data structures suffer from the basic limitation of an array: that its size cannot be increased or decreased once it is declared. As a result one ends up reserving either too much space or too less space for an array and in turn for a stack or a queue. This difficulty is eliminated when we implement these data structures using linked lists.

Before we do so let us formally define these data structures. A stack is a data structure in which addition of new element or deletion of existing element always takes place at the same end. This end is often known as 'top' of stack. This situation can be compared to a stack of plates in a cafeteria where every new plate added to the stack is added at the 'top'. Similarly, every new plate taken off the stack is also from the 'top' of the stack. There are several applications where stack can be put to use. For example, recursion, keeping track of function calls, evaluation of expressions etc. Unlike a stack, in a queue the addition of new element takes place at the end (called 'rear' of queue) whereas deletion takes place at the other end (called 'front' of queue). Figure 4.5 shows these two data structures. A stack is often called a Last-In-First-Out (LIFO) structure, whereas a queue is called a First-In-First-Out (FIFO) structure.

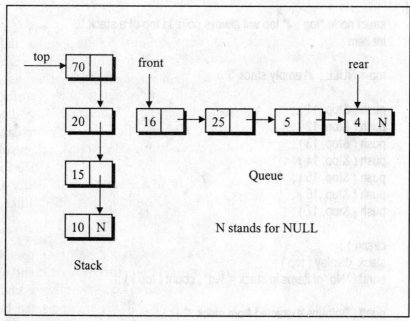

Figure 4.12

And now a program, which implements the stack and the queue using linked lists.

```
/* Program 56 */
/* Program to implement a stack as a linked list */
#include "alloc.h"

struct node
{
    int data ;
    struct node *link ;
} ;

push ( struct node **, int ) ;
pop ( struct node ** ) ;

main( )
```

```
{
    struct node *top ;  /* top will always point to top of a stack */
    int item ;

    top = NULL ;  /* empty stack */

    push ( &top, 11 ) ;
    push ( &top, 12 ) ;
    push ( &top, 13 ) ;
    push ( &top, 14 ) ;
    push ( &top, 15 ) ;
    push ( &top, 16 ) ;
    push ( &top, 17 ) ;

    clrscr( ) ;
    stack_display ( top ) ;
    printf ( "No. of items in stack = %d" , count ( top ) ) ;

    printf ( "\nItems extracted from stack : " ) ;
    item = pop ( &top ) ;
    printf ( "%d ", item ) ;

    item = pop ( &top ) ;
    printf ( "%d ", item ) ;

    item = pop ( &top ) ;
    printf ( "%d ", item ) ;

    stack_display ( top ) ;
    printf ( "No. of items in stack = %d" , count ( top ) ) ;
}

/* adds a new element on the top of stack */
push ( struct node **s, int item )
{
    struct node *q ;
    q = malloc ( sizeof ( struct node ) ) ;
    q -> data = item ;
```

```
    q -> link = *s ;
    *s = q ;
}

/* removes an element from top of stack */
pop ( struct node **s )
{
    int item ;
    struct node *q ;

    /* if stack is empty */
    if ( *s == NULL )
        printf ( " stack is empty" ) ;
    else
    {
        q = *s ;
        item = q -> data ;
        *s = q -> link ;
        free ( q ) ;
        return ( item ) ;
    }
}

/* displays whole of the stack */
stack_display ( struct node *q )
{
    printf ( "\n" ) ;

    /* traverse the entire linked list */
    while ( q != NULL )
    {
        printf ( "%2d ", q -> data ) ;
        q = q -> link ;
    }
    printf ( "\n" ) ;
}
```

/* counts the number of nodes present in the linked list representing a stack */

```
count ( struct node * q )
{
    int c = 0 ;

    /* traverse the entire linked list */
    while ( q != NULL )
    {
        q = q -> link ;
        c++ ;
    }

    return c ;
}
```

If you observe carefully, you would note that, the process of pushing and popping is similar to adding a node at the beginning of a linked list and deleting a node from the beginning of the linked list.

Let us now implement the queue data structure using a linked list.

```
/* Program 57 */
/* Program to implement a queue as a linked list */
#include "alloc.h"

struct node
{
    int data ;
    struct node *link ;
};

void addq ( struct node **, struct node **, int ) ;
delq ( struct node **, struct node ** ) ;

main( )
{
    struct node *front, *rear ;
```

```
        int item ;

        front = rear = NULL ;  /* empty queue */

        addq ( &front, &rear, 11 ) ;
        addq ( &front, &rear, 12 ) ;
        addq ( &front, &rear, 13 ) ;
        addq ( &front, &rear, 14 ) ;
        addq ( &front, &rear, 15 ) ;
        addq ( &front, &rear, 16 ) ;
        addq ( &front, &rear, 17 ) ;

        clrscr( ) ;
        q_display ( front ) ;
        printf ( "\nNo. of items in queue = %d" , count ( front ) ) ;

        printf ( "\n\nItems extracted from queue : " ) ;
        item = delq ( &front, &rear ) ;
        printf ( "%d ", item ) ;

        item = delq ( &front, &rear ) ;
        printf ( "%d ", item ) ;

        item = delq ( &front, &rear ) ;
        printf ( "%d ", item ) ;

        printf ( "\n" ) ;
        q_display ( front ) ;
        printf ( "\nNo. of items in queue = %d" , count ( front ) ) ;
}

/* adds a new element at the end of queue */
void addq ( struct node **f, struct node **r, int item )
{
        struct node *q ;

        /* create new node */
        q = malloc ( sizeof ( struct node ) ) ;
```

```
        q -> data = item ;
        q -> link = NULL ;

        /* if the queue is empty */
        if ( *f == NULL )
            *f = q ;
        else
            ( *r ) -> link = q ;

        *r = q ;
}

/* removes an element from front of queue */
delq ( struct node **f, struct node **r )
{
        struct node *q ;
        int item ;

        /* if queue is empty */
        if ( *f == NULL )
            printf ( "queue is empty" ) ;
        else
        {
            /* delete the node */
            q = *f ;
            item = q -> data ;
            *f = q -> link ;
            free ( q ) ;

            /* if on deletion the queue has become empty */
            if ( *f == NULL )
                *r = NULL ;

            return ( item ) ;
        }
}

/* displays all elements of the queue */
```

```
q_display ( struct node *q )
{
    printf ( "\nfront -> " ) ;

    /* traverse the entire linked list */
    while ( q != NULL )
    {
        if ( q -> link == NULL )
            printf ( " <- rear" ) ;

        printf ( "%2d ", q -> data ) ;
        q = q -> link ;
    }
    printf ( "\n" ) ;
}

/* counts the number of nodes present in the linked list
   representing a queue */
count ( struct node * q )
{
    int c = 0 ;

    /* traverse the entire linked list */
    while ( q != NULL )
    {
        q = q -> link ;
        c++ ;
    }

    return c ;
}
```

Note that, the addition of a node to queue is similar to adding a node at the end of the linked list. After adding a new node the **rear** is made to point to this node. To begin with, **front** and **rear** both are set to NULL to indicate emptiness of the queue.

Deleting a node from the queue is same as deleting the first node from the linked list. If on deletion of the node, the queue becomes empty, then **front** as well as **rear** should be set to NULL.

A deque is a queue in which elements can be added or deleted from both the ends i.e. front and rear. The following program shows how to achieve this. Since we have discussed the addition and deletion of nodes to/from a linked list in detail in the earlier section of this chapter, I would leave it for you to understand the logic of this program.

```
/* Program 58 */
/* Program to implement a deque as a linked list */
#include "alloc.h"

struct node
{
    int data ;
    struct node *link ;
};

void addqatend ( struct node **, struct node **, int ) ;
void addqatbeg ( struct node **, struct node **, int ) ;
delqatbeg ( struct node **, struct node ** ) ;
delqatend ( struct node **, struct node ** ) ;

main( )
{
    struct node *front, *rear ;
    int item ;

    front = rear = NULL ; /* empty queue */

    addqatend ( &front, &rear, 11 ) ;
    addqatbeg ( &front, &rear, 10 ) ;
    addqatend ( &front, &rear, 12 ) ;
    addqatend ( &front, &rear, 13 ) ;
```

```
        addqatend ( &front, &rear, 14 ) ;
        addqatend ( &front, &rear, 15 ) ;
        addqatend ( &front, &rear, 16 ) ;
        addqatend ( &front, &rear, 17 ) ;

        clrscr( ) ;
        q_display ( front ) ;
        printf ( "\nNo. of items in queue = %d" , count ( front ) ) ;

        printf ( "\n\nItems extracted from queue : " ) ;
        item = delqatbeg ( &front, &rear ) ;
        printf ( "%d ", item ) ;

        item = delqatbeg ( &front, &rear ) ;
        printf ( "%d ", item ) ;

        item = delqatbeg ( &front, &rear ) ;
        printf ( "%d ", item ) ;

        item = delqatend ( &front, &rear ) ;
        printf ( "%d ", item ) ;

        printf ( "\n" ) ;
        q_display ( front ) ;
        printf ( "\nNo. of items in queue = %d", count ( front ) ) ;
}

/* adds a new element at the end of queue */
void addqatend ( struct node **f, struct node **r, int item )
{
        struct node *q ;

        /* create new node */
        q = malloc ( sizeof ( struct node ) ) ;
        q -> data = item ;
        q -> link = NULL ;

        /* if the queue is empty */
```

```
        if ( *f == NULL )
            *f = q ;
        else
            ( *r ) -> link = q ;

        *r = q ;
},

/* adds a new element at the beginning of queue */
void addqatbeg ( struct node **f, struct node **r, int item )
{
        struct node *q ;
        int *temp ;

        /* create new node */
        q = malloc ( sizeof ( struct node ) ) ;
        q -> data = item ;
        q -> link = NULL ;

        /* if the queue is empty */
        if ( *f == NULL )
            *f = *r = q ;
        else
        {
            q -> link = *f ;
            *r = *f ;
            *f = q ;
        }
}

/* removes an element from front of queue */
delqatbeg ( struct node **f, struct node **r )
{
        struct node *q ;
        int item ;

        /* if queue is empty */
        if ( *f == NULL )
```

```
                printf ( "queue is empty" ) ;
        else
        {
            /* delete the node */
            q = *f ;
            item = q -> data ;
            *f = q -> link ;
            free ( q ) ;

            /* if on deletion the queue has become empty */
            if ( *f == NULL )
                *r = NULL ;

            return ( item ) ;
        }
}

/* removes an element from rear of queue */
delqatend ( struct node **f, struct node **r )
{
    struct node *q, *rleft, *temp ;
    int item ;

    temp = *f ;
    /* if queue is empty */
    if ( *r == NULL )
        printf ( "queue is empty" ) ;
    else
    {
        /* traverse the queue to find the previous element's address */
        while ( temp != *r )
        {
            rleft = temp ;
            temp = temp -> link ;
        }

        /* delete the node */
        q = *r ;
```

```
        item = q -> data ;
        free ( q ) ;

        *r = rleft ;
        (*r) -> link = NULL ;

        /* if on deletion the queue has become empty */
        if ( *r == NULL )
            *f = NULL ;

        return ( item ) ;
    }
}

/* displays all elements of the queue */
q_display ( struct node *q )
{
    printf ( "\nfront -> " ) ;

    /* traverse the entire linked list */
    while ( q != NULL )
    {
        if ( q -> link == NULL )
            printf ( " <- rear" ) ;

        printf ( "%2d ", q -> data ) ;
        q = q -> link ;
    }
    printf ( "\n" ) ;
}

/* counts the number of nodes present in the linked list representing
   a queue */
count ( struct node * q )
{
    int c = 0 ;

    /* traverse the entire linked list */
```

```
    while ( q != NULL )
    {
        q = q -> link ;
        c++ ;
    }

    return c ;
}
```

Doubly Linked Lists

In the linked lists that we have used so far each node provides information about where is the next node in the list. It has no knowledge about where the previous node lies in memory. If we are at say the 15th node in the list, then to reach the 14th node we have to traverse the list right from the first node. To avoid this we can store in each node not only the address of next node but also the address of the previous node in the linked list. This arrangement is often known as a 'Doubly Linked List' and is shown in the following figure.

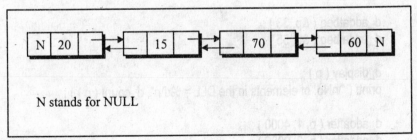

N stands for NULL

Figure 4.13

The following program implements the Doubly Linked List (DLL).

```
/* Program 59 */
/* Program to maintain a doubly linked list */
#include "alloc.h"
```

```
/* structure representing a node of the doubly linked list */
struct dnode
{
    struct dnode *prev ;
    int data ;
    struct dnode * next ;
};

main( )
{
    struct dnode *p ;

    p = NULL ;  /* empty doubly linked list */

    d_append ( &p , 11 ) ;
    d_append ( &p , 21 ) ;

    clrscr( ) ;
    d_display ( p ) ;
    printf ( "\nNo. of elements in the DLL = %d\n", d_count ( p ) ) ;

    d_addatbeg ( &p, 33 ) ;
    d_addatbeg ( &p, 55 ) ;

    d_display ( p ) ;
    printf ( "\nNo. of elements in the DLL = %d\n", d_count ( p ) ) ;

    d_addafter ( p, 1, 4000 ) ;
    d_addafter ( p, 2, 9000 ) ;

    d_display ( p ) ;
    printf ( "\nNo. of elements in the DLL = %d\n", d_count ( p ) ) ;

    d_delete ( &p, 51 ) ;
    d_delete ( &p, 21 ) ;

    d_display ( p ) ;
```

```
        printf ( "\nNo. of elements in the DLL = %d\n", d_count ( p ) ) ;
}

/* adds a new node at the end of the doubly linked list */
d_append ( struct dnode **s, int num )
{
        struct dnode *r, *q = *s ;

        /* if the linked list is empty */
        if ( *s == NULL )
        {
            /*create a new node */
            *s = malloc ( sizeof ( struct dnode ) ) ;
            ( *s ) -> prev = NULL ;
            ( *s ) -> data = num ;
            ( *s ) -> next = NULL ;
        }
        else
        {
            /* traverse the linked list till the last node is reached */
            while ( q -> next != NULL )
                q = q -> next ;

            /* add a new node at the end */
            r = malloc ( sizeof ( struct dnode ) ) ;
            r -> data = num ;
            r -> next = NULL ;
            r -> prev = q ;
            q -> next = r ;
        }
}

/* adds a new node at the begining of the linked list */
d_addatbeg ( struct dnode **s, int num )
{
        struct dnode *q ;

        /* create a new node */
```

```
    q = malloc ( sizeof ( struct dnode ) ) ;

    /* assign data and pointer to the new node */
    q -> prev = NULL ;
    q -> data = num ;
    q -> next = *s ;

    /* make new node the head node */
    ( *s ) -> prev = q ;
    *s = q ;
}

/* adds a new node after the specified number of nodes */
d_addafter ( struct dnode *q, int loc, int num )
{
    struct dnode *temp ;
    int i ;

    /* skip to desired portion */
    for ( i = 0 ; i < loc ; i++ )
    {
        q = q -> next ;
        /* if end of linked list is encountered */
        if ( q == NULL )
        {
            printf ( "\nThere are less than %d elements", loc ) ;
            return ;
        }
    }

    /* insert new node */
    q = q -> prev ;
    temp = malloc ( sizeof ( struct dnode ) ) ;
    temp -> data = num ;
    temp -> prev = q ;
    temp -> next = q -> next ;
    temp -> next -> prev = temp ;
    q -> next = temp ;
```

```
/* displays the contents of the linked list */
d_display ( struct dnode *q )
{
    printf ( "\n" ) ;

    /* traverse the entire linked list */
    while ( q != NULL )
    {
        printf ( "%2d <-->", q -> data ) ;
        q = q -> next ;
    }

    printf ( "--> NULL\n" ) ;
}

/* counts the number of nodes present in the linked list */
d_count ( struct dnode * q )
{
    int c = 0 ;

    /* traverse the entire linked list */
    while ( q != NULL )
    {
        q = q -> next ;
        c++ ;
    }

    return c ;
}

/* deletes the specified node from the doubly linked list */
d_delete ( struct dnode **s, int num )
{
    struct dnode *q = *s ;

    /* traverse the entire linked list */
```

```
while ( q != NULL )
{
    /* if node to be deleted is found */
    if ( q -> data == num )
    {
        /* if node to be deleted is the first node */
        if ( q == *s )
        {
            *s = ( *s ) -> next ;
            ( *s ) -> prev = NULL ;
        }
        else
        {
            /* if node to be deleted is the last node */
            if ( q -> next == NULL )
                q -> prev -> next = NULL ;
            else
            /* if node to be deleted is any intermediate node */
            {
                q -> prev -> next = q -> next ;
                q -> next -> prev = q -> prev ;
            }
            free ( q ) ;
        }
        return ;  /* return back after deletion */
    }
    q = q -> next ; /* go to next node */
}
printf ( "\n%d not found.", num ) ;
}
```

As you must have realised by now any operation on a linked involves adjustment of links. Instead of explaining the different operations performed on a linked list, I think it would be a better idea, if I show these operations with the help of figures. Given below is a group of such figures. Keep the program given above handy to understand the various operations performed on the linked list.

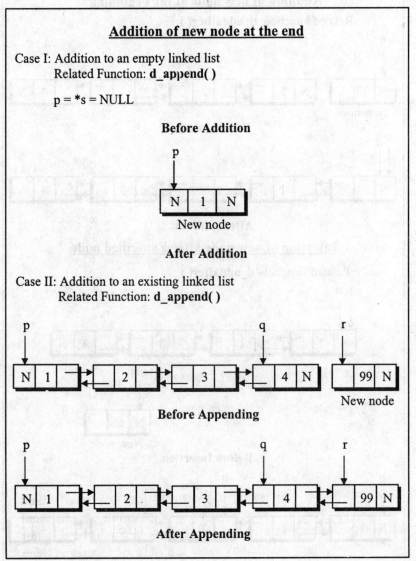

Figure 4.14

Figure 4.14 (Contd.)

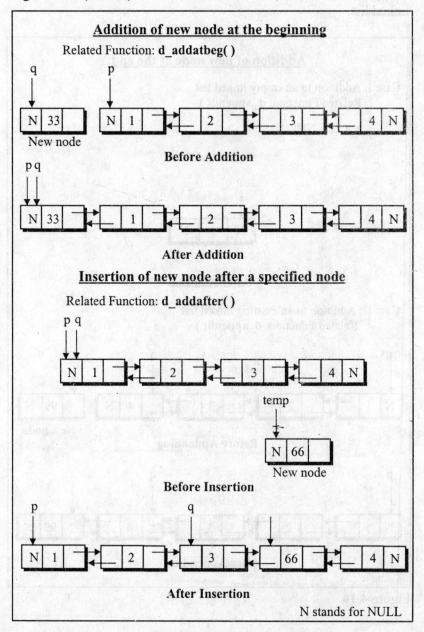

N stands for NULL

Figure 4.14 (Contd.)

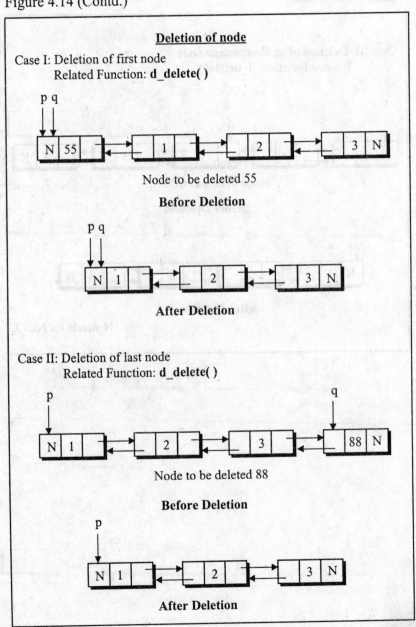

Deletion of node

Case I: Deletion of first node
    Related Function: **d_delete( )**

Node to be deleted 55

Before Deletion

After Deletion

Case II: Deletion of last node
    Related Function: **d_delete( )**

Node to be deleted 88

Before Deletion

After Deletion

Figure 4.14 (Contd.)

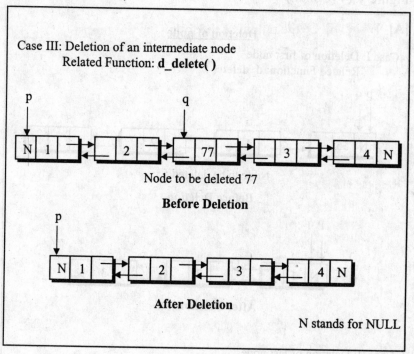

Case III: Deletion of an intermediate node
        Related Function: **d_delete( )**

Node to be deleted 77

Before Deletion

After Deletion

N stands for NULL

Solved Problems

[A] What will be the output of the following programs:

(1)
```
struct s
{
    char ch ;
    int i ;
    float a ;
} ;
main( )
{
    struct s var = { 'C', 100, 12.55 } ;
    f ( var ) ;
    g ( &var ) ;
}

f ( struct s v )
{
    printf ( "\n%c %d %f", v->ch, v->i, v->a ) ;
}

g ( struct s *v )
{
    printf ( "\n%c %d %f", v.ch, v.i, v.a ) ;
}
```

Output

Error message: Pointer required on left of -> in function f
Error message: Variable required on left of . in function g

Explanation

The function **f( )**, called from **main( )**, is sent the **struct** variable **var**, which is collected in **v**. The **printf( )** in **f( )**

attempts to print the structure elements using the arrow operator with **v**, wherein lies the first error. On the left of the arrow operator, there must always be a pointer to a structure. On the other hand, function **g( )** collects a pointer to a structure, which it uses in conjunction with the dot operator. The dot operator must always be preceded by a structure variable, never a pointer. Hence the second error message.

(2)
```
main( )
{
    struct
    {
        int num ;
        float f ;
        char mess[50] ;
    } m ;

    m.num = 1 ;
    m.f = 3.14 ;
    strcpy ( m.mess, "Everything looks rosy" ) ;

    printf ( "\n%u %u %u", &m.num, &m.f, m.mess ) ;
    printf ( "\n%d %f %s", m.num, m.f, m.mess ) ;
}
```

Output

1401 1403 1407
1 3.140000 Everything looks rosy

Explanation

In the elements **num** and **f** of the structure, 1 and 3.14 are stored. For assigning contents to the third element of the structure, i.e. the array **mess[ ]**, **strcpy( )**, the string copy function is used. Why use a string function.b for this? Could we not have said:

m.mess = "Everything looks rosy" ;

like when we assigned values to **num** and **f**? The answer is an emphatic NO! Unlike **m.num** and **m.f**, **m.mess** signifies an address, and a base address at that. Hence, it can't ever occur on the left-hand side of the assignment operator. In other words, **m.mess** is not a lvalue.

The first **printf( )** prints the addresses of the three elements within the **struct**. The output goes to show that the elements of a **struct** are stored in contiguous memory locations. Address of **m.num** is found to be 1401. Since an **int** occupies two bytes in memory, address of the **float, m.f,** is 1403. Finally, the address of the array **mess[ ]** is 1407. This is four bytes ahead of the address of **m.f**, as a **float** is a four-byte entity.

The second **printf( )** prints out the three elements of the structure.

(3) main( )
```
{
    struct a
    {
        char arr[10] ;
        int i ;
        float b ;
    } v[2] ;

    /* assume that the first structure begins at address 1004 */
    printf ( "\n%u %u %u", v[0].arr, &v[0].i, &v[0].b ) ;
    printf ( "\n%u %u %u", v[1].arr, &v[1].i, &v[1].b ) ;
}
```

Output

```
1004 1014 1016
1020 1030 1032
```

Explanation

v[ ] has been declared as an array of structures. Understand that though each structure consists of dissimilar data types, more than one similar structures are capable of forming an array. The word 'similar' is important here, as that is the only criterion Dennis Ritchie set for constructing an array of any data type.

The output verifies that elements of an array of structures, in keeping with the tradition of arrays, are stored in contiguous memory locations. The address of the zeroth element of the zeroth structure is 1004. As this is a **char** array of size 10, ten bytes are used by it. Next, at 1014, the **int** of the zeroth structure is stored. After leaving 2 bytes for **v[0].i**, the **float** **v[0].b** occupies bytes 1016 to 1019. Immediately after this, the next structure of the array is stored, as the outputted addresses 1020, 1030, and 1032, justify.

(4) main( )
```
{
    struct a
    {
        char ch[7] ;
        char *str ;
    } ;

    struct a s1 = { "Nagpur", "Bombay" } ;

    printf ( "\n%c %c", s1.ch[0], *s1.str ) ;
    printf ( "\n%s %s", s1.ch, s1.str ) ;
```

```
}
```

Output

N B
Nagpur Bombay

Explanation

struct a comprises of **char** array **ch[ ]** and a **char** pointer **str**. **s1**, a variable of type **struct a,** is initialised next. Here "Nagpur" gets stored in the array **ch[ ]**, and "Bombay" gets stored starting from the address contained in **str**.

In the first **printf( )**, **ch[0]** signifies the zeroth element of the array **ch[ ]**. Since this array is within a **struct**, a dot operator preceded by the structure variable of that type must be used. Thus, **s1.ch[0]** refers to the zeroth element of the array **ch[ ]**. As this array has been assigned the string "Nagpur", the first character 'N' is printed out.

Next, ***s1.str** signifies the value at address contained in **s1.str**. Since this is the address at which 'B' of "Bombay" is stored, the **printf( )** prints out a 'B'.

The next **printf( )** outputs both "Nagpur" and "Bombay", as **s1.ch** denotes the base address of the former, and **s1.str,** that of the latter string.

```
(5)  main( )
     {
         struct a
         {
             char ch[7] ;
             char *str ;
         };
```

```
struct b
{
    char *c ;
    struct a ss1 ;
};

struct b s2 = { "Raipur", "Kanpur", "Jaipur" } ;

printf ( "\n%s %s", s2.c, s2.ss1.str ) ;
printf ( "\n%s %s", ++s2.c, ++s2.ss1.str ) ;
}
```

Output

```
Raipur Jaipur
aipur aipur
```

Explanation

At the outset, **struct a** is declared to comprise a character array **ch[ ]** and a character pointer **str**. Next, **s2** is declared as a variable of type **struct b**, which is made up of a **char** pointer **c** and another variable **ss1** of type **struct a.** While initialising **s2**, the base address of the string "Raipur" is assigned to **s2.c**, "Kanpur" is assigned to **s2.ss1.ch[ ]**, and the base address of "Jaipur" is assigned to **s2.ss1.str**.

Coming to the **printf( )**s now, the first one is supplied **s2.c** and **s2.ss1.str**. **s2.c** gives the base address of "Raipur", and **s2.ss1.str** gives the base address of "Jaipur". Since these base addresses are passed to **printf( )**, it promptly prints out the two strings.

The second **printf( )** uses incremented values of these addresses. On incrementing **s2.c** using the **++** operator, it now points to the next element 'a' of "Raipur". Similarly, on incrementing **s2.ss1.str**, it points to 'a' of "Jaipur". With these as starting addresses, the remaining strings are printed out.

(6) main( )

```
{
    struct s1
    {
        char *z ;
        int i ;
        struct s1 *p ;
    } ;
    static struct s1 a[ ] = {
                        { "Nagpur", 1, a + 1 },
                        { "Raipur", 2, a + 2 },
                        { "Kanpur", 3, a }
                    } ;
    struct s1 *ptr = a ;

    printf ( "\n%s %s %s", a[0].z, ptr->z, a[2].p->z ) ;
}
```

Output

Nagpur Nagpur Nagpur

Explanation

The zeroth and first elements of **struct s1** are a character pointer and an **int** respectively. The second element is what's new. It is a pointer to a structure. That is, **p** stores the starting address of a structure variable of the type **struct s1**. Next, **a[ ]**, an array of such structures is declared as well as initialised. During initialisation the base address of "Nagpur" is stored in **a[0].z**, 1 is stored in the element **a[0].i**, and **a + 1** is assigned to **a[0].p**. On similar lines, the remaining two elements of the array are initialised. **a[1].z**, **a[1].i** and **a[1].p** are assigned

"Raipur", 2 and **a + 2** in that order, and "Kanpur", 3 and **a** are stored at **a[2].z, a[2].i** and **a[2].p** respectively.

What exactly do **a, a + 1** and **a + 2** signify? **a**, of course, is the base address of the array **a[ ]**. Let us assume it to be 4000, as shown in Figure 4.15. Locations 4000 and 4001 are occupied by the **char** pointer **a[0].z,** since a pointer is always two bytes long. The next two bytes are used to store the integer **a[0].i,** and then 4004 and 4005 are used by **a[0].p.** Similarly, the next 6 bytes store the first structure **a[1],** and the 6 bytes after that contain **a[2],** the second structure in the array.

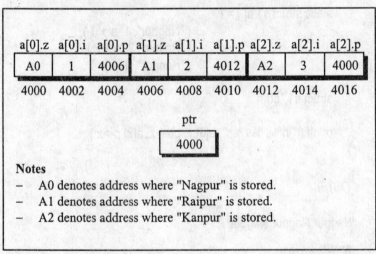

Figure 4.15

Now, when we say **a + 1**, we do not arrive at 4001, but at 4006. This is because on incrementing any pointer, it points to the next location of its type. **a** points to the zeroth structure in the array, i.e. **a[0]**. Hence, on incrementing **a**, it will point to the immediately next element of its type, i.e. the first structure **a[1]** of the array. Likewise, **a + 2** signifies the address of the second element **a[2]** of the array. Thus, **a[0].p** contains address 4006 (refer figure), **a[1].p** contains 4012, and **a[2].p** stores 4000.

A **struct** pointer **ptr** is now set up, which is assigned **a**, the base address of the array.

In the **printf( )**, **a[0].z** denotes the address where "Nagpur" is stored. Hence "Nagpur" gets printed out.

Since **ptr** contains the address of **a[0]**, **ptr->z** refers to the contents of element **z** of the array element **a[0]**. Thus **ptr->z** gives the address A0 (refer figure) and this address happens to be the base address of the string "Nagpur". Hence "Nagpur" gets printed out.

Let us now analyse the expression **a[2].p->z.** The left side of the arrow operator always represents the base address of a structure. What structure does **a[2].p** point to? Looking at the figure we can confirm that **a[2].p** contains the address 4000. which is the base address of the array **a[ ]**. Hence the expression **a[2].p->z** can also be written as **a->z.** Since **a** is the base address of the structure **a[0]**, this expression refers to the element **z** of the zeroth structure. Thus, "Nagpur" gets printed for the third time.

```
(7)  main( )
     {
         struct s1
         {
             char *str ;
             int i ;
             struct s1 *ptr ;
         } ;
         static struct s1 a[ ] = {
                                 { "Nagpur", 1, a + 1 },
                                 { "Raipur", 2, a + 2 },
                                 { "Kanpur", 3, a }
```

```
                              } ;
    struct s1 *p = a ;
    int j ;

    for ( j = 0 ; j <= 2 ; j++ )
    {
        printf ( "\n%d " , --a[j].i ) ;
        printf ( "%s" , ++a[j].str ) ;
    }
}
```

Output

```
0 agpui
1 aipur
2 anpur
```

Explanation

The example deals with a structure similar to the one we just encountered. Picking up from the **for** loop, it is executed for 3 values of **j**: 0, 1 and 2. The first time through the **for** loop, **j** is equal to zero, so the first **printf( )** prints **--a[0].i**. Since the dot operator has a higher priority, first **a[0].i** is evaluated, which is 1. As **--** precedes the value to be printed, 1 is first decremented to 0, and then printed out.

The second **printf(.)** prints the string at address **++a[0].str**. **a[0].str** gives the starting address of "Nagpur". On incrementing, it points to the next character, 'a' of "Nagpur", so starting from 'a', the remaining string "agpur" is outputted.

A similar procedure is repeated for **j = 1**, and then once again for **j = 2**, following which the execution is terminated.

```
(8)  main( )
     {
          struct s1
          {
               char *z ;
               int i ;
               struct s1 *p ;
          } ;
          static struct s1 a[] = {
                              { "Nagpur", 1, a + 1 },
                              { "Raipur", 2, a + 2 },
                              { "Kanpur", 3, a }
                         } ;
          struct s1 *ptr = a ;

          printf ( "\n%s", ++( ptr->z ) ;
          printf ( "\n%s", a[ ( ++ptr )->i ].z ) ;
          printf ( "\n%s", a [ --( ptr->p->i ) ].z ) ;
     }
```

Output

agpur
Kanpur
Kanpur

Explanation

With a similar set up as in the previous two programs, we try to print some more combinations. Let us tackle them one by one. The following figure should prove helpful in analysing these combinations.

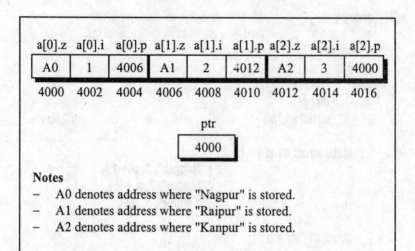

Figure 4.16

++(ptr->z)

ptr holds the base address of the array of structures. We can also think of this base address as the address of the zeroth structure in the array. **ptr->z** thus signifies the element **z** of the zeroth structure, which is the starting address of the string "Nagpur". On incrementing this using ++ operator, we get the next address, that of 'a' in "Nagpur". Therefore the string is printed out 'a' onwards.

a[(++ptr)->i].z

Intimidating? Won't seem so after we have finished dissecting it. Starting from the parentheses, **++ptr** leads to contents of **ptr** being incremented. Currently **ptr** contains the address of the zeroth structure of the array **a[ ]**. This address, as per the figure, turns out to be 4000. Adding 1 to this address takes you 6 bytes further, and not 1, as you might be led to believe. This is so because on incrementing any pointer, it points to the next location of its type. Since **ptr** is a pointer to a structure, it skips as many bytes as the structure comprises of, and points to the following location. Our structure **s1** uses 2 bytes for the **char** pointer **z**, 2 for the **int i**, and 2 for the **struct** pointer **p**. Hence, on incrementing **ptr**, we get that address where **a[1]**, the next structure of the array begins. This address as per the figure is 4006. Now, (**4006**)->**i** is 2, as has been initialised earlier. Thus the expression **a[(++ptr)->i].z** reduces to plain and simple **a[2].z,** which yields the base address of the string "Kanpur". The same is printed out by **printf( ).**

a[--(ptr->p->i)].z

Following our strategy of crossing the bridges one at a time, we start with the inner parentheses. Moving from left to right, **ptr->p** is evaluated first. **ptr**, after getting incremented in the second **printf( )**, points to the first structure, **a[1]** of the array. The element **p** of this structure stores the address 4012, or in other words, the address given by **a + 2**. This address, as you would agree, is the base address of the second structure of the array. Thus the parentheses reduce to (**a + 2**)->**i**, or **4012->i,** which is 3. 3 is decremented to 2 by the **--** operator, and we realise that the expression that almost succeeded in putting us off was only a camouflage for **a[2].z!** This again yields the starting address of "Kanpur", and the same is therefore displayed once again.

```
(9)   main( )
      {
          struct s1
          {
              char *str ;
              struct s1 *ptr ;
          };
          static struct s1 arr[ ] = {
                              { "Nikhil", arr+1 },
                              { "Aditya", arr+2 },
```

```
                              { "Sudheer", arr }
                            } ;
    struct s1 *p[3] ;
    int i ;

    for ( i = 0 ; i <= 2 ; i++ )
        p[i] = arr[i].ptr ;

    printf ( "\n%s", p[0]->str ) ;
    printf ( "\n%s", ( *p )->str ) ;
    printf ( "\n%s", ( **p ) ) ;
}
```

Output

Aditya
Aditya
Aditya

Explanation

struct s1 comprises of 2 pointers; one a **char** pointer and
another, a pointer to **struct s1**. **arr[ ]**, an array of such
structures, is declared and initialised. Next, an array of
pointers to structures, **p[3]** is declared. What this means is that
each element of array **p[ ]** will hold the address of a structure
of the type **struct s1**.

The first time in the **for** loop, **arr[0].ptr** is assigned to **p[0]**,
which is the zeroth element of the array of pointers to
structures. **arr[0].ptr** contains the address 4004 as per Figure
4.17. Likewise, **p[1]** is assigned the address 4008 and **p[2]**,
the address 4000.

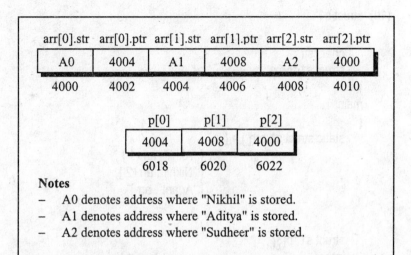

Figure 4.17

Following this, the **printf( )**s get executed. In the first one, the string at **p[0]->str** is printed. As **p[0]** is equal to 4004, the expression refers to the element **str** of the first structure, which stores A1, the starting address of "Aditya". Hence the name "Aditya" gets printed for the first time.

In the second **printf( )**, mentioning **p** gives the base address of the array **p[ ]**. This address according to the figure is 6018. Hence ***p** would give the value at address 6018, which is nothing but 4004. Thus **(*p)->str** evaluates to **4004->str,** which yields A1, the base address of "Aditya". This outputs "Aditya" once again.

Finally, let us analyse the expression ****p**. A quick glance at the figure would confirm that ***p** gives the address 4004, and ****p** therefore gives the address at 4004. This address this time too turns out to be A1. Thus "Aditya" gets printed out through this **printf( )** too.

```
(10)  struct s1
      {
          char *str ;
          struct s1 *next ;
      } ;
      main( )
      {
          static struct s1 arr[ ] = {
                                      { "Akhil", arr+1 },
                                      { "Nikhil", arr+2 },
                                      { "Anant", arr }
                                    } ;

          struct s1 *p[3] ;
          int i ;

          for ( i = 0 ; i <= 2 ; i++ )
              p[i] = arr[i].next ;

          printf ( "\n%s %s %s", p[0]->str, (*p)->str, (**p).str ) ;

          swap ( *p, arr ) ;

          printf ( "\n%s", p[0]->str ) ;
          printf ( "\n%s", ( *p )->str ) ;
          printf ( "\n%s", ( *p )->next->str ) ;

          swap ( p[0], p[0]->next ) ;

          printf ( "\n%s", p[0]->str ) ;
          printf ( "\n%s", ( *++p[0] ).str ) ;
          printf ( "\n%s", ++( *++( *p )->next ).str ) ;
      }

      swap ( struct s1 *p1, struct s1 *p2 )
      {
          char *temp ;
```

```
    temp = p1->str ;
    p1->str = p2->str ;
    p2->str = temp ;
}
```

Output

Nikhil Nikhil Nikhil
Akhil
Akhil
Anant
Anant
Akhil
nant

Explanation

You can by now take the setting up of the arrays of structures and pointers to structures in your stride. In the **for** loop the array **p[ ]** is set up with the addresses 4004, 4008 and 4000, as per Figure 4.18.

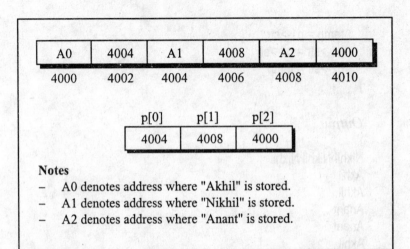

Figure 4.18

In the first **printf( )**, **p[0]->str** is same as (**4004->str**). As 4004 denotes the base address of the first structure, **str** corresponds to the address A1, which is the base address of "Nikhil". Hence this **printf( )** prints the first string "Nikhil".

*p is another way of referring to the same element **p[0]** (as you would recall that **n[i]** is equal to ***(n + i)**). Thus, corresponding to ***p->str,** "Nikhil" is outputted once again.

The third expression uses ****p,** which is equal to ***(p[0])**, i.e. ***(4004)**, which can also be expressed as ***(arr + 1)**. But the expression ***(arr + 1)** is same as **arr[1]**. Thus the expression ****p.str** can also be thought of as **arr[1].str**. As can be confirmed from the figure, **arr[1].str** gives A1, which is the base address of the string "Nikhil". Hence "Nikhil" gets printed through the **printf( )**.

After this, a function **swap( )** is called, which takes as its arguments the base addresses of two structures, **arr + 1** (as ***p** equals **arr + 1**) and **arr**. Hence, in **swap( )**, **p1** and **p2** have been declared as **struct** pointers. Using an auxiliary pointer **temp**, the strings at (**arr + 1**)->**str** and **arr->str** are exchanged. Thus, "Akhil" is now present where "Nikhil" was and vice versa. The current contents of the array **arr[ ]** are now changed to:

```
{
    { "Nikhil", arr + 1 },
    { "Akhil", arr + 2 },
    { "Anant", arr }
}
```

Thus, "Akhil" shows up for the next two **printf( )**s.

Let us now analyse the expression (***p**) -> **next->str**. ***p->next** is same as **p[0]->next.** Since **p[0]** contains the address 4004, the term can be expressed as **4004->next**, which yields the address 4008. Next, **4008->str** yields A2, the base address of "Anant". Hence the **printf( )** outputs "Anant".

After this, **swap( )** is called once again with arguments **p[0]** and **p[0]->next**. This time **p[0]** contains the address 4004, while **p[0]->next** contains the address 4008. 4004 and 4008 represent the base addresses of the first and second structures of the array **arr[ ]**. In the function **swap( )** the strings in these two structures are interchanged. So the array now looks like:

```
{
    { "Nikhil", arr + 1 },
    { "Anant", arr + 2 },
    { "Akhil", arr }
}
```

With this changed array, let's look at the last set of **printf( )**s. The first of these is quite simple. **p[0]->str**, i.e. **4004->str** yields "Anant" in keeping with the latest contents of the array.

Next is the expression (*++p[0]).str. In the parentheses p[0] is incremented by the ++ operator. Thus, **p[0]**, storing (**arr + 1**), now contains (**arr + 2**). Now, *(**arr + 2**) can be expressed as **arr[2]**. Hence the **printf( )** prints **arr[2].str**, which yields "Akhil".

Not allowing ourselves to be impressed by the length of the last **printf( )**'s argument, we start within the parentheses, on the left of the arrow operator. ***p**, i.e. **p[0]**, having been incremented in the preceding **printf( )**, currently contains (**arr + 2**). Since the -> operator enjoys a higher priority than the ++, (**arr + 2**)->**next** gets evaluated next, yielding address **arr**. Now the ++ operator goes to work and we get the address **arr + 1**.

The expression can now be rewritten as ++(*(**arr + 1**)).str. As *(**arr + 1**) is same as **arr[1]**, the expression is reduced to **++arr[1].str**. **arr[1].str** gives the starting address of "Anant". The ++ operator increments this so that the address of the first 'n' of "Anant" is reached. Since this is the address supplied to **printf( )**, the string is printed 'n' onwards. This corresponds to the last output "nant".

(11)
```
#include "alloc.h"
main( )
{
    struct node
    {
        int data ;
        struct node *link ;
    };
    struct node *p, *q ;

    p = malloc ( sizeof ( struct node ) ) ;
    q = malloc ( sizeof ( struct node ) ) ;
    printf ( "\n%d %d", sizeof ( p ), sizeof ( q ) ) ;
}
```

Output

2 2

Explanation

p and **q** have been declared as pointers to structures of the type **struct node**. In the next statement we come across **malloc( )**, which is a standard library function. It reserves as many locations in memory as its argument specifies. Unlike arrays, which put aside a fixed number of bytes specified at the time of declaration, **malloc( )** can be given a variable as an argument, thus allowing flexibility in the size of memory to be allocated.

The **struct node** engages two bytes for **data** and two for **link**, hence the size of **struct node** is 4. Therefore when the calls to **malloc( )** are made, the argument that is passed is 4. Hence each time, **malloc( )** reserves 4 bytes in memory. These bytes would always be in contiguous memory locations. Having successfully reserved the bytes, **malloc( )** returns the base address of these 4 bytes. The base address returned during the first call to **malloc( )** is collected in **p** and the one returned during the second call, in **q**. As **p** and **q** are both 2-byte addresses, saying **sizeof (p)** and **sizeof (q)** results in 2 and 2 being outputted.

(12)
```
#include "alloc.h"
main( )
{
    struct node
    {
        int data ;
        struct node *link ;
    };
```

```
struct node *p, *q ;

p = malloc ( sizeof ( struct node ) ) ;
q = malloc ( sizeof ( struct node ) ) ;
p->data = 30 ;
p->link = q ;
q->data = 40 ;
q->link = NULL ;

printf ( "\n%d ", p->data ) ;
p = p->link ;
printf ( "%d", p->data ) ;
}
```

Output

30 40

Explanation

p and **q** are returned the starting addresses of two slots of memory allocated by the two **malloc( )**s for structures of the type **struct node.** When we say **p->data,** we are referring to the first two bytes starting from the address in **p**, where 30 is assigned. In **p->link** is stored the address present in **q**, which is the base address of the area of memory allocated by the second **malloc( )**. In the structure starting from address contained in **q**, 40 and NULL are stored. NULL is defined as 0 in the file 'alloc.h'. On printing **p->data,** we find the 30 stored there. Now we change the contents of **p** to **p->link,** so that **p** is now equal to **q**. Thus **p->data** now evaluates to 40, and on printing the same this time we get 40.

The arrangement of the data types in this problem conforms to the popular 'linked list' data structure. This arrangement is shown in Figure 4.19, where the arrow represents the pointer to the next node.

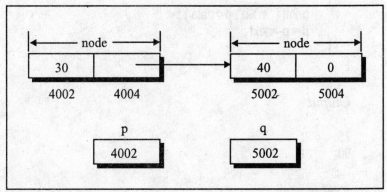

Figure 4.19

(13)
```
#include "alloc.h"
main( )
{
    struct node
    {
        struct node *previous ;
        int data ;
        struct node *next ;
    }

    struct node *p, *q ;

    p = malloc ( sizeof ( struct node ) ) ;
    q = malloc ( sizeof ( struct node ) ) ;

    p->data = 75 ;
    q->data = 90 ;
    p->previous = NULL ;
    p->next = q ;
    q->previous = p ;
    q->next = NULL ;
```

```
while ( p != NULL )
{
    printf ( "\n%d", p->data ) ;
    p = p->next ;
}
}
```

Output

75
90

Explanation

The structure comprises of an integer **data** and two **struct** pointers, **previous** and **next**. The **malloc( )**s allocate 2 blocks of memory starting at addresses 4002 and 5002 as per Figure 4.20. The whole arrangement can be thought of as a chain of 2 structures. As the variable names suggest, **previous** of **p**, assigned NULL, indicates there is no structure prior to the one at **p**. **next** of **p** stores the address of the structure at **q**. Similarly, **previous** of **q** points to the structure preceding it in the chain, which is present at **p**, and **next** of **q** is assigned NULL, signifying that there are no more structures after the one at **q**. This arrangement is nothing but a 'doubly linked list'.

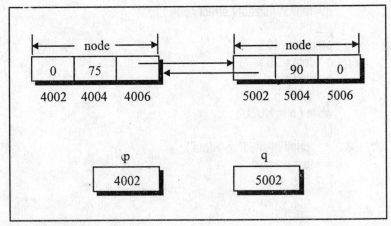

Figure 4.20

The body of the **while** loop is executed subject to the condition that **p** is not equal to NULL, i.e. 0. Since **p** contains 4002, this condition is satisfied for the first time, hence **p->data,** which is 75, gets outputted. Next **p** is assigned **p->next,** which is equal to 5002. This is as good as shifting **p** so that it now points to the next node. Since **p** now contains 5002, the condition in the loop would once again be satisfied, and this time around the **printf( )** prints out 90. In the next statement, **p->next** is assigned to **p.** But this time **p->next** contains 0 (NULL), so **p** is assigned the value 0. The condition in **while** now fails, and the program is terminated.

```
(14)  #include "alloc.h"
      main( )
      {
          struct node
          {
              int data ;
              struct node *next ;
```

```
} ;
struct node *p, *q ;

p = malloc ( sizeof ( struct node ) ) ;
q = malloc ( sizeof ( struct node ) ) ;

p->data = 10 ;
q->data = 20 ;
p->next = q ;
q->next = p ;
while ( p != NULL )
{
    printf ( "\n%d", p->data ) ;
    p = p->next ;
}
}
```

Output

```
10
20
10
20
10
20
...
...
...
```

Explanation

p and **q** are declared as pointers to structures of the type
struct node. With the use of **malloc( )**, two areas in memory,
each of the same size as that of **struct node** are reserved. **p**
and **q** collect the starting addresses of these areas. According
to Figure 4.21, these addresses are 4002 and 5002. Now 10

and 20 are assigned to the **data** parts within the two structures. Next, **p->next** is assigned the contents of **q**, i.e. the address 5002, and **q->next** is assigned the contents of **p**, which is the address 4002.

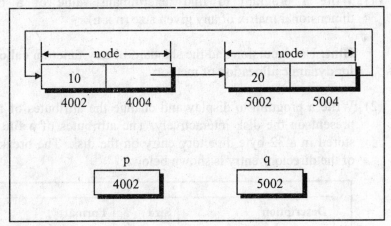

Figure 4.21

The **while** checks the contents of **p** for its execution. The first time since the condition is satisfied, **p->data**, which is 10, gets printed. Now **p** is assigned **p->next**, which is 5002. Thus **p** now points to the second structure. Hence the condition in **while** gets satisfied, and so this time **p->data** yields 20. After this **p** is assigned the value of **p->next**. Since **p** right now contains 5002, **p->next** this time turns out to be 4002 (refer figure). Thus **p** is assigned the address 4002, and **p** now points to the first structure. The integer **data** within the first structure stores 10, which again gets printed when the **printf( )** is executed. Once again the address 5002 is assigned to **p** through the statement **p = p->next**. Thus contents of **p** toggle between 4002 and 5002. And since **p** never becomes NULL, defined earlier as 0, the loop is an indefinite one.

Exercise

[A] Attempt the following:

(1) Write a program to find determinant value of a two-dimensional matrix of any given size (n x n).

   Hint: Use recursion and the standard library function **calloc( )** for dynamic allocation of memory.

(2) Write a program to display and change the attributes of files present on the disk interactively. The attributes of a file are stored in a 32-byte directory entry on the disk. The break-up of the directory entry is shown below.

Description	Size	Format
Filename	8 bytes	ASCII characters
Extension	3 bytes	ASCII characters
Attribute	1 bytes	bit coded
Reserved for future use	10 bytes	unused, zeroes
Time	2 bytes	encoded
Date	2 bytes	encoded
Starting cluster number	2 bytes	integer
Size	4 bytes	long integer

Figure 4.22

The individual bits of the attribute byte in the directory entry control the current attributes of the file. The break-up of the attribute byte is shown below

Bit numbers	Meaning
7 6 5 4 3 2 1 0	
. . . . 1	Read-only
. . . . . . 1 .	Hidden
. . . . . 1 . .	System
. . . . 1 . . .	Volume label entry
. . . 1	Sub-directory entry
. . 1	Archive bit
. 1	Unused
1	Unused

Figure 4.23

Hint: Use standard library Turbo C function **absread( )** to read the existing attribute byte settings and the function **abswrite( )** to overwrite them with new attributes.

(3) Write a program to list the current directory in alphabetical order using a linked list.

Hints:

— Use standard library functions **findfirst( )** and **findnext( )** in Turbo C to read the directory entries.

— Define a structure **struct node**, which contains the standard structure **struct ffblk** defined in file "dos.h" as data part, and add another element **next** as link to the next node.

— When all the directory entries are read and stored in the linked list, sort the linked list and then display the sorted linked list.

(4) Write a program to display contents of boot sector of floppy / hard disk. The structure of the boot sector is as follows:

Description	Length
Jump instruction	3 bytes
System ID	8 bytes
Number of bytes per sector	2 bytes
Number of sectors per cluster	1 byte
Number of sectors in reserved area	2 bytes
Number of copies of FAT	1 byte
Number of root directory entries	2 bytes
Total number of sectors	2 bytes
Media descriptor	1 byte
Number of sectors per FAT	2 bytes
Number of sectors per track	2 bytes
Number of sides	2 bytes
Number of hidden sectors	2 bytes

Figure 4.24

Hint: Use standard library function **absread( )** in Turbo C.

(5) Write a program to display contents of the Partition Table present on the hard disk. The structure of the partition table is as shown below:

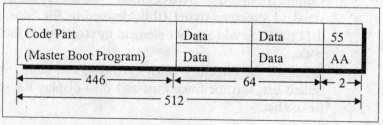

Figure 4.25(a)

Bytes	Meaning
0	Boot indicator. Contains 80h for the active partition, 0 for all others. Only one partition can be active at a time
1	Side where the partition begins.
2	The low six bits are the sectors where the partition begins. The high two bits are the two high bits of the track where the partition begins.
3	Low order eight bits of the track where the partition begins.
4	Partition type indicator. The contents of this byte indicate the type of the partition. The following values may exist. 0 - Unused partition 1 - DOS partition that uses a 12-bit FAT 2 - Unix partition 4 - DOS partition that uses a 16-bit FAT 5 - Extended partition 6 - Huge partition
5	Side where the partition ends.
6	Low order six bits are the sector where the partition ends. The high two bits are the high two bits of the ending track number.
7	Low eight bits of the track number where the partition ends.
8-11	Double word containing the number of sectors preceding the partition. Low order word is stored first.
12-15	Double word containing the number of sectors in the partition. Low order word is stored first.

Figure 4.25(b)

Hint: Use the **biosdisk( )** library function in Turbo C/C++.

[B] What will be the output of the following program segments:

(1)
```
main( )
{
    struct a
    {
        char *str ;
        struct a *ptr ;
    } ;
    static struct a arr[ ] = {
                                { "Niranjan", arr+2 },
                                { "Praveen", arr },
                                { "Ashish", arr+1 }
                             } ;
    struct a *p[3] ;
    int i ;

    for ( i = 0 ; i <= 2 ; i++ )
        p[i] = arr[i].ptr ;
    printf ( "%s\n", p[0]->str ) ;
    printf ( "%s\n", (*p)->str ) ;
    printf ( "%s\n", (**p) ) ;
}
```

(2)
```
#include "alloc.h"
main( )
{
    struct a
    {
        struct a *next ;
        int data ;
    } ;
    struct a *ptr[3] ;
    int i ;
```

```
        ptr[0] = malloc ( sizeof ( struct a ) ) ;
        ptr[1] = malloc ( sizeof ( struct a ) ) ;
        ptr[2] = malloc ( sizeof ( struct a ) ) ;

        ptr[0]->data = 10 ;
        ptr[1]->data = 20 ;
        ptr[2]->data = 50 ;
        ptr[0]->next = ptr[1] ;
        ptr[1]->next = ptr[2] ;
        ptr[2]->next = NULL ;

        while ( ptr[0] != NULL )
        {
            printf ( "\n%d", ptr[0]->data ) ;
            ptr[0] = ptr[0]->next ;
        }
    }
```

(3)   ```
       struct a
       {
           char city[3][20] ;
           char state[3][20] ;
       } ;

       main( )
       {
           struct a arr = {
                           {
                               "Nagpur",
                               "Mumbai",
                               "Bangalore"
                           },
                           {
                               "Maharashtra",
                               "Maharashtra",
                               "Karnataka"
                           }
       ```
       ```

```
                        } ;
        printf ( "\n%s %s", arr.city, arr.state ) ;
        printf ( "\n%s %s", arr.city + 2, arr.state + 2 ) ;
    }


(4)  main( )
    {
        struct a
        {
            struct b
            {
                char name[10] ;
                int age ;
            } bb ;
            struct c
            {
                char address[50] ;
                int sal ;
            } cc ;
        } ;

        struct a *ptr ;
        struct a aa = {
                        { "George", 30 },
                        { "86, Vermalayout, Nagpur", 4000 }
                    } ;
        ptr = &aa ;
        printf ( "\n%s %s %d %d", ptr->bb.name, ptr->cc.address,
                    ptr->bb.age, ptr->cc.sal ) ;
    }

(5)  struct b
    {
        char name[10] ;
        char address[50] ;
    } ;
    main( )
```

```
{
    struct b bb = {
                        "Niranjan",
                        "Samarth Apartment, TTnagar, Nagpur"
                    } ;
    print ( &bb ) ;
}
print ( struct b *bb )
{
    printf ( "\n%s", bb->name ) ;
    printf ( "\n%s", bb->address ) ;
}
```

No Pointers, No Data Structures.

5 Pointers and Data Structures

In Computer Science linked lists are extensively used in Data Base Management Systems, Process Management, Operating Systems, Editors etc. In the last chapter, we saw how a singly linked list and a doubly linked list can be implemented using pointers. We also saw that while using arrays very often the list of items to be stored in an array is either too short or too big as compared to the declared size of the array. Moreover, during program execution the list cannot grow beyond the size of the declared array. Also, operations like insertion and deletion at a specified location in a list requires a lot of movement of data, thereby leading to an inefficient and time consuming algorithm.

The primary advantage of linked list over an array is that the linked list can grow and shrink in size during its lifetime. In particular, the linked list's maximum size need not be known in advance. In practical applications this often makes it possible to have several data structures share the same space, without paying particular attention to their relative size at any time.

The second advantage of linked lists is that they provide flexibility in allowing the items to be rearranged efficiently. This flexibility is gained at the expense of quick access to any arbitrary item in the list.

In this chapter we would write programs to perform more complicated operations on the linked list. We would also find out how linked lists can be used to maintain polynomials and manipulate them. Let us begin with merging of two linked lists.

Merging of Linked Lists

Suppose we have two linked lists pointed to by two independent pointers and we wish to merge the two lists into a third list. While carrying out this merging we wish to ensure that those elements which are common to both the lists occur only once in the third list. The program to achieve this is given below. It is assumed that within a list all elements are unique.

```
/* Program 60 */
/* Program to merge two linked lists, restricting the common elements to
   occur only once */
#include "alloc.h"

struct node
{
    int data ;
    struct node *link ;
};

main( )
{
    struct node *first, *second, *third ;
    first = second = third = NULL ;  /* empty linked lists */
```

```
        add ( &first, 1 ) ;
        add ( &first, 2 ) ;
        add ( &first, 3 ) ;
        add ( &first, 4 ) ;
        add ( &first, 5 ) ;
        add ( &first, 6 ) ;
        add ( &first, 7 ) ;

        clrscr( ) ;
        printf ( "First linked list : " ) ;
        display ( first ) ;
        printf ( "\nNo. of elements in Linked List : %d" , count ( first ) ) ;

        add ( &second, 8 ) ;
        add ( &second, 9 ) ;
        add ( &second, 3 ) ;
        add ( &second, 4 ) ;
        add ( &second, 5 ) ;
        add ( &second, 6 ) ;
        add ( &second, 7 ) ;

        printf ( "\n\nSecond linked list : " ) ;
        display ( second ) ;
        printf ( "\nNo. of elements in Linked List : %d" , count ( second ) ) ;

        merge ( first, second, &third ) ;

        printf ( "\n\nThe concatenated list : " ) ;
        display ( third ) ;
        printf ( "\nNo. of elements in Linked List : %d", count ( third ) ) ;
}

/* adds node to an ascending order linked list */
add ( struct node **q, int num )
{
        struct node *r, *temp = *q ;
```

```
r = malloc ( sizeof ( struct node ) ) ;
r -> data = num ;

/* if list is empty or if new node is to be inserted before the first node */
if ( *q == NULL || ( *q ) -> data > num )
{
    *q = r ;
    ( *q ) -> link = temp ;
}
else
{
    /* traverse the entire linked list to search the position to insert
       the new node */
    while ( temp != NULL )
    {
        if ( temp -> data < num && ( temp -> link -> data > num ||
            temp -> link == NULL ))
        {
            r -> link = temp -> link ;
            temp -> link = r ;
            return ;
        }
        temp = temp -> link ;  /*go to next node */
    }

    r -> link = NULL ;
    temp -> link = r ;
}
}

/* displays the contents of the linked list */
display ( struct node *q )
{
    printf ( "\n" ) ;

    /* traverse the entire linked list */
    while ( q != NULL )
    {
```

```
            printf ( "%d ", q -> data ) ;
            q = q -> link ;
        }
    }

/* counts the number of nodes present in the linked list */
count ( struct node * q )
{
    int c = 0 ;

    /* traverse the entire linked list */
    while ( q != NULL )
    {
        q = q -> link ;
        c++ ;
    }

    return c ;
}

/* merges the two linked lists, restricting the common elements to occur
   only once in the final list */
merge ( struct node *p, struct node *q, struct node **s )
{
    struct node *z ;

    z = NULL ;

    /* if both lists are empty */
    if ( p == NULL && q == NULL )
        return ;

    /* traverse both linked lists till the end. If end of any one list is reached
       loop is terminated */
    while ( p != NULL && q != NULL )
    {
        /* if node being added in the first node */
        if ( *s == NULL )
```

```
{
    *s = malloc ( sizeof ( struct node ) ) ;
    z = *s ;
}
else
{
    z -> link = malloc ( sizeof ( struct node ) ) ;
    z = z -> link ;
}

if ( p -> data < q -> data )
{
    z -> data = p -> data ;
    p = p -> link ;
}
else
{
    if ( q -> data < p -> data )
    {
        z -> data = q -> data ;
        q = q -> link ;
    }
    else
    {
        if ( p -> data == q -> data )
        {
            z -> data = q -> data ;
            p = p -> link ;
            q = q -> link ;
        }
    }
}
}

/* if end of first list has not been reached */
while ( p != NULL )
{
    z -> link = malloc ( sizeof ( struct node ) ) ;
```

```
        z = z -> link ;
        z -> data = p -> data ;
        p = p -> link ;
    }

    /* if end of second list has been reached */
    while ( q != NULL )
    {
        z -> link = malloc ( sizeof ( struct node ) ) ;
        z = z -> link ;
        z -> data = q -> data ;
        q = q -> link ;
    }
    z -> link = NULL ;
}
```

In this program, as usual, we begin by building a structure to accommodate the data and link, which together represent a node. We have used pointers **first**, **second** and **third** to point to the three linked lists. Since to begin with all the three linked lists are empty, these pointers contain NULL. Next, by calling the function **add( )** repeatedly two linked lists are built, one being pointed to by **first** and other by the pointer **second**. Finally, the **merge( )** function is called to merge the two lists into one. This merged list is pointed to by the pointer **third**. While merging the two lists it is assumed that the lists themselves are in ascending order. While building the two lists the **add( )** function makes sure that when a node is added the elements in the lists are maintained in ascending order. While merging the two lists the **merge( )** functions accounts for the possibility of any of the two lists being empty.

Linked Lists and Polynomials

Polynomials like $5x^4+2x^3+7x^2+10x-8$ can be maintained using a linked list. To achieve this each node should consists of three elements, namely coefficient, exponent and a link to the next term. While maintaining the polynomial it is assumed that the exponent of each successive term is less than that of the previous term. Once we build a linked list to represent a polynomial we can use such lists to perform common polynomial operations like addition and multiplication. The program that can perform these operations is given below.

```
/* Program 61 */
/* Program to add two polynomials maintained as linked lists */
#include "alloc.h"

/* structure representing a node of a linked list. The node can store term of a
   polynomial */
struct polynode
{
    float coeff ;
    int exp ;
    struct polynode *link ;
};

void poly_append ( struct polynode **, float, int ) ;
void poly_addition ( struct polynode *, struct polynode *,
                            struct polynode ** ) ;

main( )
{
    struct polynode *first, *second, *total ;
    int i = 0 ;

    first = second = total = NULL ;  /* empty linked lists */

    poly_append ( &first, 1.4, 5 ) ;
    poly_append ( &first, 1.5, 4 ) ;
    poly_append ( &first, 1.7, 2 ) ;
    poly_append ( &first, 1.8, 1 ) ;
    poly_append ( &first, 1.9, 0 ) ;

    clrscr( ) ;
```

```
        display_poly ( first ) ;

        poly_append ( &second, 1.5, 6 ) ;
        poly_append ( &second, 2.5, 5 ) ;
        poly_append ( &second, -3.5, 4 ) ;
        poly_append ( &second, 4.5, 3 ) ;
        poly_append ( &second, 6.5, 1 ) ;

        printf ( "\n\n" ) ;
        display_poly ( second ) ;

        /* draws a dashed horizontal line */
        printf ( "\n" ) ;
        while ( i++ < 79 )
            printf ( "-" ) ;
        printf ( "\n\n" ) ;

        poly_addition ( first, second, &total ) ;
        display_poly ( total ) ;   /* displays the resultant polynomial */
}

/* adds a term to a polynomial */
void poly_append ( struct polynode **q, float x, int y )
{
        struct polynode *temp ;
        temp = *q ;

        /* creates a new node if the list is empty */
        if ( *q == NULL )
        {
            *q = malloc ( sizeof ( struct polynode ) ) ;
            temp = *q ;
        }
        else
        {
            /* traverse the entire linked list */
            while ( temp -> link != NULL )
                temp = temp -> link ;
```

```
                /* create new nodes at intermediate stages */
                temp -> link = malloc ( sizeof ( struct polynode ) ) ;
                temp = temp -> link ;
        }

        /* assign coefficient and exponent */
        temp -> coeff = x ;
        temp -> exp = y ;
        temp -> link = NULL ;
}

/* displays the contents of linked list representing a polynomial */
display_poly ( struct polynode *q )
{
        /* traverse till the end of the linked list */
        while ( q != NULL )
        {
                printf ( "%.1f x^%d  :  ", q -> coeff, q -> exp ) ;
                q = q -> link ;
        }

        printf ( "\b\b\b " ) ;  /* erases the last colon */
}

/* adds two polynomials */
void poly_addition ( struct polynode *x, struct polynode *y,
                        struct  polynode **s )
{
        struct polynode *z ;

        /* if both linked lists are empty */
        if ( x == NULL && y == NULL )
                return ;

        /* traverse till one of the list ends */
        while ( x != NULL && y != NULL )
        {
```

```
/* create a new node if the list is empty */
if ( *s == NULL )
{
    *s = malloc ( sizeof ( struct polynode ) ) ;
    z = *s ;
}
/* create new nodes at intermediate stages */
else
{
    z -> link = malloc ( sizeof ( struct polynode ) ) ;
    z = z -> link ;
}

/* store a term of the larger degree polynomial */
if ( x -> exp < y -> exp )
{
    z -> coeff = y -> coeff ;
    z -> exp = y -> exp :
    y = y -> link ;  /* go to the next node */
}
else
{
    if ( x -> exp > y -> exp )
    {
        z -> coeff = x -> coeff ;
        z -> exp = x -> exp ;
        x = x -> link ;  /* go to the next node */
    }
    else
    {
        /* add the coefficients, when exponents are equal */
        if ( x -> exp == y -> exp )
        {
            /* assigning the added coefficient */
            z -> coeff = x -> coeff + y -> coeff ;
            z -> exp = x -> exp ;
            /* go to the next node */
            x = x -> link ;
```

```
                    y = y -> link ;
               }
          }
     }
}
```

```
/* assign remaining terms of the first polynomial to the result */
while ( x != NULL )
{
     if ( *s == NULL )
     {
          *s = malloc ( sizeof ( struct polynode ) ) ;
          z = *s ;
     }
     else
     {
          z -> link = malloc ( sizeof ( struct polynode ) ) ;
          z = z -> link ;
     }

     /* assign coefficient and exponent */
     z -> coeff = x -> coeff ;
     z -> exp = x -> exp ;
     x = x -> link ;  /* go to the next node */
}

/* assign remaining terms of the second polynomial to the result */
while ( y != NULL )
{
     if ( *s == NULL )
     {
          *s = malloc ( sizeof ( struct polynode ) ) ;
          z = *s ;
     }
     else
     {
          z -> link = malloc ( sizeof ( struct polynode ) ) ;
          z = z -> link ;
```

```
        }

        /* assign coefficient and exponent */
        z -> coeff = y -> coeff ;
        z -> exp = y -> exp ;
        y = y -> link ; /* go to the next node */
    }

    z -> link = NULL ; /* assign NULL at end of resulting linked list */
}
```

In this program the **poly_append( )** function is called several times to build the two polynomials which are pointed to by the pointers **first** and **second**. Next the function **poly_addition( )** is called to carry out the addition of two polynomials. In this function the linked lists representing the two polynomials are traversed till the end of one of them is reached. While doing this traversal the polynomials are compared on term by term basis. If the exponents of the two terms being compared are equal then their coefficients are added and the result is stored in the third polynomial. If the exponents of two terms are not equal then the term with the bigger exponent is added to the third polynomial. During the traversal if the end of one of the list is reached the control breaks out of the **while** loop. Now the remaining terms of that polynomial whose end has not been reached are simply appended to the resulting polynomial. Lastly, the terms of the resulting polynomials are displayed using the function **display_poly( )**.

And now a program to carry out multiplication of the two polynomials

```
/* Program 62 */
/* Program to multiply two polynomials maintained as linked lists */
#include "alloc.h"
/* structure representing a node of a linked list. The node can store a term of
   a polynomial */
struct polynode
```

```
{
    float coeff ;
    int exp ;
    struct polynode *link ;
} ;

void poly_append ( struct polynode **, float, int ) ;
void poly_multiply ( struct polynode *, struct polynode *,
                                  struct polynode ** ) ;
padd ( float, int, struct polynode ** ) ;

main( )
{
    struct polynode *first, *second, *mult ;
    int i = 1 ;

    first = second = mult = NULL ;  /* empty linked lists */

    poly_append ( &first, 3, 5 ) ;
    poly_append ( &first, 2, 4 ) ;
    poly_append ( &first, 1, 2 ) ;

    clrscr( ) ;
    display_poly ( first ) ;

    poly_append ( &second, 1, 6 ) ;
    poly_append ( &second, 2, 5 ) ;
    poly_append ( &second, 3, 4 ) ;

    printf ( "\n\n" ) ;
    display_poly ( second ) ;

    printf ( "\n" ) ;
    while ( i++ < 79 )
        printf ( "-" ) ;

    poly_multiply ( first, second, &mult ) ;
```

```
    printf ( "\n\n" ) ;
    display_poly ( mult ) ;
}

/* adds a term to a polynomial */
void poly_append ( struct polynode **q, float x, int y )
{
    struct polynode *temp ;
    temp = *q ;

    /* create a new node if the list is empty */
    if ( *q == NULL )
    {
        *q = malloc ( sizeof ( struct polynode ) ) ;
        temp = *q ;
    }
    else
    {
        /* traverse the entire linked list */
        while ( temp -> link != NULL )
            temp = temp -> link ;

        /* create new nodes at intermediate stages */
        temp -> link = malloc ( sizeof ( struct polynode ) ) ;
        temp = temp -> link ;
    }

    /* assign coefficient and exponent */
    temp -> coeff = x ;
    temp -> exp = y ;
    temp -> link = NULL ;
}

/* displays the contents of linked list representing a polynomial */
display_poly ( struct polynode *q )
{
    /* traverse till the end of the linked list */
    while ( q != NULL )
```

```
    {
        printf ( "%.1f x^%d  : ", q -> coeff, q -> exp ) ;
        q = q -> link ;
    }

    printf ( "\b\b\b " ) ;  /* erases the last colon(:) */
}

/* multiplies the two polynomials */
void poly_multiply ( struct polynode *x, struct polynode *y,
                     struct polynode **m )
{
    struct polynode *y1 ;
    float coeff1, exp1 ;

    y1 = y ;  /* point to the starting of the second linked list */

    if ( x == NULL && y == NULL )
        return ;

    /* if one of the list is empty */
    if ( x == NULL )
        *m = y ;
    else
    {
        if ( y == NULL )
            *m = x ;
        else  /* if both linked lists exist */
        {
            /* for each term of the first list */
            while ( x != NULL )
            {
                /* multiply each term of the second linked list with a
                   term of the first linked list */
                while ( y != NULL )
                {
                    coeff1 = x -> coeff * y -> coeff ;
                    exp1 = x -> exp + y -> exp ;
```

```
                    y = y -> link ;

                    /* add the new term to the resultant polynomial */
                    padd ( coeff1, exp1, m ) ;
                }

                y = y1 ; /* reposition the pointer to the starting of
                            the second linked list */

                x = x -> link ; /* go to the next node */
            }
        }
    }
}

/* adds a term to the polynomial in the descending order of the exponent */
padd ( float c, int e, struct polynode **s )
{
    struct polynode *r, *temp = *s ;

    /* if list is empty or if the node is to be inserted before the first node */
    if ( *s == NULL || e > ( *s ) -> exp )
    {
        *s = r = malloc ( sizeof ( struct polynode ) ) ;
        ( *s ) -> coeff = c ;
        ( *s ) -> exp = e ;
        ( *s ) -> link = temp ;
    }
    else
    {
        /* traverse the entire linked list to search the position to insert a new
           node */
        while ( temp != NULL )
        {
            if ( temp -> exp == e )
            {
                temp -> coeff += c ;
                return ;
```

```
            }

            if ( temp -> exp > e && ( temp -> link -> exp < e ||
                temp -> link == NULL ) )
            {
                r = malloc ( sizeof ( struct polynode ) ) ;
                r -> coeff = c;
                r -> exp = e ;
                r -> link = temp -> link ;
                temp -> link = r ;
                return ;
            }

            temp = temp -> link ;  /* go to next node */
        }

        r -> link = NULL ;
        temp -> link = r ;
    }
}
```

In this program once again the **poly_append( )** function is called
to build the two polynomials. Followed by this, the
poly_multiply( ) function is called to carry out the multiplication
of the two polynomials. In this function if it is found that both the
linked lists (representing the two polynomials being multiplied)
are non-empty then the control goes in a pair of **while** loops. Here
each term of the second polynomial is multiplied with every term
of the first polynomial. As this proceeds and a new term is built,
the function **p_add( )** is called to add this term to the resulting
polynomial. In **p_add( )** each term of the existing resulting
polynomial is scanned to find whether there exists a term in this
polynomial whose exponent is same as that of the term to be
added. If it is so, then the corresponding coefficient of the existing
polynomial is updated, otherwise the new term is simply appended
to the end of the existing polynomial. Yet again the resulting
polynomial is displayed using the function **display_poly( )**.

Sorting a Linked List

Suppose, we wish to sort the elements of a linked list. We can use any of the standard sorting algorithms for carrying out the sorting. While performing the sorting, when it is time to exchange two elements, we can adopt any of the following two strategies:

(a) Exchange the data part of two nodes, keeping the links intact. This is shown in Figure 5.1.

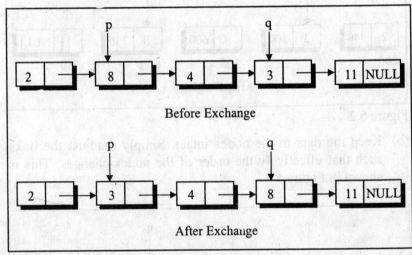

Before Exchange

After Exchange

Figure 5.1

Suppose the elements 8 and 3 are to be exchanged. While carrying out the exchange only 8 gets exchanged with 3. The link part of node being pointed to by **p** and the link part of node being pointed to by **q** remains unchanged. To make this absolutely clear take a look at Figure 5.2. In this instead of showing links I have shown the actual addresses of nodes. Referring to Figure 5.2 you can observe that after the exchange of 8 and 3 the addresses stored in nodes pointed to by **p** and **q** (i.e. addresses 500 and 750) have remained intact.

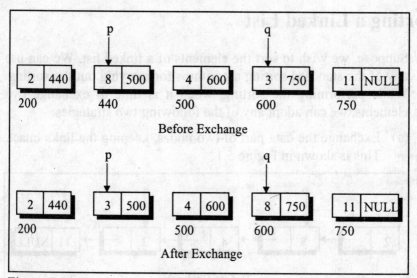

Figure 5.2

(b) Keep the data in the nodes intact. Simply readjust the links such that effectively the order of the nodes changes. This is shown in Figure 5.3.

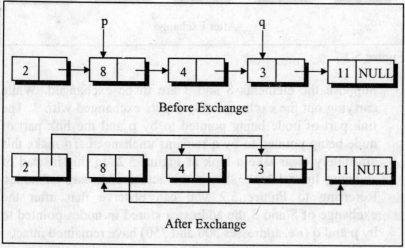

Figure 5.3

Instead of links if you look at actual physical addresses stored in the link part you may get a clearer idea about how the links are being readjusted. This is shown in Figure 5.4.

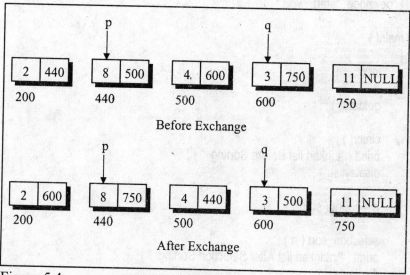

Figure 5.4

Of the two methods suggested above, the first one is easier to implement, but the second one is likely to be more efficient. This is because if the data part contains an employee record (containing name, age, salary etc.) then to carry out exchange of this record would be inefficient time wise as well as space wise. Instead if we adopt second method, since we are readjusting only the links this would involve only pointers and not the bulky structures representing records.

In this chapter we would implement both the methods to sort a linked list. Here is a program for the first one.

```
/* Program 63 */
#include "alloc.h"
```

```
struct node
{
    int data ;
    struct node *link ;
} *newnode, *start, *visit ;

main( )
{
    int n ;

    getdata( ) ;

    clrscr( ) ;
    printf ( "Linked list Before Sorting: " ) ;
    displaylist( ) ;

    n = count ( start ) ;

    selection_sort ( n ) ;
    printf ( "\nLinked list After Selection Sorting: " ) ;
    displaylist( ) ;
    getch( ) ;

    getdata( ) ;
    clrscr( ) ;
    printf ( "Linked list Before Sorting: " ) ;
    displaylist( ) ;

    n = count ( start ) ;

    bubble_sort ( n ) ;
    printf ( "\nLinked list After Bubble Sorting: " ) ;
    displaylist( ) ;
    getch( ) ;
}

getdata( )
{
```

```
    int val, n ;
    char ch ;
    struct node *new ;

    clrscr( ) ;

    new = NULL ;
    do
    {
        printf ( "\nEnter a value: " ) ;
        scanf ( "%d", &val ) ;

        append ( &new, val ) ;

        printf ("\nAny More Nodes (Y/N): " ) ;
        ch = getche( ) ;
    } while ( ch == 'y' || ch == 'Y' ) ;

    start = new ;
}

/* adds a node at the end of a linked list */
append ( struct node **q, int num )
{
    struct node *temp ;
    temp = *q ;

    if ( *q == NULL ) /* if the list is empty, create first node */
    {
        *q = malloc ( sizeof ( struct node ) ) ;
        temp = *q ;
    }
    else
    {
        /* go to last node */
        while ( temp -> link != NULL )
        temp = temp -> link ;
```

```
                /* add node at the end */
                temp -> link = malloc ( sizeof ( struct node ) ) ;
                temp = temp -> link ;
        }

        /* assign data to the last node */
        temp -> data = num ;
        temp -> link = NULL ;
}

/* displays the contents of the linked list */
displaylist( )
{

        visit = start ;

        /* traverse the entire linked list */
        while ( visit != NULL )
        {
                printf ( "%d ", visit -> data ) ;
                visit = visit -> link ;
        }
}

/* counts the number of nodes present in the linked list */
count ( struct node * q )
{
        int c = 0 ;

        /* traverse the entire linked list */
        while ( q != NULL )
        {
                q = q -> link ;
                c++ ;
        }

        return c ;
}
```

```
selection_sort ( int n )
{
    int i, j, k, temp ;
    struct node *p, *q ;

    p = start ;
    for ( i = 0 ; i < n - 1 ; i++ )
    {
        q = p -> link ;

        for ( j = i + 1 ; j < n ; j++ )
        {
            if ( p -> data > q -> data )
            {
                temp = p -> data ;
                p -> data = q -> data ;
                q -> data = temp ;
            }
            q = q -> link ;
        }
        p = p -> link ;
    }
}

bubble_sort ( int n )
{
    int i, j, k, temp ;
    struct node *p, *q ;

    k = n ;
    for ( i = 0 ; i < n - 1 ; i++, k-- )
    {
        p = start ;
        q = p -> link ;

        for ( j = 1 ; j < k ; j++ )
        {
```

```
            if ( p -> data > q -> data )
            {
                temp = p -> data ;
                p -> data = q -> data ;
                q -> data = temp ;
            }
            p = p -> link ;
            q = q -> link ;
        }
    }
}
```

In the above program, we have added nodes to the linked list using **getdata( )**, which in turn calls **append( )**. After accepting the data, we have sorted the linked list using **selection_sort( )** function. The same procedure of receiving data, building a linked list and sorting is repeated again; the only difference being, this time we have used the **bubble_sort( )** function to carry out the sorting. Both the functions are pretty straightforward as they use the same logic as is used while sorting an array.

Both the functions suffer from the limitation that they swap the data part of the node. Consider a case where we have to sort records. In this case, to perform one exchange of records, we need to copy the entire record thrice using the following statements:

```
struct emp
{
    char name ;
    int age ;
    float salary ;
} temp ;

struct empl
{
    char name ;
    int age ;
```

```
        float salary ;
        struct empl *link ;
} *p, *q ;

strcpy ( temp.name, p -> name ) ;
strcpy ( p -> name, q -> name ) ;
strcpy ( q -> name, temp.name )

temp.age = p -> age ;
p -> age = q -> age ;
q -> age = temp.age ;

temp.sal = p -> sal ;
p -> sal = q -> sal ;
q -> sal = temp.sal ;
```

Thus a great deal of time would be lost in swapping the records.

This limitation can be overcome if we readjust links instead of exchanging data. This has been achieved through the following program.

```
/* Program 64 */
#include "alloc.h"

struct node
{
        int data ;
        struct node *link ;
} *start, *visit ;

main( )
{
        getdata( ) ;
        clrscr( ) ;
        printf ( "\nLinked List Before Sorting:\n" ) ;
        displaylist( ) ;
```

```
        selection_sort( ) ;
        printf ( "\nLinked List After Selection Sorting:\n" ) ;
        displaylist( ) ;
        getch( ) ;

        getdata( ) ;
        clrscr( ) ;
        printf ( "\nLinked List Before Sorting:\n" ) ;
        displaylist( ) ;

        bubble_sort( ) ;
        printf ( "\nLinked List After Bubble Sorting:\n" ) ;
        displaylist( ) ;
        getch( ) ;
}

getdata( )
{
        int val, n ;
        char ch ;
        struct node *newnode;

        clrscr( ) ;

        newnode = NULL ;
        do
        {
            printf ( "\nEnter a value: " ) ;
            scanf ( "%d", &val ) ;

            append ( &newnode, val ) ;

            printf ( "\nAny More Nodes (Y/N): " ) ;
            ch = getche( ) ;
        } while ( ch == 'y' || ch == 'Y' ) ;

        start =  newnode ;
}
```

```
/* adds a node at the end of a linked list */
append ( struct node **q, int num )
{
    struct node *temp ;
    temp = *q ;

    if ( *q == NULL ) /* if the list is empty, create first node */
    {
        *q = malloc ( sizeof ( struct node ) ) ;
        temp = *q ;
    }
    else
    {
        /* go to last node */
        while ( temp -> link != NULL )
        temp = temp -> link ;

        /* add node at the end */
        temp -> link = malloc ( sizeof ( struct node ) ) ;
        temp = temp -> link ;
    }

    /* assign data to the last node */
    temp -> data = num ;
    temp -> link = NULL ;
}

/* displays the contents of the linked list */
displaylist( )
{
    visit = start ;

    /* traverse the entire linked list */
    while ( visit != NULL )
    {
        printf ( "%d ", visit -> data ) ;
        visit = visit -> link ;
```

```
        }
}

selection_sort( )
{
    struct node *p, *q, *r, *s, *temp ;

    p = r = start ;
    while ( p -> link != NULL )
    {
        s = q = p -> link ;
        while ( q != NULL )
        {
            if ( p -> data > q -> data )
            {
                if ( p -> link == q ) /* Adjacent Nodes */
                {
                    if ( p == start )
                    {
                        p -> link = q -> link ;
                        q -> link = p ;

                        temp = p ;
                        p = q ;
                        q = temp ;

                        start = p ;
                        r = p ;
                        s = q ;
                        q = q -> link ;
                    }
                    else
                    {
                        p -> link = q -> link ;
                        q -> link = p ;
                        r -> link = q ;

                        temp = p ;
```

```
                    p = q ;
                    q = temp ;


                    s = q ;
                    q = q -> link ;
                }
        }
        else
        {
            if ( p == start )
            {
                    temp = q -> link ;
                    q -> link = p -> link ;
                    p -> link = temp ;

                    s -> link = p ;

                    temp = p ;
                    p = q ;
                    q = temp ;


                    s = q ;
                    q = q -> link ;
                    start = p ;
            }
            else
            {
                    temp = q -> link ;
                    q -> link = p -> link ;
                    p -> link = temp ;

                    r -> link = q ;
                    s -> link = p ;

                    temp = p ;
                    p = q ;
                    q = temp ;
```

```
                        s = q ;
                        q = q -> link ;
                    }
                }
            }
            else
            {
                s = q ;
                q = q -> link ;
            }
        }
        r = p ;
        p = p -> link ;
    }
}

bubble_sort( )
{
    struct node *p, *q, *r, *s, *temp ;
    s = NULL ;

    /* r precedes p and s points to the node up to which comparisons are to
       be made */
    while ( s != start -> link )
    {
        r = p = start ;
        q = p -> link ;

        while ( p != s )
        {
            if ( p -> data > q -> data )
            {
                if ( p == start )
                {
                    temp = q -> link ;
                    q -> link = p ;
                    p -> link = temp ;
```

```
                            start = q ;
                            r = q ;
                        }
                    else
                        {
                            temp = q -> link ;
                            q -> link = p ;
                            p -> link = temp ;

                            r -> link = q ;
                            r = q ;
                        }
                }
            else
                {
                    r = p ;
                    p = p -> link ;
                }
            q = p -> link ;
            if ( q == s )
                s = p ;
        }
    }
}
```

Unlike the previous program we have omitted the **count( )** function. Instead we have traversed the entire linked list while carrying out the sorting.

Let us understand the **selection_sort( )** and the **bubble_sort( )** functions one by one. In **selection_sort( )**, pointers **p** and **q** point to the nodes being compared and the pointers **r** and **s** point to the node prior to **p** and **q** respectively. Initially, **p** and **r** are set to **start**, where **start** is a pointer to the first node in the list. Also, to begin with **q** and **s** are set to **p -> link**. The outer loop is controlled by the condition **p -> link != NULL** and the inner loop is controlled by the condition **q != NULL**.

While adjusting the links of the nodes being compared, we would encounter one of the following four cases:

(a) Nodes being compared are adjacent to one another and **p** is pointing to the first node in the list.
(b) Nodes being compared are adjacent to one another and **p** is not pointing to the first node.
(c) Nodes being compared are not adjacent to one another and **p** is pointing to the first node.
(d) Nodes being compared are not adjacent to one another and **p** is not pointing to the first node.

Let us now understand these cases one by one.

Case (a):

When the nodes being compared are adjacent and **p** is pointing to the first node, the following operations are performed:

```
p -> link = q -> link ;
q -> link = p ;

temp = p ;
p = q ;
q = temp ;

start = p ;
r = p ;
s = q ;
q = q -> link ;
```

You can trace these operations with the help of following figure.

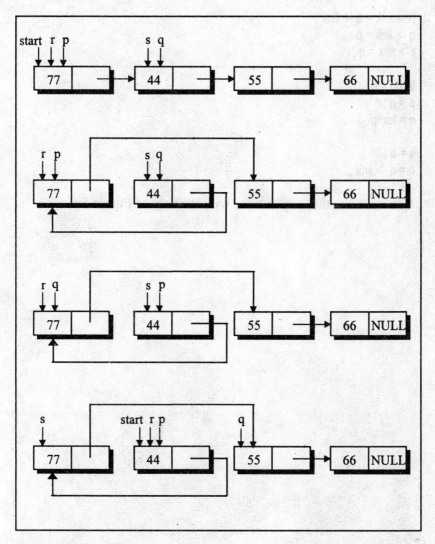

Figure 5.5

Case (b):

When the nodes being compared are adjacent and **p** is not pointing
to the first node, the following operations are performed:

```
p -> link = q -> link ;
q -> link = p ;
r -> link = q ;

temp = p ;
p = q ;
q = temp ;

s = q ;
q = q -> link ;
```

You can trace these operations with the help of Figure 5.6.

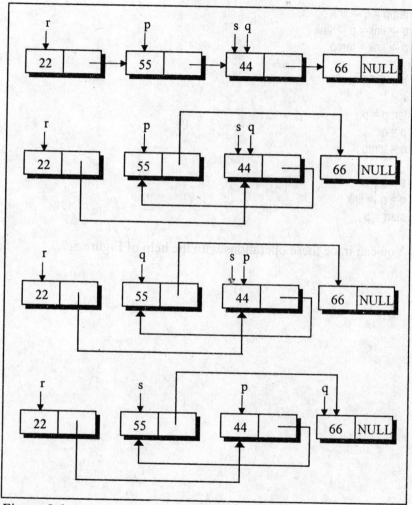

Figure 5.6

Case (c):

When the nodes being compared are not adjacent and **p** is pointing
to the first node, the following operations are performed:

```
temp = q -> link ;
q -> link = p -> link ;
p -> link = temp ;

s -> link = p ;

temp = p ;
p = q ;
q = temp ;

s = q ;
q = q -> link ;
start = p ;
```

You can trace these operations with the help of Figure 5.7.

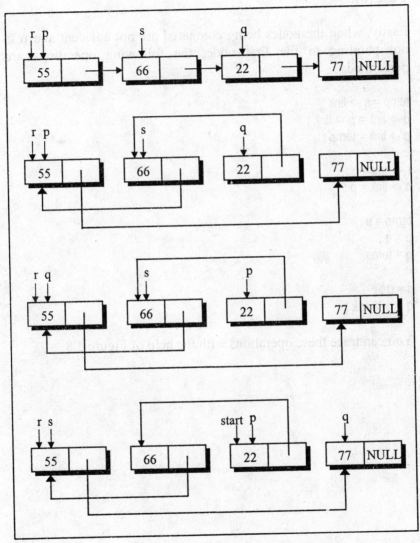

Figure 5.7

Case (d):

Lastly, when the nodes being compared are not adjacent and **p** is not pointing to the first node, the following operations are performed:

```
temp = q -> link ;
q -> link = p -> link ;
p -> link = temp ;

r -> link = q ;
s -> link = p ;

temp = p ;
p = q ;
q = temp ;

s = q ;
q = q -> link ;
```

You can trace these operations with the help of Figure 5.8.

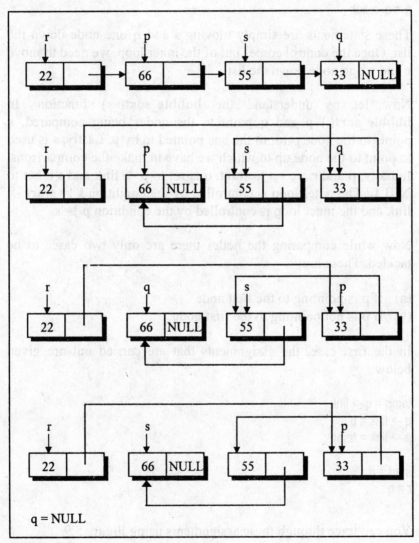

Figure 5.8

If **p -> data** is not greater than **q ->** data then the only changes required are:

s = q ;

```
q = q -> link ;
```

These statements are simply moving **s** and **q** one node down the list. Once the control comes out of the inner loop, we need to move **r** and **p** one node down the list.

Now let us understand the **bubble_sort( )** function. In **bubble_sort( )** **p** and **q** point to the nodes being compared, **r** points to the node prior to the one pointed to by **p**. Lastly, **s** is used to point to the node up to which we have to make the comparisons. Initially, **p** and **r** are set to **start**, **q** is set to **p -> link** and **s** is set to **NULL**. The outer loop is controlled by the condition **s != start -> link** and the inner loop is controlled by the condition **p != s**.

Now while comparing the nodes there are only two cases to be tackled. These are:

(a) If **p** is pointing to the first node
(b) If **p** is not pointing to the first node

In the first case, the assignments that are carried out are given below:

```
temp = q -> link ;
q -> link = p ;
p -> link = temp ;

start = q ;
r = q ;
```

You can trace through these assignments using Figure 5.9.

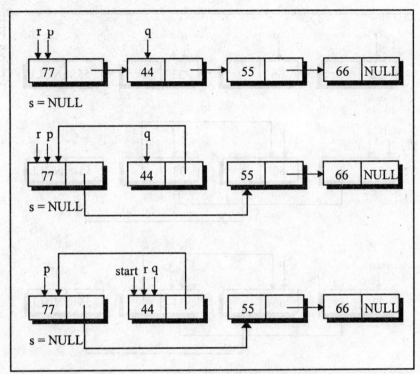

Figure 5.9

On the other hand, when **p** is not pointing to **start**, the following operations should be performed:

```
temp = q -> link ;
q -> link = p ;
p -> link = temp ;

r -> link = q ;
r = q ;
```

Once again referring to Figure 5.10 would help you understand these operations easily.

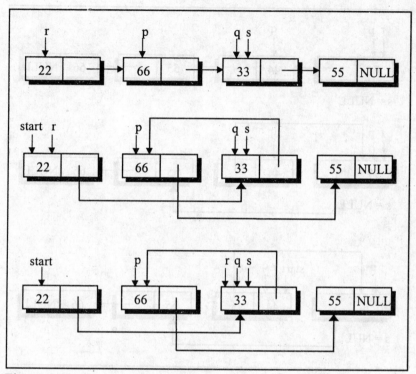

Figure 5.10

When the condition **p->data > q->data** becomes false, we need to store the address of node currently being pointed to by **p** in **r** and then shift **p** and **q** one node down the list.

In every iteration of the outer loop, the biggest element gets stored at the end. This element naturally should not be used to carry out the comparisons during the next iteration of the outer loop. That is, during every iteration of the outer loop, the inner loop should be executed one time less. The pointer **s** is used to keep track of the node up to which the comparisons should be made during the next iteration.

Circular Linked List

The linked lists that we have seen so far are often known as linear linked lists. All elements of such a linked list can be accessed by first setting up a pointer pointing to the first node in the list and then traversing the entire list using this pointer. Although a linked linear list is a useful data structure, it has several shortcomings. For example, given a pointer **p** to a node in a linear list, we cannot reach any of the nodes that precede the node to which **p** is pointing. This disadvantage can be overcome by making a small change to the structure of a linear list such that the **link** field in the last node contains a pointer back to the first node rather than a **NULL**. Such a list is called a **circular linked list** and is illustrated in Figure 5.11.

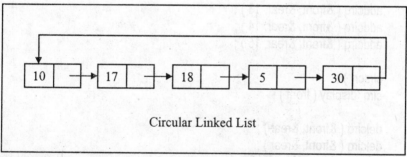

Circular Linked List

Figure 5.11

From any point in such a list it is possible to reach any other point in the list. If we begin at a given node and traverse the entire list, we ultimately end up at the starting point. A circular linked list does not have a first or last node. We must, therefore, establish a first and last node by convention. A circular linked list can be used to represent a stack and a queue. The following program implements a queue as a circular linked list.

```
/* Program 65*/
/* Program to implement a circular queue as a linked list */
#include "alloc.h"
```

```
struct node
{
    int data ;
    struct node * link ;
} ;

main( )
{
    struct node *front, *rear ;

    front = rear = NULL ;

    addcirq ( &front, &rear, 10 ) ;
    addcirq ( &front, &rear, 11 ) ;
    addcirq ( &front, &rear, 12 ) ;
    addcirq ( &front, &rear, 13 ) ;
    addcirq ( &front, &rear, 14 ) ;
    addcirq ( &front, &rear, 15 ) ;

    clrscr( ) ;
    cirq_display ( front ) ;

    delcirq ( &front, &rear ) ;
    delcirq ( &front, &rear ) ;
    delcirq ( &front, &rear ) ;

    printf ( "\n\nAfter deletion :\n" ) ;
    cirq_display ( front ) ;
}

/* adds a new element at the end of queue */
addcirq ( struct node **f, struct node **r, int item )
{
    struct node *q ;

    /* create new node */
    q = malloc ( sizeof ( struct node ) ) ;
```

```
    q -> data = item ;

    /* if the queue is empty */
    if ( *f == NULL )
        *f = q ;
    else
        ( *r ) -> link = q ;

    *r = q ;
    ( *r ) -> link = *f ;
}

/* removes an element from front of queue */
delcirq ( struct node **f, struct node **r )
{
    struct node *q ;
    int item ;

    /* if queue is empty */
    if ( *f == NULL )
        printf ( "queue is empty" ) ;
    else
    {
        if ( *f == *r )
        {
            item = ( *f ) -> data ;
            free ( *f ) ;
            *f = NULL ;
            *r = NULL ;
        }
        else
        {
            /* delete the node */
            q = *f ;
            item = q -> data ;
            *f = ( *f ) -> link ;
            ( *r ) -> link = *f ;
            free ( q ) ;
```

```
        }
        return ( item ) ;
    }
}

/* displays whole of the queue */
cirq_display ( struct node *f )
{
    struct node *q = f, *p = NULL ;

    printf ( "\nfront --> " ) ;

    /* traverse the entire linked list */
    while ( q != p )
    {
        printf ( "%2d ", q -> data ) ;

        q = q -> link ;
        p = f ;
    }
    printf ( " --> .... front" ) ;
}
```

Trees

The data structures that we have seen so far (such as linked lists, stacks, and queues) were linear data structures. As against this, trees are non-linear data structures. Trees are encountered frequently in everyday life.

In a linked list each node has a link which points to another node. In a tree structure, however, each node may point to several other nodes (which may then point to several other nodes, etc.). Thus a tree is a very flexible and powerful data structure that can be used for a wide variety of applications. For example, suppose we wish to use a data structure to represent a person and all of his or her descendants. Assume that the person's name is **Rahul** and that he has 3 children, **Sanjay**, **Sameer** and **Nisha**. Also suppose that **Sameer** has 3 children, **Abhay**, **Ajit** & **Madhu** and **Nisha** has one child **Neha**. We can represent **Rahul** and his descendants quite naturally with the tree structure shown in Figure 5.12.

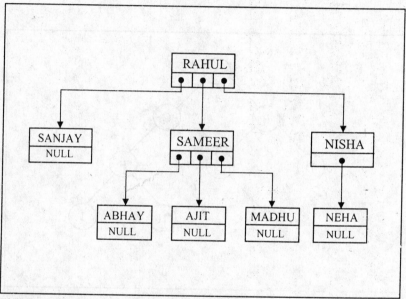

Figure 5.12

Notice that each tree node contains a name for data and one or more pointers to the other tree nodes.

Although the nodes in a general tree may contain any number of pointers to the other tree nodes, a large number of data structures have at the most two pointers to the other tree nodes. This type of a tree is called a **binary tree**. In this chapter we would restrict our discussion of trees to only binary trees.

Binary Trees

Let us begin our study of binary trees by discussing some basic concepts and terminology. A simple binary tree is shown in Figure 5.13.

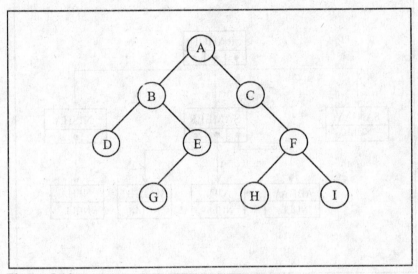

Figure 5.13

A binary tree is a finite set of elements that is either empty or is partitioned into three disjoint subsets. The first subset contains a single element called the **root** of the tree. The other two subsets are themselves binary trees, called the **left** and **right subtrees** of the original tree. A left or right subtree can be empty. Each element of a binary tree is called a **node** of the tree and the tree consists of nine nodes with **A** as its root. Its left subtree is rooted at **B** and its right subtree is rooted at **C**. This is indicated by the two branches emanating from **A** to **B** on the left and to **C** on the right. The absence of a branch indicates an empty subtree. For example, the left subtree of the binary tree rooted at **C** and the right subtree of the binary tree rooted at **E** are both empty. The binary trees rooted at **D, G, H** and **I** have empty right and left subtrees.

Figure 5.14 illustrates some structures that are not binary trees. Be sure that you understand why each of them is not a binary tree as just defined.

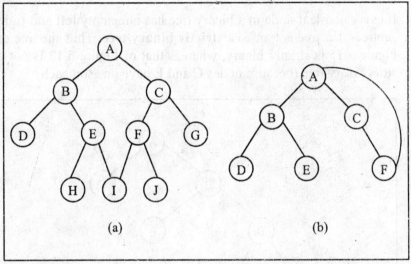

(a)   (b)

Figure 5.14

Let us now get used to some more terminology used in association with binary trees. If **A** is the root of a binary tree and **B** is the root of its left or right subtree, then **A** is said to be the **father** of **B** and **B** is said to be the **left** or **right son** of **A**. A node that has no sons (such as **D**, **G**, **H**, or **I** of Figure 5.13) is called a **leaf**. In general any node say **n1**, is an **ancestor** of node **n2** (and **n2** is a **descendant** of **n1**) if **n1** is either the father of **n2** or the father of some ancestor of **n2**. For example, in the tree of Figure 5.13, **A** is an ancestor of **C**. A node **n2** is a **left descendant** of node **n1** if **n2** is either the left son of **n1** or a descendant of the left son of **n1**. A **right descendant** may be similarly defined. Two nodes are **brothers** if they are left and right sons of the same father.

Although natural trees grow with their roots in the ground and their leaves in the air, computer scientists almost universally portray tree data structures with the root at the top and the leaves at the bottom. The direction from the root to the leaves is "down" and the opposite direction is "up". Going from the leaves to the root is called **climbing** the tree, and going from the root to the leaves is called **descending** the tree.

If every non-leaf node in a binary tree has nonempty left and right subtrees, the tree is termed a **strictly binary tree**. Thus the tree of Figure 5.15 is strictly binary, whereas that of Figure 5.13 is not a strict binary tree (because nodes **C** and **E** have one son each).

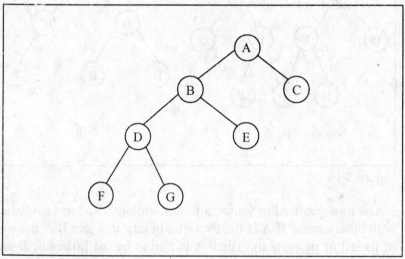

Figure 5.15

The **level** of a node in a binary tree is defined as follows. The root of the tree has level **0**, and the level of any other node in the tree is one more than the level of its father. For example, in the binary tree of Figure 5.13, node **E** is at level 2 and node **H** is at level 3. The **depth** of a binary tree is the maximum level of any leaf in the tree. This equals the length of the longest path from the root to any leaf. Thus the depth of the tree of Figure 5.13 is 3. A **complete binary tree** of depth **d** is a strictly binary tree all of whose leaves are at level **d**. Figure 5.16 illustrates the complete binary tree of depth 3.

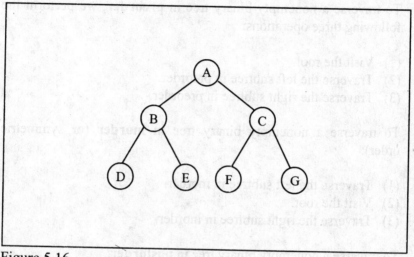

Figure 5.16

Traversal of a Binary Tree

The traversal of a binary tree is to visit each node in the tree exactly once. Binary tree traversal is useful in many applications. The order in which nodes of a linear list are visited is clearly from first to last. However, there is no such natural linear order for the nodes of a tree. The methods differ primarily in the order in which they visit the nodes. There are three popular methods of binary tree traversal. These methods are known as **inorder** traversal, **preorder** traversal and **postorder** traversal. In each of these methods nothing need be done to traverse an empty binary tree. The functions used to traverse a tree using these methods can be kept quite short if we understand the recursive nature of the binary tree. Recall that a binary tree is recursive in that each subtree is really a binary tree itself. Thus traversing a binary tree involves visiting the root node and traversing its left and right subtrees. The only difference among the methods is the order in which these three operations are performed.

To traverse a nonempty binary tree in **preorder**, we perform the following three operations:

(1) Visit the root.
(2) Traverse the left subtree in preorder.
(3) Traverse the right subtree in preorder.

To traverse a nonempty binary tree in **inorder** (or symmetric order):

(1) Traverse the left subtree in inorder.
(2) Visit the root.
(3) Traverse the right subtree in inorder.

To traverse a nonempty binary tree in **postorder**:

(1) Traverse the left subtree in postorder.
(2) Traverse the right subtree in postorder.
(3) Visit the root.

Many algorithms that use binary trees proceed in two phases. The first phase builds a binary tree, and the second traverses the tree. As an example of such an algorithm, consider the following sorting method. Given a list of numbers in an input file, we wish to print them in ascending order. As we read the numbers, they can be inserted into a binary tree such as the one of Figure 5.17. When a number is compared with the contents of a node in the tree, a left branch is taken if the number is smaller than the contents of the node and a right branch if it is greater or equal to the contents of the node. Thus if the input list is

20 17 6 8 10 7 18 13 12 5

the binary tree of Figure 5.17 is produced.

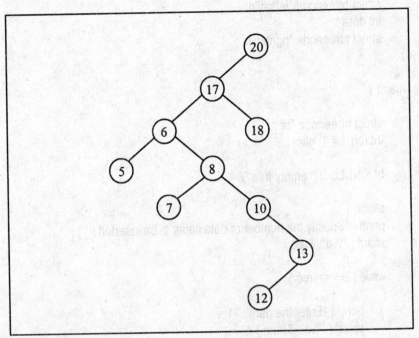

Figure 5.17

Such a binary tree has the property that all elements in the left subtree of a node **n** are less than the contents of **n**, and all elements in the right subtree of **n** are greater than or equal to the contents of **n**. A binary tree that has these properties is called a **Binary Search tree**. If a binary search tree is traversed in inorder (left, root, right) and the contents of each node are printed as the node is visited, the numbers are printed in ascending order. Convince yourself that this is the case for the binary search tree of Figure 5.17. The program to implement this algorithm is given below.

```
/* Program 66 */
/* Program to implement a binary tree */
#include "alloc.h"

struct btreenode
{
```

```
        struct btreenode *leftchild ;
        int data ;
        struct btreenode *rightchild ;
} ;

main( )
{
        struct btreenode *bt ;
        int req, i = 1, num ;

        bt = NULL ;  /* empty tree */

        clrscr( ) ;
        printf ( "Specify the number of data items to be inserted : " ) ;
        scanf ( "%d", &req ) ;

        while ( i++ <= req )
        {
                printf ( "Enter the data : " ) ;
                scanf ( "%d", &num ) ;
                insert ( &bt, num ) ;
        }

        clrscr( ) ;
        printf ( "\nInorder Traversal: " ) ;
        inorder ( bt ) ;

        printf ( "\nPreorder Traversal: " ) ;
        preorder ( bt ) ;

        printf ( "\nPostorder Traversal: " ) ;
        postorder ( bt ) ;
}

/* inserts a new node in a binary search tree */
insert ( struct btreenode **sr, int num )
{
        if ( *sr == NULL )
```

```
    {
        *sr = malloc ( sizeof ( struct btreenode ) ) ;

        ( *sr ) -> leftchild = NULL ;
        ( *sr ) -> data = num ;
        ( *sr ) -> rightchild = NULL ;
        return ;
    }
    else   /* search the node to which new node will be attached */
    {
        /* if new data is less, traverse to left */
        if ( num < ( *sr ) -> data )
            insert ( &( ( *sr ) -> leftchild ), num ) ;
        else
            /* else traverse to right */
            insert ( &( ( *sr ) -> rightchild ), num ) ;
    }
    return ;
}

/* traverse a binary search tree in a LDR (Left-Data-Right) fashion */
inorder ( struct btreenode *sr )
{
    if ( sr != NULL )
    {
        inorder ( sr -> leftchild ) ;

        /* print the data of the node whose leftchild is NULL or the path
           has already been traversed */
        printf ( "%d ", sr -> data ) ;

        inorder ( sr -> rightchild ) ;
    }
    else
        return
}

/* traverse a binary search tree in a DLR (Data-Left-right) fashion */
```

```
preorder ( struct btreenode *sr )
{
    if ( sr != NULL )
    {
        /* print the data of a node */
        printf ( "%d ", sr -> data ) ;
        /* traverse till leftchild is not NULL */
        preorder ( sr -> leftchild ) ;
        /* traverse till rightchild is not NULL */
        preorder ( sr -> rightchild ) ;
    }
    else
        return ;
}

/* traverse a binary search tree in LRD (Left-Right-Data) fashion */
postorder ( struct btreenode *sr )
{
    if ( sr != NULL )
    {
        postorder ( sr -> leftchild ) ;
        postorder ( sr -> rightchild ) ;
        printf ( "%d ", sr -> data ) ;
    }
    else
        return ;
}
```

Deletion from a Binary Tree

In addition to techniques for inserting data in a binary tree and traversing the tree, practical examples call for deleting data from the binary tree. Assuming that we will pass the specified data item that we wish to delete to the delete function, there are four possible cases that we need to consider:

(a)   No node in the tree contains the specified data.

(b) The node containing the data has no children.
(c) The node containing the data has exactly one child.
(d) The node containing the data has two children.

For **case (a)** we merely need to print the message that the data item is not present in the tree.

In **case (b)** since the node to be deleted has no children the memory occupied by this should be freed and either the left link or the right link of the parent of this node should be set to **NULL**. Which of these to set to **NULL** depends upon whether the node being deleted is a left child or a right child of its parent.

In **case (c)** since the node to be deleted has one child the solution is again rather simple. We have to adjust the pointer of the parent of the node to be deleted such that after deletion it points to the child of the node being deleted. This is illustrated in Figure 5.18.

For **case (d)**, in which the node to be deleted has two children the solution is more complex. Consider node **C** in Figure 5.18 **Before Deletion**. From the figure the inorder successor of the node **C** is node **J**. The data of this inoder successor should now be copied into the node to be deleted and a pointer should be set up pointing to the inorder successor (node **J**). This inorder successor would have one or zero children. This node should then be deleted using the same procedure as for deleting a one child or a zero child node. Thus the whole logic of deleting a node with two children is to locate the inorder successor, copy its data and reduce the problem to a simple deletion of a node with one or zero children. A program to implement this deletion procedure is given below.

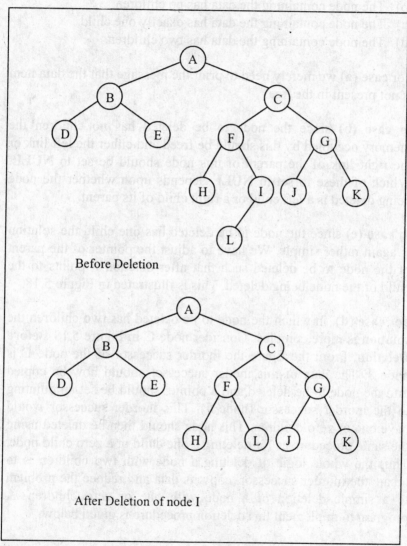

Before Deletion

After Deletion of node I

Figure 5.18

/* Program 67 */
/* Program to to delete a node form a binary search tree */
#include "alloc.h"
#define TRUE 1

```
#define FALSE 0

struct btreenode
{
    struct btreenode *leftchild ;
    int data ;
    struct btreenode *rightchild ;
} ;

main( )
{
    struct btreenode *bt ;
    int req, i = 0, num, a[ ]= { 11, 9, 13, 8, 10, 12, 14, 15, 7 } ;

    bt = NULL ;  /* empty tree */

    clrscr( ) ;

    while ( i <= 8 )
    {
        insert ( &bt, a[i] ) ;
        i++ ;
    }

    clrscr( ) ;
    printf ( "Binary tree before deletion: " ) ;
    inorder ( bt ) ;

    delete ( &bt, 10 ) ;
    printf ( "\nBinary tree after deletion: " ) ;
    inorder ( bt ) ;

    delete ( &bt, 14 ) ;
    printf ( "\nBinary tree after deletion: " ) ;
    inorder ( bt ) ;

    delete ( &bt, 8 ) ;
    printf ( "\nBinary tree after deletion: " ) ;
```

```
        inorder ( bt ) ;

        delete ( &bt, 13 ) ;
        printf ( "\nBinary tree after deletion: " ) :
        inorder ( bt ) ;
}

/* inserts a new node in a binary search tree */
insert ( struct btreenode **sr, int num )
{
    if ( *sr == NULL )
    {
        *sr = malloc ( sizeof ( struct btreenode ) ) ;

        ( *sr ) -> leftchild = NULL ;
        ( *sr ) -> data = num ;
        ( *sr ) -> rightchild = NULL ;
        return ;
    }
    else   /* search the node to which new node will be attached */
    {
        /* if new data is less, traverse to left */
        if ( num < ( *sr ) -> data )
            insert ( &( ( *sr ) -> leftchild ), num ) ;
        else
            /* else traverse to right */
            insert ( &( ( *sr ) -> rightchild ), num ) ;
    }
    return ;
}

/* deletes a node from the binary search tree */
delete ( struct btreenode **root, int num )
{
    int found ;
    struct btreenode *parent, *x, *xsucc ;

    /* if tree is empty */
```

```
if ( *root == NULL )
{
    printf ( "\nTree is empty" ) ;
    return ;
}

parent = x = NULL ;

/* call to search function to find the node to be deleted */
search ( root, num, &parent, &x, &found ) ;

/* if the node to deleted is not found */
if ( found == FALSE )
{
    printf ( "\nData to be deleted, not found" ) ;
    return ;
}

/* if the node to be deleted has two children */
if ( x -> leftchild != NULL && x -> rightchild != NULL )
{
    parent = x ;
    xsucc = x -> rightchild ;

    while ( xsucc -> leftchild != NULL )
    {
        parent = xsucc ;
        xsucc = xsucc -> leftchild ;
    }

    x -> data = xsucc -> data ;
    x = xsucc ;
}

/* if the node to be deleted has no child */
if ( x -> leftchild == NULL && x -> rightchild == NULL )
{
    if ( parent -> rightchild == x )
```

```
            parent -> rightchild = NULL ;
        else
            parent -> leftchild = NULL ;

        free ( x ) ;
        return ;
    }

    /* if the node to be deleted has only rightchild */
    if ( x -> leftchild == NULL && x -> rightchild != NULL )
    {
        if ( parent -> leftchild == x )
            parent -> leftchild = x -> rightchild ;
        else
            parent -> rightchild = x -> rightchild ;

        free ( x ) ;
        return ;
    }

    /* if the node to be deleted has only left child */
    if ( x -> leftchild != NULL && x -> rightchild == NULL )
    {
        if ( parent -> leftchild == x )
            parent -> leftchild = x -> leftchild ;
        else
            parent -> rightchild = x -> leftchild ;

        free ( x ) ;
        return ;
    }
}

/* returns the address of the node to be deleted, address of its parent
   and whether the node is found or not */
search ( struct btreenode **root, int num, struct btreenode **par,
         struct btreenode **x, int *found )
{
```

```
struct btreenode *q ;

q = *root ;
*found = FALSE ;
*par = NULL ;

while ( q != NULL )
{
    /* if the node to be deleted is found */
    if ( q -> data == num )
    {
        *found = TRUE ;
        *x = q ;
        return ;
    }

    if ( q -> data > num )
    {
        *par = q ;
        q = q -> leftchild ;
    }
    else
    {
        *par = q ;
        q = q -> rightchild ;
    }
}
}

/* traverse a binary search tree in a LDR (Left-Data-Right) fashion */
inorder ( struct btreenode *sr )
{
    if ( sr != NULL )
    {
        inorder ( sr -> leftchild ) ;

        /* print the data of the node whose leftchild is NULL or the path
           has already been traversed */
```

```
        printf ( "%d ", sr -> data ) ;

        inorder ( sr -> rightchild ) ;
    }
    else
        return ;

}
```

Threaded Binary Trees

Both the recursive and non-recursive procedures for binary tree traversal require that pointers to all of the free nodes be kept temporarily on a stack. It is possible to write binary tree traversal procedure that do not require that any pointers to the nodes be put on the stack. Such procedures eliminate the overhead (time and memory) involved in initialising, pushing and popping the stack.

In order to get an idea of how such binary-tree-traversal procedures work, let us look at the tree in Figure 5.19. First we follow the left pointers until we reach node **C**, without, however, pushing the pointers to **A**, **B** and **C** onto a stack. For inorder traversal the data for node **C** is then printed, after which **C**'s right pointer is followed to node **E**. Then the data from node **E** is printed. The next step in our inorder traversal is to go back to node **B** and print its data; however, we did not save any pointers. But suppose that when we created the tree we had replaced the **NULL** right pointer in node **E** with a pointer back to node **B**. We could then easily follow this pointer back to node **B** (see Figure 5.20).

Similarly, suppose we replace the normal **NULL** right pointer of **D** with a pointer back up to **A**, as in Figure 5.21. Then after printing the data in **D**, we can easily jump up to **A** and print its data. These pointers which point inorder successor of a node are called **right threads**. Each **right thread** replaces a normal right pointer in a tree node. Likewise, we can have **left threads** which point to the inorder predecessor of a node.

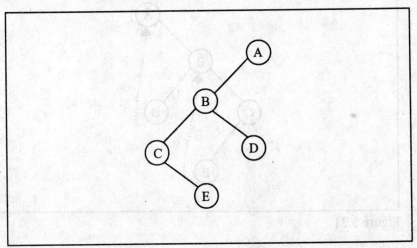

Figure 5.19

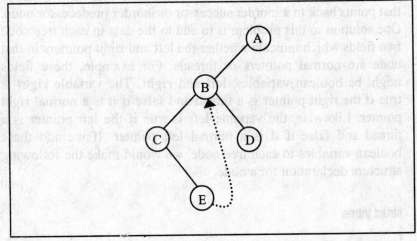

Figure 5.20

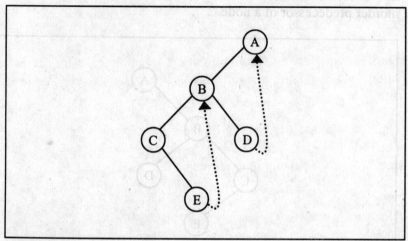

Figure 5.21

The only problem with threads is that the coding requires that we know whether a pointer is a normal pointer to a child or a thread that points back to a inorder successor or inorder predecessor node. One solution to this problem is to add to the data in each tree node two fields which indicate whether the left and right pointers in that node are normal pointers or threads. For example, these fields might be boolean variables, **left** and **right**. The variable **right** is true if the right pointer is a thread and false if it is a normal right pointer. Likewise, the variable **left** is true if the left pointer is a thread and false if it is a normal left pointer. If we add these boolean variables to each tree node, we would make the following structure declaration for a node.

```
struct thtree
{
    enum boolean left ;
    struct thtree *leftchild ;
    int data ;
    struct thtree *rightchild ;
    enum boolean right ;
```

```
};
```

Thus each node would contain data, a left pointer, a true or false value for left thread, a right pointer and a true or false value for right thread.

The program to implement a threaded binary tree is given below. The program also shows how to insert nodes in a threaded binary tree, delete nodes from it and traverse it in inorder traversal.

```
/* Program 68 */
/* Program to implement a threaded binary tree */
#include "alloc.h"

enum boolean
{
    false = 0 ,
    true = 1 ,
};

struct thtree
{
    enum boolean left ;
    struct thtree *leftchild ;
    int data ;
    struct thtree *rightchild ;
    enum boolen right ;
};

main( )
{
    struct thtree *th_head ;

    th_head = NULL ;  /* empty tree */

    insert ( &th_head, 11 ) ;
    insert ( &th_head, 9 ) ;
```

```
        insert ( &th_head, 13 ) ;
        insert ( &th_head, 8 ) ;
        insert ( &th_head, 10 ) ;
        insert ( &th_head, 12 ) ;
        insert ( &th_head, 14 ) ;
        insert ( &th_head, 15 ) ;
        insert ( &th_head, 7 ) ;

        clrscr( ) ;
        printf ( "Threaded binary tree before deletion: " ) ;
        inorder ( th_head ) ;

        delete ( &th_head, 10 ) ;
        printf ( "\nThreaded binary tree after deletion: " ) ;
        inorder ( th_head ) ;

        delete ( &th_head, 14 ) ;
        printf ( "\nThreaded binary tree after deletion: " ) ;
        inorder ( th_head ) ;

        delete ( &th_head, 8 ) ;
        printf ( "\nThreaded binary tree after deletion: " ) ;
        inorder ( th_head ) ;

        delete ( &th_head, 13 ) ;
        printf ( "\nThreaded binary tree after deletion: " ) ;
        inorder ( th_head ) ;
}

/* inserts a node in a threaded binary tree */
insert ( struct thtree **s, int num )
{
        struct thtree *head = *s , *p, *z ;

        /* allocating a new node */
        z = malloc ( sizeof ( struct thtree ) ) ;

        z -> left = true ; /* indicates a thread */
```

```
z -> data = num ; /* assign new data */
z -> right = true ; /* indicates a thread */

/* if tree is empty */
if ( *s == NULL )
{
    head = malloc ( sizeof ( struct thtree ) ) ;

    /* the entire tree is treated as a left subtree of the head node */
    head -> left = false ;
    head -> leftchild = z ;  /* z becomes leftchild of the head node */
    head -> data = -9999 ;  /* no data */
    head -> rightchild = head ;  /* right link will always be pointing
                                        to itself */

    head -> right = false ;

    *s = head ;

    z -> leftchild = head ;  /* left thread to head */
    z -> rightchild = head ;  /* right thread to head */
}
else /* if tree is non-empty */
{
    p = head -> leftchild ;

    /* traverse till the thread is found attached to the head */
    while ( p != head )
    {
        if ( p -> data > num )
        {
            if ( p -> left != true ) /* checking for a thread */
                p = p -> leftchild ;
            else
            {
                z -> leftchild = p -> leftchild ;
                p -> leftchild = z ;
                p -> left = false ; /* indicates a link */
                z -> right = true ;
```

```
                        z -> rightchild = p ;
                        return ;
                    }
                }
            else
            {
                if ( p -> data < num )
                {
                    if ( p -> right != true )
                        p = p -> rightchild ;
                    else
                    {
                        z -> rightchild = p -> rightchild ;
                        p -> rightchild = z ;
                        p -> right = false ;  /* indicates a link */
                        z -> left = true ;
                        z -> leftchild = p ;
                        return ;
                    }
                }
            }
        }
    }
}

/* deletes a node from the binary search tree */
delete ( struct thtree **root, int num )
{
    int found ;
    struct thtree *parent, *x, *xsucc ;

    /* if tree is empty */
    if ( *root == NULL )
    {
        printf ( "\nTree is empty" ) ;
        return ;
    }
```

```
parent = x = NULL ;

/* call to search function to find the node to be deleted */
search ( root, num, &parent, &x, &found ) ;

/* if the node to deleted is not found */
if ( found == false )
{
    printf ( "\nData to be deleted, not found" ) ;
    return ;
}

/* if the node to be deleted has two children */
if ( x -> left == false && x -> right == false )
{
    parent = x ;
    xsucc = x -> rightchild ;

    while ( xsucc -> left == false )
    {
        parent = xsucc ;
        xsucc = xsucc -> leftchild ;
    }

    x -> data = xsucc -> data ;
    x = xsucc ;
}

/* if the node to be deleted has no child */
if ( x -> left == true && x -> right == true )
{
    if ( parent -> rightchild == x )
    {
        parent -> right = true ;
        parent -> rightchild = x -> rightchild ;
    }
    else
    {
```

```
            parent -> left = true ;
            parent -> leftchild = x -> leftchild ;
        }

    free ( x ) ;
    return ;
}

/* if the node to be deleted has only rightchild */
if ( x -> left == true && x -> right == false )
{
    if ( parent -> leftchild == x )
    {
        parent -> leftchild = x -> rightchild ;
        x -> rightchild -> leftchild = x -> leftchild ;
    }
    else
    {
        parent -> rightchild = x -> rightchild ;
        x -> rightchild -> leftchild = parent ;
    }

    free ( x ) ;
    return ;
}

/* if the node to be deleted has only left child */
if ( x -> left == false && x -> right == true )
{
    if ( parent -> leftchild == x )
    {
        parent -> leftchild = x -> leftchild ;
        x -> leftchild -> rightchild = parent ;
    }
    else
    {
        parent -> rightchild = x -> leftchild ;
        x -> leftchild -> rightchild = x -> rightchild ;
```

```
            }

            free ( x ) ;
            return ;
        }
}

/* returns the address of the node to be deleted, address of its parent
   and whether the node is found or not */
search ( struct thtree **root, int num, struct thtree **par,
         struct thtree **x, int *found )
{
        struct thtree *q ;

        q = ( *root ) -> leftchild ;
        *found = false ;
        *par = NULL ;

        while ( q != root )
        {
            /* if the node to be deleted is found */
            if ( q -> data == num )
            {
                *found = true ;
                *x = q ;
                return ;
            }

            if ( q -> data > num )
            {
                *par = q ;
                q = q -> leftchild ;
            }
            else
            {
                *par = q ;
                q = q -> rightchild ;
            }
```

```
        }
    }

/* traverses the threaded binary tree in inorder */
inorder ( struct thtree *root )
{
    struct thtree *p ;

    p = root -> leftchild ;

    while ( p != root )
    {
        while ( p -> left == false )
            p = p -> leftchild ;

        printf ( "%d ", p -> data ) ;

        while ( p -> right == true )
        {
            p = p -> rightchild ;

            if ( p == root )
                break ;

            printf ( "%d ", p -> data ) ;

        }
        p = p -> rightchild ;
    }
}
```

And now a brief explanation about the program.

We have used an enumerated data type **boolean** to store information whether the thread is present or not. If **left** is true it means that there is a left thread and the node has no left child, if **right** is true it shows the presence of right thread and the node has no right child.

To insert a new node in a threaded tree, the **insert( )** function is called which first checks for the empty tree. If the tree is found to be empty a head node is created and the node is joined as its left subtree with both links converted to threads by making **left** and **right** both true and **leftchild** and **rightchild** pointing back to the head node. Otherwise, the node is inserted into the tree so that a threaded binary search tree is created.

Deletion of a node from the threaded binary tree is similar to that of a normal binary tree. That is, we have to identify the four possibilities about the node being deleted:

(a) No node in the tree contains the specified data.
(b) The node has no children.
(c) The node has exactly one child.
(d) The node has two children.

The treatment given to these possibilities is same as the one discussed in the previous section on binary trees except for some minor readjustment of threads.

The threaded binary tree's inorder traversal is different than a normal tree in the sense that we do not have to stack the pointers to nodes visited earlier so as to reach them later. This is avoided by using the threads to ancestors. The procedure to achieve this is as follows.

This procedure begins by first going to the left subtree of the head node using the statement

p = root -> leftchild ;

Then through a **while** loop we follow the leftmost pointers until a thread to a predecessor is found. On encountering this thread we print the data for the leftmost node. Next, through another **while** loop we check the boolean value of the right thread. If this value is true, we follow the thread back up to the ancestor node and print this ancestor node's data. This way we continue to move up till the right thread is true. When the right thread is found to be false we again proceed by going to the right child and checking it left subtree.

As we follow these steps we are sometimes likely to reach the head node, and that is the time to stop the procedure. This is what is being achieved by the statements:

```
if ( p == root )
    break ;
```

Graphs

The only non-linear data structure that we have seen so far is tree. A tree in fact is a special type of graph. Graphs are data structures which have wide-ranging applications in real life like, Analysis of electrical circuits, Finding shortest routes, Statistical analysis, etc. To be able to understand and use the graph data structure one must first get familiar with the definitions and terms used in association with graphs. There are discussed below.

Definitions and Terminology

A graph consists of two sets **v** and **e** where, **v** is a finite, non-empty set of vertices and **e** is a set of pairs of vertices. The pairs of vertices are called edges. A Graph can be of two types: Undirected graph and Directed graph.

In an undirected graph the pair of vertices representing any edge is unordered. Thus, the pairs (**v1, v2**) and (**v2, v1**) represent the same edge.

In a directed graph each edge is represented by a directed pair <**v1, v2**>. **v1** is the tail and **v2** the head of the edge. Therefore

<v2, v1> and <v1, v2> represent two different edges. A directed graph is also called Digraph. In Figure 5.22 the graph **G1** is an undirected graph whereas graph **G2** is a directed graph.

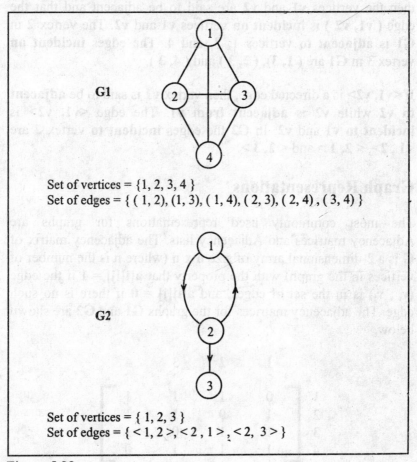

Set of vertices = {1, 2, 3, 4 }
Set of edges = { (1, 2), (1, 3), (1, 4), (2, 3), (2, 4) , (3, 4) }

Set of vertices = { 1, 2, 3 }
Set of edges = { < 1, 2 >, < 2 , 1 >, < 2, 3 > }

Figure 5.22

Note that the edges of a directed graph are drawn with an arrow from the tail to the head.

Adjacent Vertices & Incident Edges

In an undirected graph if (**v1, v2**) is an edge in the set of edges, then the vertices **v1** and **v2** are said to be adjacent and that the edge (**v1, v2**) is **incident on** vertices **v1** and **v2**. The vertex 2 in **G1** is **adjacent to** vertices 1, 3, and 4. The edges **incident on** vertex 3 in **G1** are (1, 3), (2, 3) and (4, 3).

If <**v1, v2**> is a directed edge, then vertex **v1** is said to be **adjacent to v2** while **v2** is **adjacent from v1**. The edge <**v1, v2**> is **incident to v1** and **v2**. In **G2** the edges **incident to** vertex 2 are <1 , 2>, < 2, 1 > and < 2, 3 >.

Graph Representations

The most commonly used representations for graphs are Adjacency matrices and Adjacency lists. The adjacency matrix of **G** is a 2-dimensional array of size **n x n** (where n is the number of vertices in the graph) with the property that **a[i][j] = 1** if the edge (v_i , v_j) is in the set of edges, and **a[i][j] = 0** if there is no such edge. The adjacency matrices for the graphs **G1** and **G2** are shown below.

	1	2	3	4
1	0	1	1	1
2	1	0	1	1
3	1	1	0	1
4	1	1	1	0

	1	2	3
1	0	1	0
2	1	0	1
3	0	0	0

As can be seen from above, thé adjacency matrix for an undirected graph is symmetric. The adjacency matrix for a directed graph need not be symmetric. The space needed to represent a graph using its adjacency matrix is n^2 locations. About half this space can be saved in the case of undirected graphs by storing only the upper or lower triangle of the matrix.

Adjacency Lists

In this representation the **n** rows of the adjacency matrix are represented as **n** linked lists. There is one list for each vertex in the graph. The nodes in list **i** represent the vertices that are adjacent from vertex **i**. Each list has a head node. The head nodes are sequential providing easy random access to the adjacency list for any particular vertex. The adjacency lists for graphs **G1** and **G2** are shown below.

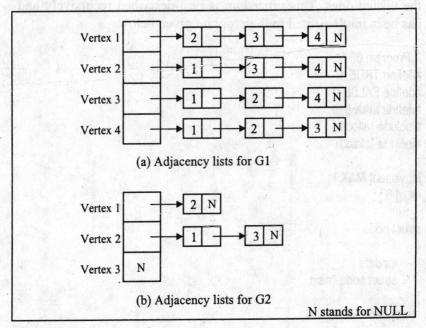

(a) Adjacency lists for G1

(b) Adjacency lists for G2

N stands for NULL

Figure 5.23

Given the root node of a binary tree, one of the most common operation performed is visiting every node of the tree in some order. Similarly, given a vertex in a directed or undirected graph we may wish to visit all vertices in the graph that are reachable from this vertex. This can be done in two ways—using the Depth First Search and the Breadth First Search algorithm.

Depth First Search

Depth first search of an undirected graph proceeds as follows. The start vertex **v** is visited. Next an unvisited vertex **w** adjacent to **v** is selected and a depth first search from **w** is initiated. When a vertex **u** is reached such that all its adjacent vertices have been visited, we back up to the last vertex visited which has an unvisited vertex **w** adjacent to it and initiate a depth first search from **w**. The search terminates when no unvisited vertex can be reached from any of the visited ones. This procedure is best-described recursively and has been implemented in the program given below.

```
/* Program 69 */
#define TRUE 1
#define FALSE 0
#define MAX 8
#include "alloc.h"
#include "stdio.h"

int visited[ MAX ] ;
int q[ 8 ] ;

struct node
{
    int data ;
    struct node *next ;
};
struct node *newnode ;

main( )
```

```
{
    struct node *arr[MAX] ;
    struct node * getnode_write ( int val ) ;
    struct node *v1, *v2, *v3, *v4, *v5, *v6, *v7, *v8 ;

    clrscr( ) ;

    v1 = getnode_write ( 2 ) ;
    arr[ 0 ] = v1 ;
    v1 -> next = v2 = getnode_write ( 3 ) ;
    v2 -> next = NULL ;

    v1 = getnode_write ( 1 ) ;
    arr[ 1 ] = v1 ;
    v1 -> next = v2 = getnode_write ( 4 ) ;
    v2 -> next = v3 = getnode_write ( 5 ) ;
    v3 -> next = NULL ;

    v1 = getnode_write ( 1 ) ;
    arr[ 2 ] = v1 ;
    v1 -> next = v2 = getnode_write ( 6 ) ;
    v2 -> next = v3 = getnode_write ( 7 ) ;
    v3 -> next = NULL ;

    v1 = getnode_write ( 2 ) ;
    arr[ 3 ] = v1 ;
    v1 -> next = v2 = getnode_write ( 8 ) ;
    v2 -> next = NULL ;

    v1 = getnode_write ( 2 ) ;
    arr[ 4 ] = v1 ;
    v1 -> next = v2 = getnode_write ( 8 ) ;
    v2 -> next = NULL ;

    v1 = getnode_write ( 3 ) ;
    arr[ 5 ] = v1 ;
    v1 -> next = v2 = getnode_write ( 8 ) ;
    v2 -> next = NULL ;
```

```
    v1 = getnode_write ( 3 ) ;
    arr[ 6 ] = v1 ;
    v1 -> next = v2 = getnode_write ( 8 ) ;
    v2 -> next = NULL ;

    v1 = getnode_write ( 4 ) ;
    arr[ 7 ] = v1 ;
    v1 -> next = v2 = getnode_write ( 5 ) ;
    v2 -> next = v3 = getnode_write ( 6 ) ;
    v3 -> next = v4 = getnode_write ( 7 ) ;
    v4 -> next = NULL ;

    clrscr( ) ;
    dfs ( 1, arr, 8 ) ;
    getch( ) ;
}

dfs ( int v, struct node **p, int n )
{
    struct node *q ;
    visited [ v - 1 ] = TRUE ;

    printf ( " %d", v ) ;

    q = * ( p + v - 1 ) ;

    while ( q != NULL )
    {
        if ( visited [ q -> data - 1 ] == FALSE )
            dfs ( q -> data, p, n ) ;
        else
            q = q -> next ;
    }
}

struct node * getnode_write ( int val )
{
```

```
newnode = ( struct node * ) malloc ( sizeof ( struct node ) ) ;
newnode -> data = val ;
return newnode ;
}
```

The graph **G** in Figure 5.24 (a) is represented by its adjacency lists shown in Figure 5.24 (b). If a depth first search is initiated from vertex **v1**, then the vertices of **G** are visited in the order: v_1, v_2, v_4, v_8, v_5, v_6, v_3, v_7.

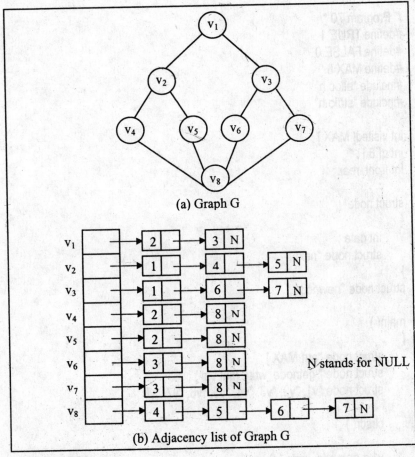

(a) Graph G

(b) Adjacency list of Graph G

N stands for NULL

Figure 5.24

Breadth First Search

Starting at vertex **v** and marking it as visited, breadth first search differs from depth first search in that all unvisited vertices adjacent to **v**, are visited next. Then unvisited vertices adjacent to these vertices are visited and so on. A breadth first search beginning at vertex v_1 of Figure 5.24 would first visit v_1 and then v_2 and v_3. Next vertices v_4, v_5, v_6 and v_7 will be visited and finally v_8. The following program implements this algorithm.

```
/* Program 70 */
#define TRUE 1
#define FALSE 0
#define MAX 8
#include "alloc.h"
#include "stdio.h"

int visited[ MAX ] ;
int q[ 8 ] ;
int front, rear ;

struct node
{
    int data ;
    struct node *next ;
} ;
struct node *newnode ;

main( )
{
    struct node *arr[ MAX ] ;
    struct node * getnode_write ( int val ) ;
    struct node *v1, *v2, *v3, *v4, *v5, *v6, *v7, *v8 ;

    clrscr( ) ;

    v1 = getnode_write ( 2 ) ;
```

```
arr[ 0 ] = v1 ;
v1 -> next = v2 = getnode_write ( 3 ) ;
v2 -> next = NULL ;

v1 = getnode_write ( 1 ) ;
arr[ 1 ] = v1 ;
v1 -> next = v2 = getnode_write ( 4 ) ;
v2 -> next = v3 = getnode_write ( 5 ) ;
v3 -> next = NULL ;

v1 = getnode_write ( 1 ) ;
arr[ 2 ] = v1 ;
v1 -> next = v2 = getnode_write ( 6 ) ;
v2 -> next = v3 = getnode_write ( 7 ) ;
v3 -> next = NULL ;

v1 = getnode_write ( 2 ) ;
arr[ 3 ] = v1 ;
v1 -> next = v2 = getnode_write ( 8 ) ;
v2 -> next = NULL ;

v1 = getnode_write ( 2 ) ;
arr[ 4 ] = v1 ;
v1 -> next = v2 = getnode_write ( 8 )
v2 -> next = NULL ;

v1 = getnode_write ( 3 ) ;
arr[ 5 ] = v1 ;
v1 -> next = v2 = getnode_write ( 8 ) ;
v2 -> next = NULL ;

v1 = getnode_write ( 3 ) ;
arr[ 6 ] = v1 ;
v1 -> next = v2 = getnode_write ( 8 ) ;
v2 -> next = NULL ;

v1 = getnode_write ( 4 ) ;
arr[ 7 ] = v1 ;
```

```
    v1 -> next = v2 = getnode_write ( 5 ) ;
    v2 -> next = v3 = getnode_write ( 6 ) ;
    v3 -> next = v4 = getnode_write ( 7 ) ;
    v4 -> next = NULL ;

    clrscr( ) ;
    front = rear = -1 ;
    bfs ( 1, arr, 8 ) ;
    getch( ) ;
}

bfs ( int v, struct node **p, int n )
{
    struct node *u ;

    visited[ v - 1 ] = TRUE ;
    printf ( " %d", v ) ;
    addqueue ( v ) ;

    while ( isempty( ) == FALSE )
    {
        v = deletequeue( ) ;
        u = * ( p + v - 1 ) ;

        while ( u != NULL )
        {
            if ( visited [ u -> data - 1 ] == FALSE )
            {
                addqueue ( u -> data ) ;
                visited [ u -> data - 1 ] = TRUE ;
                printf ( " %d", u -> data ) ;
            }
            u = u -> next ;
        }
    }
}

struct node * getnode_write ( int val )
```

```
{
    newnode = ( struct node * ) malloc ( sizeof ( struct node ) ) ;
    newnode -> data = val ;
    return newnode ;
}

addqueue ( int vertex )
{
    if ( rear == MAX - 1 )
    {
        printf ( "\nQueue Overflow" ) ;
        exit( ) ;
    }

    rear++ ;
    q[ rear ] = vertex ;

    if ( front == -1 )
        front = 0 ;
}

deletequeue( )
{
    int data ;

    if ( front == -1 )
    {
        printf ( "\nQueue Underflow" ) ;
        exit( ) ;
    }

    data = q[ front ] ;
    if ( front == rear )
        front = rear = -1 ;
    else
        front++ ;

    return data ;
```

```
}

isempty( )
{
    if ( front == -1 )
        return TRUE ;
    return FALSE ;
}
```

Solved Problems

[A] Attempt the following:

(1) Write a program to concatenate one linked list at the end of another.

Program

```
/* Program to concatenate one linked list at end of another */
#include "alloc.h"

struct node
{
    int data ;
    struct node *link ;
};

main( )
{
    struct node *first, *second ;

    first = second = NULL ;  /* empty linked lists */

    append ( &first, 1 ) ;
    append ( &first, 2 ) ;
    append ( &first, 3 ) ;
    append ( &first, 4 ) ;

    clrscr( ) ;
    printf ( "\nFirst List : " ) ;
    display ( first ) ;
    printf ( "\nNo. of elements in Linked List = %d", count ( first ) ) ;

    append ( &second, 5 ) ;
    append ( &second, 6 ) ;
    append ( &second, 7 ) ;
```

```
        append ( &second, 8 ) ;

        printf ( "\n\nSecond List : " ) ;
        display ( second ) ;
        printf ( "\nNo. of elements in Linked List = %d", count ( second ) ) ;

        /* the result obtained after concatenation is in the first list */
        concat ( &first, &second ) ;

        printf ( "\n\nConcatenated List : " ) ;
        display ( first ) ;
        printf ( "\nNo. of elements in Linked List = %d", count ( first ) ) ;
}

/* adds a node at the end of a linked list */
append ( struct node **q, int num )
{
        struct node *temp ;
        temp = *q ;

        if ( *q == NULL )  /* if the list is empty, create first node */
        {
            *q = malloc ( sizeof ( struct node ) ) ;
            temp = *q ;
        }
        else
        {
            /* go to last node */
            while ( temp -> link != NULL )
                temp = temp -> link ;

            /* add node at the end */
            temp -> link = malloc ( sizeof ( struct node ) ) ;
            temp = temp -> link ;
        }

        /* assign data to the last node */
        temp -> data = num ;
```

```
        temp -> link = NULL ;
}

/* concatenates two linked lists */
concat ( struct node **p, struct node **q )
{
    struct node *temp ;

    /* if the first linked list is empty */
    if ( *p == NULL )
        *p = *q ;
    else
    {
        /* if both linked lists are non-empty */
        if ( *q != NULL )
        {
            temp = *p ;  /* points to the starting of the first list */

            /* traverse the entire first linked list */
            while ( temp -> link != NULL )
                temp = temp -> link ;

            temp -> link = *q ;  /* concatenate the second list after the
                                    first */
        }
    }
}

/* displays the contents of the linked list */
display ( struct node *q )
{
    printf ( "\n" ) ;

    /* traverse the entire linked list */
    while ( q != NULL )
    {
        printf ( "%d ", q -> data ) ;
        q = q -> link ;
```

```
        }
}

/* counts the number of nodes present in the linked list */
count ( struct node *q )
{
    int c = 0 ;

    /* traverse the entire linked list */
    while ( q != NULL )
    {
        q = q -> link ;
        c++ ;
    }

    return c ;
}
```

(2) Write a program to erase all the nodes of a linked list.

Program

```
/* Program to erase all nodes present in a linked list   */
#include "alloc.h"

struct node
{
    int data ;
    struct node *link ;
};

struct node *erase ( struct node * ) ;

main( )
{
    struct node *first ;
```

```
    first = NULL ;

    append ( &first, 0 ) ;
    append ( &first, 1 ) ;
    append ( &first, 2 ) ;
    append ( &first, 3 ) ;
    append ( &first, 4 ) ;
    append ( &first, 5 ) ;

    clrscr( ) ;
    display ( first ) ;
    printf ( "\nNo. of elements in Linked List before erasing = %d",
            count ( first ) ) ;

    first = erase ( first ) ;
    printf ( "\nNo. of elements in Linked List after erasing = %d",
            count ( first ) ) ;
}

/* adds a node at the end of a linked list */
append ( struct node **q, int num )
{
    struct node *temp ;
    temp = *q ;

    if ( *q == NULL )  /* if the list is empty, create first node */
    {
        *q = malloc ( sizeof ( struct node ) ) ;
        temp = *q ;
    }
    else
    {
        /* go to last node */
        while ( temp -> link != NULL )
            temp = temp -> link ;

        /* add node at the end */
```

```
            temp -> link = malloc ( sizeof ( struct node ) ) ;
            temp = temp -> link ;
    }

    /* assign data to the last node */
    temp -> data = num ;
    temp -> link = NULL ;
}

/* displays the contents of the linked list */
display ( struct node *q )
{
    printf ( "\n" ) ;

    /* traverse the entire linked list */
    while ( q != NULL )
    {
        printf ( "%d ", q -> data ) ;
        q = q -> link ;
    }
}

/* counts the number of nodes present in the linked list */
count ( struct node *q )
{
    int c = 0 ;

    /* traverse the entire linked list */
    while ( q != NULL )
    {
        q = q -> link ;
        c++ ;
    }

    return c ;
}

/* erases all the nodes from a linked list */
```

```
struct node *erase ( struct node *q )
{
    struct node *temp ;

    /* traverse till the end erasing each node */
    while ( q != NULL )
    {
        temp = q ;
        q = q -> link ;
        free ( temp ) ;  /* free the memory occupied by the node */
    }

    return NULL ;
}
```

(3) Write a program to find number of nodes in a linked list using recursion.

Program

```
/* Program to find the number of nodes in the linked list
   using recursion */
#include "alloc.h"

/* structure containing a data part and link part */
struct node
{
    int data ;
    struct node *link ;
};

main( )
{
    struct node *p ;
    p = NULL ;  /* empty linked list */

    append ( &p, 1 ) ;
```

```
        append ( &p, 2 ) ;
        append ( &p, 3 ) ;
        append ( &p, 4 ) ;
        append ( &p, 5 ) ;

        clrscr( ) ;
        printf ( "Length of linked list = %d", length ( p ) ) ;
}

/* adds a node at the end of a linked list */
append ( struct node **q, int num )
{
        struct node *temp ;
        temp = *q ;

        if ( *q == NULL )  /* if the list is empty, create first node */
        {
                *q = malloc ( sizeof ( struct node ) ) ;
                temp = *q ;
        }
        else
        {
                /* go to last node */
                while ( temp -> link != NULL )
                        temp = temp -> link ;

                /* add node at the end */
                temp -> link = malloc ( sizeof ( struct node ) ) ;
                temp = temp -> link ;
        }

        /* assign data to the last node */
        temp -> data = num ;
        temp -> link = NULL ;
}

/* counts the number of nodes in a linked list */
length ( struct node *q )
```

```
{
    static int l ;

    /* if list is empty or if NULL is encountered */
    if ( q == NULL )
        return ( 0 ) ;
    else
    {
        /* go to next node */
        l = 1 + length ( q -> link ) ;
        return ( l ) ;
    }
}
```

(4) Write a program to compare two linked lists using recursion.

Program

```
/* Program to compare two linked lists using recursion */
#include "alloc.h"

struct node
{
    int data ;
    struct node *link ;
};

main( )
{
    struct node *first, *second ;
    first = second = NULL ;  /* empty linked lists */

    append ( &first, 1 ) ;
    append ( &first, 2 ) ;
    append ( &first, 3 ) ;

    append ( &second, 1 ) ;
```

```
    append ( &second, 2 ) ;
    append ( &second, 3 ) ;

    clrscr( ) ;
    if ( compare ( first, second ) )
        printf ( "Both linked lists are EQUAL" ) ;
    else
        printf ( "Linked lists are DIFFERENT" ) ;
}

/* adds a node at the end of a linked list */
append ( struct node **q, int num )
{
    struct node *temp ;
    temp = *q ;

    if ( *q == NULL )  /* if the list is empty, create first node */
    {
        *q = malloc ( sizeof ( struct node ) ) ;
        temp = *q ;
    }
    else
    {
        /* go to last node */
        while ( temp -> link != NULL )
            temp = temp -> link ;

        /* add node at the end */
        temp -> link = malloc ( sizeof ( struct node ) ) :
        temp = temp -> link ;
    }

    /* assign data to the last node */
    temp -> data = num ;
    temp -> link = NULL ;
}

/* compares 2 linked lists and returns 1 if linked lists are equal and 0 if
```

```
    unequal */
compare ( struct node *q, struct node *r )
{
    static int flag ;

    if ( ( q == NULL ) && ( r == NULL ) )
        flag = 1 ;
    else
    {
        if ( q == NULL || r == NULL )
            flag = 0 ;

        if ( q -> data != r -> data )
            flag = 0 ;
        else
            compare ( q -> link, r -> link ) ;
    }
    return ( flag ) ;
}
```

(5) Write a program to copy one linked list into another using recursion.

Program

```
/* Program to copy one linked list into another using recursion */
#include "alloc.h"

/* structure containing a data part and link part */
struct node
{
    int data ;
    struct node *link ;
} ;

main( )
{
```

```
    struct node *first, *second ;
    first = second = NULL ;  /* empty linked lists */

    append ( &first, 1 ) ;
    append ( &first, 2 ) ;
    append ( &first, 3 ) ;
    append ( &first, 4 ) ;
    append ( &first, 5 ) ;
    append ( &first, 6 ) ;
    append ( &first, 7 ) ;

    clrscr( ) ;
    display ( first ) ;

    copy ( first, &second ) ;

    display ( second ) ;
}

/* adds a node at the end of the linked list */
append ( struct node **q, int num )
{
    struct node *temp ;
    temp = *q ;

    if ( *q == NULL )  /* if the list is empty, create first node */
    {
        *q = malloc ( sizeof ( struct node ) ) ;
        temp = *q ;
    }
    else
    {
        /* go to last node */
        while ( temp -> link != NULL )
            temp = temp -> link ;

        /* add node at the end */
        temp -> link = malloc ( sizeof ( struct node ) ) ;
```

```
            temp = temp -> link ;
        }

    /* assign data to the last node */
    temp -> data = num ;
    temp -> link = NULL ;
}

/* copies a linked list into another */
copy ( struct node *q, struct node **s )
{
    if ( q != NULL )
    {
        *s = malloc ( sizeof ( struct node ) ) ;

        ( *s ) -> data = q -> data ;
        ( *s ) -> link = NULL ;

        copy ( q -> link, &( ( *s ) -> link ) ) ;
    }
}

/* displays the contents of the linked list */
display ( struct node *q )
{
    printf ( "\n" ) ;

    /* traverse the entire linked list */
    while ( q != NULL )
    {
        printf ( "%d ", q -> data ) ;
        q = q -> link ;
    }
}
```

(6) Using recursion write a program to add a new node at the end of the linked list.

Program

```
/* Program to add a new node at the end of linked list using recursion*/
#include "alloc.h"

struct node
{
    int data ,
    struct node *link ;
} ;

main( )
{
    struct node *p ;

    p = NULL ;

    addatend ( &p, 1 ) ;
    addatend ( &p, 2 ) ;
    addatend ( &p, 3 ) ;
    addatend ( &p, 4 ) ;
    addatend ( &p, 5 ) ;
    addatend ( &p, 6 ) ;
    addatend ( &p, 10 )

    clrscr( ) ;
    display ( p ) ;
}

/* adds a new node at the end of the linked list */
addatend ( struct node **s, int num )
{
    if ( *s == NULL )
    {
        *s = malloc ( sizeof ( struct node ) ) ;
        ( *s ) -> data = num ;
        ( *s ) -> link = NULL ;
    }
```

```
        else
            addatend ( &( ( *s ) -> link ), num ) ;
    }

    /* displays the contents of the linked list */
    display ( struct node *q )
    {
        printf ( "\n" ) ;

        /* traverse the entire linked list */
        while ( q != NULL )
        {
            printf ( "%d ", q -> data ) ;
            q = q -> link ;
        }
    }
```

(7) Write a program to traverse a binary tree using inorder traversal method without using recursion.

Program

```
/* Program to traverse a binary search tree using inorder traversal
    without recursion */
#include "alloc.h"
#define MAX 10

struct btreenode
{
    struct btreenode *leftchild ;
    int data
    struct btreenode *rightchild ;
} ;
main( )
{
    struct btreenode *bt ;
    int req, i = 1, num ;
```

```
        bt = NULL ;  /* empty tree */

        clrscr( ) ;
        printf ( "Specify the number of data to be inserted : " ) ;
        scanf ( "%d", &req ) ;

        while ( i++ <= req )
        {
            printf ( "Enter the data : " ) ;
            scanf ( "%d", &num ) ;
            insert ( &bt, num ) ;
        }

        clrscr( ) ;
        inorder ( bt ) ;
}

/* inserts a new node in a binary search tree */
insert ( struct btreenode **sr, int num )
{
    if ( *sr == NULL )
    {
        *sr = malloc ( sizeof ( struct btreenode ) ) ;

        ( *sr ) -> leftchild = NULL ;
        ( *sr ) -> data = num ;
        ( *sr ) -> rightchild = NULL ;
        return ;
    }
    else   /* search the node to which new node will be attached */
    {
        /* if new data is less, traverse to left */
        if ( num < ( *sr ) -> data )
            insert ( &( ( *sr ) -> leftchild ), num ) ;
        else
            /* else traverse to right */
            insert ( &( ( *sr ) -> rightchild ), num ) ;
```

```
        }
        return ;
}

/* traverses a binary search tree in a LDR fashion */
inorder ( struct btreenode *currentnode )
{
    int top = 0 ;
    struct btreenode *nodestack[MAX] ;

    while ( 1 )
    {
        while ( currentnode != NULL )
        {
            top++ ;

            if ( top > MAX )
            {
                printf ( "\n stack is full..... " ) ;
                exit( ) ;
            }
            else
            {
                /* remembers the previous nodes whose right side is
                   yet to be traversed */
                nodestack[top] = currentnode ;
                currentnode = currentnode -> leftchild ;
            }
        }

        /* pop previous nodes one by one */
        if ( top != 0 )
        {
            currentnode = nodestack[top] ;
            top-- ;

            /* print the data field */
            printf ( "%d ", currentnode -> data ) ;
```

```
                  currentnode = currentnode -> rightchild ;
            }
            else
                break ;
        }
    }
```

(8) Write a program to swap the contents of a binary tree.

Program

```
/* program to swap a binary tree */
#include "alloc.h"

struct btreenode
{
    struct btreenode *leftchild ;
    int data ;
    struct btreenode *rightchild ,
};

void insert ( struct btreenode **, int ) ;
void insert ( struct btreenode **, int ) ;
void inorder ( struct btreenode * ) ;
void swap(struct btreenode ** ) ;

main( )
{
    struct btreenode *bt ;
    int req, i = 1, num ;

    bt = NULL ; /* empty tree */

    clrscr( ) ;

    printf ( "Specify the number of data items to be inserted: " ) ;
    scanf ( "%d", &req ) ;
```

```
        while ( i++ <= req )
        {
            printf ( "Enter the data: " ) ;
            scanf ( "%d", &num ) ;
            insert ( &bt, num ) ;
        }

        clrscr( ) ;

        printf ( "\nInorder Traversal before swaping: " ) ;
        inorder ( bt ) ;

        swap ( &bt ) ;

        printf ( "\nInorder Traversal after swaping: " ) ;
        inorder ( bt ) ;
    }

    /* inserts a new node in a binary search tree */
    void insert ( struct btreenode **sr, int num )
    {
        if ( *sr == NULL )
        {
            *sr = malloc ( sizeof ( struct btreenode ) ) ;

            ( *sr ) -> leftchild = NULL ;
            ( *sr ) -> data = num ;
            ( *sr ) -> rightchild = NULL ;
            return ;
        }
        else /* search the node to which new node will be attached */
        {
            /* if new data is less, traverse to left */
            if ( num < ( *sr ) -> data )
                insert ( &( ( *sr ) -> leftchild ), num ) ;
            else
                insert ( &( ( *sr ) -> rightchild ), num ) ;
        }
    }
```

```
        return ;
    }

/*traverse a binary search tree in a LDR ( Left-Data-Right) fashion*/
void inorder( struct btreenode *sr )
{
    if( sr != NULL )
    {
        inorder ( sr -> leftchild ) ;

        /*print the data of the node whose leftchild is NULL or the path
          has already been traversed */
        printf ( "%d ", sr -> data ) ;

        inorder ( sr -> rightchild ) ;

    }
    else
        return ;
}

void swap ( struct btreenode **sr )
{
    struct btreenode *tmp ;
    if ( *sr != NULL )
    {
        /* swap both childs */
        tmp = ( *sr ) -> leftchild ;
        ( *sr ) -> leftchild = ( *sr ) -> rightchild ;
        ( *sr ) -> rightchild = tmp ;

        swap ( &( ( *sr ) -> leftchild ) ) ;
        swap ( &( ( *sr ) -> rightchild ) ) ;
    }
    else
        return ;
}
```

Exercise

[A] Attempt the following:

(1) Write a program to implement stack as a circular linked list.

(2) Write a program to implement a doubly linked list as a circular linked list.

(3) Write a program to traverse a binary tree using preorder traversal method without using recursion.

(4) Write a program to traverse a binary tree using postorder traversal method without using recursion.

(5) Write a program to copy a binary search tree using recursion.

(6) Write a program to compare two binary search trees using recursion.

(7) Write a function to insert a node **t** as a left child of **s** in a threaded binary tree.

Know Pointers, Will travel!

6 Pointers Miscellany

or those of you who have reached this far, it's time to exploit
the immense potential of pointers. We wouldn't be able to do
so unless we know things like file pointers, far, near & huge
pointers, pointers to functions, pointers and variable number of
arguments etc. In this chapter we intend to look at these and a few
more miscellaneous topics. Let's begin with file pointers.

File Pointers

Consider the following program. It opens a file, reads it character
by character till the time its end is not encountered. On reaching
the end of file, the file is closed and the count of characters present
in it is printed.

```
/* Program 71 */
/* Count chars */
# include "stdio.h"
main( )
```

```
{
    FILE *fp ;
    char ch ;
    int nol, noc = 0 ;
    fp = fopen ( "PR1.C", "r" ) ;
    while ( 1 )
    {
        ch = fgetc ( fp ) ;
        if (ch == EOF )
            break ;

        noc++ ;
        if (ch ==EOF )
            break ;

        noc++ ;
    }
    fclose ( fp ) ;
    printf ( "\nNumber of characters = %d", noc ) ;
}
```

Here is a sample run...

Number of characters = 125

What is **fp** in our program? Most of the time it is known as a file pointer. However, it is actually a pointer to a structure. This structure has been **typedef**ed into **FILE** in the header file **stdio.h**. This structure is shown below:

```
typedef struct
{
    int             level ;       /* fill/empty level of buffer   */
    unsigned        flags ;       /* File status flags            */
    char            fd ;          /* File descriptor              */
    unsigned char   hold ;        /* Ungetc char if no buffer     */
    int             bsize ;       /* Buffer size                  */
```

```
unsigned char    *buffer ;    /* Data transfer buffer      */
unsigned char    *curp ;      /* Current active pointer     */
unsigned         istemp ;     /* Temporary file indicator   */
short            token ;      /* Used for validity checking */
} FILE ;  /* This is the FILE object */
```

When we open a file for reading two things happen:

(a) The contents of the file are loaded into buffer.

(b) A **FILE** structure is created in memory, its elements are setup and address of this structure is returned.

This address we have collected in **fp**. Thus, **fp** is not pointing to the file's buffer. Within the structure to which **fp** is pointing there is a character pointer called **buffer**. It is this pointer which is pointing to the buffer. This arrangement is shown in Figure 6.1.

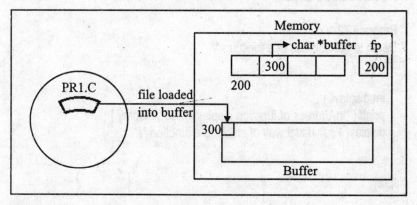

Figure 6.1

When we read a character from the file using **getc( )** we need to pass the file pointer **fp** to it. Why? Because **getc( )** must know from which file should it do the reading. Also, on reading a character using **getc( )** we never have to increment the pointer pointing to the buffer. This is because **getc( )** does this for us. Assuming that the file pointer **fp** that we have passed to **getc( )** is collected by **getc( )** in say **p**, then to increment the buffer pointer **getc( )** internally must be doing an operation of the from **p -> buffer = p -> buffer + 1**.

When we close the file using **fclose( )** the buffer associated with the file is freed along with the structure being pointed to by **fp**.

The above discussion is also relevant for a file opened for writing.

Pointers to Functions

Every type of variable, with the exception of register, has an address. We have seen how we can reference variables of type **char, int, float** etc. through their addresses—that is by using pointers. Pointers can also point to C functions. And why not? C functions have addresses. If we know the function's address we can point to it, which provides another way to invoke it. Let us see how this can be done.

```
/* Program 72 */
/* Demo to get address of a function */
main( )
{
    int display( ) ;
    printf ( "\nAddress of function display is %u", display ) ;
    display( ) ;   /* usual way of invoking a function */
}

display( )
{
    printf ( "\nLong live viruses!!" ) ;
}
```

The output of the program would be:

```
Address of function display is 1125
Long live viruses!!
```

Note that to obtain the address of a function all that we have to do is to mention the name of the function, as has been done in the **printf( )** statement above. This is similar to mentioning the name of the array to get its base address.

Now let us see how using the address of a function we can manage to invoke it. This is shown in the program given below:

```
/* Program 73 */
/* Invoking function using pointer to a function */
main( )
{
    int display( ) ;
    int ( *func_ptr )( ) ;

    func_ptr = display ;  /* assign address of function */
    printf ( "\nAddress of function display is %u", func_ptr )
    ( *func_ptr )( ) ;  /* invokes the function display( ) */
}

display( )
{
    printf ( "\nLong live viruses!!" ) ;
}
```

The output of the program would be:

```
Address of function display is 1125
Long live viruses!!
```

In **main( )** we have declared the function **display( )** as a function returning an **int**. But what are we to make of the declaration,

```
int ( *func_ptr )( ) ;
```

that comes in the next line? We are obviously declaring something which, like **display( )**, will return an **int**. But what is it? And why is ***func_ptr** enclosed in parentheses?

If we glance down a few lines in our program, we see the statement,

func_ptr = display ;

So we know that **func_ptr** is being assigned the address of **display( )**. Therefore, **func_ptr** must be a pointer to the function **display( )**.

Thus, all that the declaration

int (*func_ptr)( ) ;

means is, that **func_ptr** is a pointer to a function, which returns an **int**. And to invoke the function we are just required to write the statement,

(*func_ptr)( ) ;

Pointers to functions are certainly awkward and off-putting. And why use them at all when we can invoke a function in a much simpler manner? What is the possible gain of using this esoteric feature of C? There are several possible uses:

(a) in writing memory resident programs
(b) in writing viruses, or vaccines to remove the viruses
(c) in developing COM / DCOM components
(d) in VC++ programming to connect events to function calls

All these topics form interesting and powerful applications and would call for separate chapters on each if full justice is to be given to them. Much as I would have liked to, for want of space I would have to exclude these topics.

typedef with Function Pointers

We know that **typedef** is used to give convenient names to complicated datatypes. It is immensely useful when using pointers to functions. Given below are a few examples of its usage.

(1)   typedef int (*funcptr)( );
       funcptr fptr ;

       fptr is a pointer to a function returning **an int**.

(2)   typedef int (*fret_int)(char *, char *) ;
       fret_int fri1, fri2 ;

       fri1 and **fri2** are pointers to function that accepts two **char** pointers and returns an **int**.

(3)   typedef void (*complex)( ) ;
       complex c ;

       c is a pointer to a function that doesn't accept any parameter and doesn't return anything.

(4)   typedef char (* (*frpapfrc( )) [ ])( ) ;
       frpapfrc f ;

       f is a function returning a pointer to an array of pointers to functions returning a **char**.

(5)   typedef int (* (* arr2d_ptr)( )) [3][4] ;
       arr2d_ptr p ;

       p is a pointer to a function returning a pointer to a 2-D **int** array.

(6)   typedef int (* (* (* ptr2d_fptr)( )) [10])( ) ;
       ptr2d_fptr p ;

p is a pointer to a function returning a pointer to an array of 10 pointers to function returning an **int**.

(7) typedef char (* (* arr_fptr[3])( )) [10] ;
arr_fptr x ;

x is an array of 3 pointers to function returning a pointer to an array of 10 **char**s.

(8) typedef float* (* (* (* ptr_fptr)( )) [10])( ) ;
ptr_fptr q ;

q is a pointer to function returning a pointer to an array of 10 pointers to functions returning a **float** pointer.

argc and *argv*—Arguments to *main( )*

Can we not pass arguments to **main( )** the way we pass them to other functions? We can. For this we specify the arguments at command prompt when we execute the program. For example, suppose 'PR1.EXE' is the name of the executable file, and we wish to pass the arguments 'Cat', 'Dog' and 'Parrot' to **main( )** in this file. We can do so through the following command at the command prompt:

C> PR1.EXE Cat Dog Parrot

Now if we are passing arguments to **main( )**, it must collect them in variables. Usually only two variables are used to collect these arguments. These are called **argc** and **argv**. Of these, **argc** contains the count (number) of arguments being passed to **main( )**, whereas **argv** contains addresses of strings passed to **main( )**. In the above example **argc** would contain 4, whereas **argv[0]**, **argv[1]**, **argv[2]**, and **argv[3]** would contain base addresses of PR1.EXE, Cat, Dog and Parrot respectively. If we so desire we can print these arguments from within **main( )** as shown in the following program.

```
/* Program 74 */
main ( int argc, char *argv[ ] )
{
    int i ;

    for ( i = 0 ; i < argc ; i++ )
        printf ( "\n%s", argv[i] ) ;
}
```

Note the declaration of **argv[ ]**. It has been declared as an array of pointers to strings. Also observe the format specification used in **printf( )**. We are using **%s** because we wish to print out the various strings that are being passed to **main( )**.

It is not necessary that we should always use the variable names **argc** and **argv**. In place of them any other variable names can as well be used.

Pointers and Variable Number of Arguments

We use **printf( )** so often without realising how it works correctly irrespective of how many arguments we pass to it. How do we go about writing such routines, which can take variable number of arguments? And what have pointers got to do with it? There are three macros available in the file "stdarg.h" called **va_start**, **va_arg** and **va_list**, which allow us to handle this situation. These macros provide a method for accessing the arguments of the function when a function takes a fixed number of arguments followed by a variable number of arguments. The fixed number of arguments are accessed in the normal way, whereas the optional arguments are accessed using the macros **va_start** and **va_arg**. Out of these macros **va_start** is used to initialise a pointer to the beginning of the list of optional arguments. On the other hand the macro **va_arg** is used to advance the pointer to the next argument. Let us put these concepts into action using a program. Suppose we wish to write a function **findmax( )** which would find out the maximum value from a set of values, irrespective of the number of values passed to it.

```
/* Program 75 */
#include "stdarg.h"
main( )
{
    int max ;

    max = findmax ( 5, 23, 15, 1, 92, 50 ) ;
    printf ( "\nMax = %d", max ) ;

    max = findmax ( 3, 100, 300, 29 ) ;
    printf ( "\nMax = %d", max ) ;
}

findmax ( int tot_num )
{
    int max, count, num ;

    va_list ptr ;

    va_start ( ptr, tot_num ) ;
    max = va_arg ( ptr, int ) ;

    for ( count = 1 ; count < tot_num ; count++ )
    {
        num = va_arg ( ptr, int ) ;
        if ( num > max )
            max = num ;
    }

    return ( max ) ;
}
```

Here we are making two calls to **findmax( )** first time to find maximum out of 5 values and second time to find maximum out of

3 values. Note that for each call the first argument is the count of arguments that are being passed after the first argument. The value of the first argument passed to **findmax( )** is collected in the variable **tot_num**. **findmax( )** begins with a declaration of pointer **ptr** of the type **va_list**. Observe the next statement carefully:

```
va_start ( ptr, tot_num ) ;
```

This statement sets up **ptr** such that it points to the first variable argument in the list. If we are considering the first call to **findmax( )**, **ptr** would now point to 23. The next statement **max = va_arg (ptr, int)** would assign the integer being pointed to by **ptr** to **max**. Thus 23 would be assigned to **max**, and **ptr** would now start pointing to the next argument i.e., 15. The rest of the program is fairly straightforward. We just keep picking up successive numbers in the list and keep comparing them with the latest value in **max**, till all the arguments in the list have been scanned. The final value in **max** is then returned to **main( )**.

How about another program to fix your ideas? This one calls a function **display( )** which is capable of printing any number of arguments of any type.

```
/* Program 76 */
#include "stdarg.h"
main( )
{
    printf ( "\n" ) ;
    display ( 1, 2, 5, 6 ) ;
    printf ( "\n" ) ;
    display ( 2, 4, 'A', 'a', 'b', 'c' ) ;
    printf ( "\n" ) ;
    display ( 3, 3, 2.5, 299.3, -1.0 ) ;
}

display ( int type, int num )
{
    int i, j ;
```

```
char c ;
float f ;
va_list ptr ;

va_start ( ptr, num ) ;

switch ( type )
{
    case 1 :
        for ( j = 1 ; j <= num ; j++ )
        {
            i = va_arg ( ptr, int ) ;
            printf ( "%d ", i ) ;
        }
        break ;

    case 2 :
        for ( j = 1 ; j <= num ; j++ )
        {
            c = va_arg ( ptr, char ) ;
            printf ( "%c ", c ) ;
        }
        break ;

    case 3 :
        for ( j = 1 ; j <= num ; j++ )
        {
            f = ( float ) va_arg ( ptr, double ) ;
            printf ( "%f ", f ) ;
        }
}
}
```

Here we are passing two fixed arguments to the function
display( ). The first one indicates the data type of the arguments to
be printed and the second indicates the number of such arguments
to be printed. Once again through the statement **va_start (ptr,**

num) we have set up **ptr** such that it points to the first argument in the variable list of arguments. Then depending upon whether the value of **type** is 1, 2 or 3 we have printed out the arguments as **int**s, **char**s or **float**s.

near, *far* and *huge* **Pointers**

To understand **near**, **far** and **huge** pointers it's necessary to know the details about memory organisation, memory addressing scheme and various memory models. Let us begin with the basics.

To enable the flow of data between the microprocessor and the memory there is a set of wires. This set of wires is called a 'data bus'. Each wire in this bus carries a bit of data at a time (either zero or one in the form of an electric pulse). If the data bus has 8 wires then 8 bits or 1 byte of data can flow in it at a time and this is called a 8-bit data bus. Similarly, we have 16-bit and 32-bit data buses that can respectively carry 16 and 32 bits at a time.

A microprocessor with a 32-bit data bus is faster than the one with a 16-bit data bus. This is because in the former, four bytes of data are brought to the microprocessor at a time; while in the latter only 2 bytes of data are brought at a time.

If a microprocessor with a 32-bit data bus is faster than the one with a 16-bit data bus, then why not have a 32-bit data bus instead of a 16-bit data bus? This is not possible because the microprocessors are designed that way. A microprocessor with a provision for connecting only a 16-bit data bus cannot be connected with a 32-bit data bus. Hence, each type of microprocessor can be distinguished by the width of the data bus that it is connected to. A microprocessor with a provision for 16-bit data bus is called a 16-bit microprocessor; the one with a provision for 32 bits is called a 32-bit microprocessor and so on.

The way the data bus width tells how many bits the bus can move at a time, there is another bus called address bus whose width tells how many addresses the microprocessor can access. For example, if the address bus width of a microprocessor is 20 bits then it can access 2^{20} locations (1 mb) in memory. The following figure shows the data and address bus width for different microprocessors.

Microprocessor	Data bus	Add. Bus	Max. Mem.	Mode of operation
8088 (PC, XT)	8	20	1 mb	Real
8086 (PC, XT)	16	20	1 mb	Real
80286 (AT)	16	24	16 mb	Real/Protected
80386 (AT386)	32	32	4096 mb	Real/Protected
80486 (AT486)	32	32	4096 mb	Real/Protected
Pentium	64	64	2^{44} mb	Real/Protected

Figure 6.2

As can be seen from the above figure the microprocessors have different modes of operation that determines how much memory they can handle. These modes are part of hardware but dictate the kind of software that runs on the microprocessor. The 8088 and 8086 chips (of the old PC and XT) operate only in real mode, and so can address only 1024 kb or 1 mb memory.

The 286, 386, 486 and pentium can work in real as well as protected mode. In real mode they work just like an 8088 or 8086 but successively faster because the microprocessor speeds are increasingly faster, from 286 to pentium. The protected mode has features to help protect multiple programs from stepping into each other's areas of memory. The MS-DOS operating system has been written for real mode, whereas, Unix has been written for protected mode. So if an AT (80286) has 16 mb installed in it, while running under DOS only 1 mb out of these 16 mb can be accessed. This is because even though the 80286 have a 24-bit address bus in real mode it acts as a 20-bit address bus. Similarly, on 80386, 80486 or pentium running under DOS only 1 mb memory can be accessed.

Thus, if you are going to work in DOS on an AT with 16 mb memory, 15 mb memory will remain unused. It's like building homes without any streets. Sure you have got the buildings, but there are no streets to get there.

There are two major schemes for slipping around this pesky DOS 1 mb limit: expanded memory and extended memory. The details of these are beyond the scope of this book. All that we would say is to be able to use these memories one needs special driver programs like EMM386 or such.

Let's now see how to access the various memory locations. As we said earlier when running an application under DOS on any of the microprocessors a 16-bit data bus and a 20-bit address bus would be used. To access any of the 2^{20} (10,48,576 bytes) locations the microprocessors use 16-bit CPU registers. However in 16 bit registers the maximum value that can be stored is 65,536. Then how do we access memory locations beyond 65535th byte? By using two registers (segment and offset) in conjunction. For this the total memory (1 mb) is divided into a number of units each comprising 65,536 (64 kb) locations. Each such unit is called a segment. Each segment always begins at a location number, which is exactly divisible by 16. The segment register contains the address where a segment begins, whereas the offset register contains the offset of the data/code from where the segment begins. For example, if the number contained in segment register is 2 and that in the offset register is 5, the address of the data/code will be (16 * 2) + 5 = 37. Let us now consider a more complicated example - the address of the first byte in VGA video memory. The segment address of video memory is B0000h (20-bit address), whereas the offset value of the first VGA byte in this segment is 8000h. This is shown in the following figure.

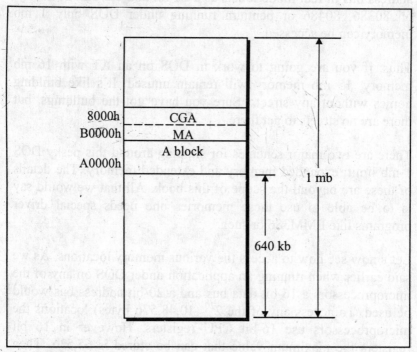

Figure 6.3

Here 8000h (16 bit address) can be easily placed in offset register, but how do we store the 20 bit B0000h address in 16 bit segment register? What is done is out of B0000h only the first four hex digits (16 bits) are stored in segment register. DOS can afford to do this because a segment address is always a multiple of 16 and hence always contains a 0 as the last digit. Therefore, the first byte in CGA video memory is referred using segment:offset format as B000h:8000h. Thus, the offset register works relative to segment register. Using both these, we can point to a specific location anywhere in the 1 mb address space.

Suppose we want to write a character 'A' at location B000h:8000h. We must convert this address into a form, which C understands. This is done by simply writing the segment and offset addresses side by side to obtain a 32-bit address. In our example this address would be B0008000. Now whether C would support this 32-bit address or not depends upon the memory model in use. The C compiler understands many kinds of memory models. The responsibility of choosing the correct memory model for your needs, though, lies squarely at your door. For example, if we are using a large data model (compact, large, huge) the above address is acceptable. This is because in these models all pointers to data are 32 bits long. As against this if we are using a small data model (tiny, small, medium) the above address won't work since in these models each pointer is 16 bits long.

What if we are working in small data model and still want to access the first byte of CGA video memory? In such cases both Microsoft C and Turbo C provide a keyword called far, which is used as shown below,

```
char far *s ;
s = 0xB0008000 ;
```

A **far** pointer is always treated as a 32-bit pointer and contains both a segment address and an offset address.

A **huge** pointer is also 32 bits long, again containing a segment address and an offset. However, there are a few differences between a **far** pointer and a **huge** pointer. We would look at these differences as we go along.

A **near** pointer is only 16 bits long. It uses the current contents of the CS (Code Segment) register (if the pointer is pointing to code) or current contents of DS (Data Segment) register (if the pointer is pointing to data) for the segment part, whereas the offset part is stored in the 16 bit **near** pointer. Using **near** pointer limits your data/code to current 64 kb segment.

As against this a **far** pointer (32 bit) contains the segment as well as the offset. By using **far** pointers we can have multiple code segments, which in turn allow you to have programs longer than 64 kb. Likewise, with **far** data pointers we can address more than 64 kb worth of data. However, while using **far** pointers some problems may crop up which are discussed later. The limitations of **far** pointers are overcome if we use **huge** pointers instead of **far** pointers.

The following figure captures the essence of these different types of pointers along with the pointer type supported by each memory model.

Memory model	Code Pointer	Data Pointer	Code Size	Data Size
Tiny	near	near	◄──── 64 kb ────►	
Small	near	near	64 kb	64 kb
Medium	far	near	1 mb	64 kb
Compact	near	far	64 kb	1 mb
Large	far	far	1 mb	1 mb
Huge	far	huge	1 mb	*

* Single data element (say an array) can occupy more than one segment

Figure 6.4

Which Pointers to Use?

Now that we have understood the **far** and the **huge** pointers let us now go into their intricacies. A clear understanding of these details lets you make a correct decision in selecting the pointer type in many an application. Let us begin with a simple program.

```
/* Program 77 */
main( )
{
    char far *a = 0x00000120 ;
    char far *b = 0x00100020 ;
    char far *c = 0x00120000 ;

    if ( a == b )
        printf ( "Hello" ) ;
    if ( a == c )
        printf ( "Hi" ) ;
    if ( b == c )
        printf ( "Hello Hi" ) ;
    if ( a > b && a > c && b > c )
        printf ( "Bye" ) ;
}
```

Note that all the 32-bit addresses stored in variables **a**, **b** and **c** refers to the same memory location. This deduces from the method of obtaining the 20-bit physical address from the segment:offset pair. This is shown below for the three addresses used in the program.

```
00000   segment address left shifted by 4 bits
 0120   offset address
----------
00120   resultant 20-bit address

00100   segment address left shifted by 4 bits
 0020   offset address
----------
00120   resultant 20-bit address

00120   segment address left shifted by 4 bits
 0000   offset address
----------
00120   resultant 20-bit address
```

Now if **a**, **b** and **c** refer to same location in memory we expect the first three **if**s to be satisfied. However this doesn't happen. This is because while comparing the **far** pointers using == (and !=) the full 32-bit value is used and since the 32-bit values are different the **if**s fail. The last **if** however gets satisfied, because while comparing using > (and >=, <, <=) only the offset value is used for comparison. And the offset values of **a**, **b** and **c** are such that the last condition is satisfied.

These limitations are overcome if we use **huge** pointers instead of **far** pointers. Unlike **far** pointers **huge** pointers are 'normalized' to avoid these problems. What is a normalized pointer? It is a 32- bit pointer, which has as much of its value in the segment address as possible. Since a segment can start every 16 bytes, this means that the offset will only have a value from 0 to F.

How do we normalize a pointer? Simple. Convert it to its 20-bit address then use the left 16 bits for the segment address and the right 4 bits for the offset address. For example, given the pointer 500D:9407, we convert it to a 20-bit absolute address 594D7, which we then normalize to 594D:0007.

huge pointers are always kept normalized. As a result for any given memory address there is only one possible **huge** address—segment:offset pair—for it. Run the above program using **huge** instead of **far** and now you would find that the first three **if**s are satisfied, whereas the fourth fails. This is more logical than the result obtained while using **far** pointers.

But then there is a price to be paid for using **huge** pointers. Huge pointer arithmetic is done with calls to special subroutines. Because of this, **huge** pointer arithmetic is significantly slower than that of **far** or **near** pointers.

Physical Address to Segment:Offset

We might often be required to convert a segment:offset address to a physical address or vice-versa. For achieving this there are standard macros available. Thus, to make a **far** pointer point to a given memory location (a specific segment:offset address) we can use the macro **MK_FP**, which takes a segment and an offset and returns a **far** pointer. For example:

MK_FP (segment_value, offset_value)

Similarly, given a **far** pointer, **fp**, we can get the segment component with **FP_SEG (fp)** and the offset component with **FP_OFF (fp)**. Both these macros return an **unsigned int** representing the segment or the offset value. The following program demonstrates the usage of these macros.

```
/* Program 78 */
#include "dos.h"
main( )
{
    char far *ptr ;
    unsigned seg, off ;

    ptr = MK_FP ( 0xb000, 0 ) ;
    seg = FP_SEG ( ptr ) ;
    off = FP_OFF ( ptr ) ;

    printf ( "\nfar ptr = %Fp", ptr ) ;
    printf ( "segment = %04X offset = %04X", seg, off ) ;
}
```

And here is the output...

```
far ptr = B000:0000
segment = B000, offset 0000
```

Having discussed **near**, **far**, and **huge** pointers at length it's time for a little bit of practice. Can you make out what the following declarations stand for? Try your hand at them.

```
int f1( ) ;
int *p1 ;
int *f2( ) ;
int ( *fp1 ) ( int ) ;
int ( *fp2 ) ( int *ip ) ;
int ( far * list[5] ) ( int far *ip ) ;
int ( huge * a[10] ) ( char far *j ) ;
```

The Dancing Dolls

Let us now put the knowledge of **far** pointers to use. Look at the following program.

```
/* Program 79 */
main( )
{
    char far *scr ;
    int i ;

    scr = 0xB0008000 ;
    while ( 1 )
    {
        for ( i = 0 ; i <<= 3999 ; i = i + 2 )
        {
            if ( *( scr + i ) >>= 'A' && *( scr + i ) <<= 'Z' )
                *( scr + i ) = *( scr + i ) + 32 ;
            else
            {
                if ( *( scr + i ) >>= 'a'  && *( scr + i ) <<= 'z' )
                    *( scr + i ) = *( scr + i ) - 32 ;
            }
        }
    }
}
```

}

B0008000h is the address of video memory. A character written at this address appears on the screen at 0th row, 0th column. Address B0008000h + 1 contains a number, which determines the colour of the character at row 0, column 0. Thus, every character present on the screen has 2 bytes in video memory, one containing the ASCII value of the character and another containing its colour. The above program makes use of this fact and goes to every byte in video memory, which contains the ASCII values of the characters on the screen and appropriately changes those, which are capital to small case and vice-versa. Since this entire logic is within an indefinite loop the characters change from capital to small case to capital to small case at such a fast rate that they appear to be dancing on the screen.

On similar lines can you now try a program, which will change the colour of the characters on the screen. Note that the colour byte can take 256 different values in the range 0 to 255.

Caps Locked!

Having tinkered with the screen using **far** pointers let us now turn our attention to the keyboard. At location 417h in memory is stored the current status of several interesting keys is stored. Figure 6.5 shows the meaning of each bit in 417h.

What if we wish to put the caps lock on through our program. All that we have to do is to ensure that bit number 6 of 417h is put on. This can be achieved by writing a binary number 01000000 (or its decimal equivalent, 64) at 417h.

7	6	5	4	3	2	1	0	Meaning
1								Insert state
	1							Caps lock state
		1						Num lock state
			1					Scroll lock state
				1				Alt pressed
					1			Ctrl pressed
						1		Left shift pressed
							1	Right shift pressed

Figure 6.5

The following program demonstrates this.

```
/* Program 80*/
main( )
{
    char far *kb ;
    kb = 0x417 ;
    *kb = 64 ;
}
```

Can you figure out why **kb** has been declared a **far** pointer here? Figure 6.6 would possibly clarify it. Had **kb** pointed to some location in the data segment of our program we would have declared it as a **near** pointer. But since **kb** points to a location outside the data segment we need to declare it as a **far** pointer.

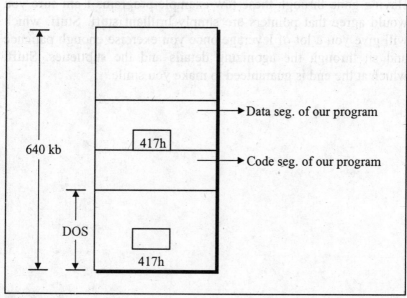

Figure 6.6

How Much Memory Do You Have?

The base memory size of any computer gets stored at locations 413h and 414h on booting the computer. We can access these two locations and print out the base memory size of the computer. Here is a program, which does this.

```
/* Program 81 */
main( )
{
    unsigned int far *mem ;

    mem = 0x413 ;
    printf ( "Base memory size = %u kb", *mem ) ;
}
```

Having gone through these few example programs I am sure you would agree that pointers are simply brilliant stuff. Stuff, which will give you a lot of leverage once you exercise enough patience and sit through the agonizing details and the subtleties. Stuff, which at the end is guaranteed to make you smile.

Exercise

[A] Attempt the following:

(1) For every character present on the screen there is a two-byte sequence in VDU memory. The first byte contains ASCII value of the character whereas the second byte contains the color of the character. The VDU memory begins at address B8000000h for monochrome adapters and at B8000000h for others. Write a program to continuously change the color of the characters present on the screen.

(2) Write a program, which on execution makes the characters present in the top-most row of the screen to fall down one by one. During the fall those characters that come in the path of the falling characters should get wiped out. As these characters reach the bottom of the screen they should construct a message in the last row: 'It's raining, it's pouring, while the old PC is snoring'.

(3) The system time of computer in terms of clock ticks passed since midnight is stored as a 4-byte entity starting from address 46Ch in BIOS Data Area. The number of clock ticks that occur per second is 18.2.

For example, if system time is 01:04:44 (HH:MM:SS format), then its equivalent 4-byte entity would be:

```
    44 * 18.2              (seconds part)
+   4 * 60 * 18.2          (minutes part)
+   1 * 60 * 60 * 18.2     (hours part)
-------------------------------
    70688
```

Write a program to print the current system time in HH:MM:SS format. Also write a program to change the system time.

(4) Write a program to display list of equipment attached to your computer. This list is stored in two bytes 410h and 411h in BIOS Data Area in bitwise-encoded format. It's break-up is as follows.

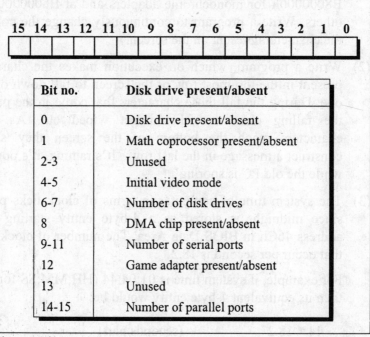

15	14	13	12	11	10	9	8	7	6	5	4	3	2	1	0

Bit no.	Disk drive present/absent
0	Disk drive present/absent
1	Math coprocessor present/absent
2-3	Unused
4-5	Initial video mode
6-7	Number of disk drives
8	DMA chip present/absent
9-11	Number of serial ports
12	Game adapter present/absent
13	Unused
14-15	Number of parallel ports

Figure 6.7

(5) Write a function, which arranges the numbers passed to it in ascending/descending order making use of a variable argument list. The fixed arguments to the function should be:

(1) an integer indicating whether to sort numbers in ascending or descending order.

(2) an integer to indicate number of arguments to follow (the arguments being the numbers to be sorted).

[B] What will be the output of the following programs:

(1)
```
main( )
{
    void ( *message )( ) ;
    void print( ) ;
    print( ) ;
    message = print ;
    ( *message )( ) ;
}
void print( )
{
    printf ( "\nNever trouble trouble till trouble troubles you" ) ;
}
```

(2)
```
main( )
{
    long far *a ;

    printf ( "\nLove makes life lovely" ) ;
    printf ( "\nPress any key..." ) ;
    a = 36 ;
    *a = 0 ;
    getch( ) ;
    printf ( "... except when you hit a key" ) ;

}
```

(3)
```
/* Compile this program and run the executable file from command
   prompt as: PR5 aabbcc */

main ( int argc, char *argv[ ] )
{
```

```
        printf ( "\n%c", ++( *( ++( *++argv ) ) ) ) ;
    }

(4)  main( )
    {
        int i, fun1( ), fun2( ), fun3( ) ;
        int ( *f[3] )( ) ;

        f[0] = fun1 ;
        f[1] = fun2 ;
        f[2] = fun3 ;
        for ( i = 0 ; i <= 2 ; i++ )
            ( *f[i] )( ) ;
    }
    fun1( )
    {
        printf ( "\nHail" ) ;
    }
    fun2( )
    {
        printf ( "\nthe" ) ;
    }
    fun3( )
    {
        printf ( "\nviruses!" ) ;
    }

(5)  main( )
    {
        char huge *a = 0x00000120 ;
        char huge *b = 0x00100020 ;
        char huge *c = 0x00120000 ;

        if ( a == b )
                printf ( "\nHello" ) ;
        if ( a == c )
                printf ( "\nHi" ) ;
```

```
        if ( b == c )
                printf ( "\nHello Hi" ) ;
        if ( a > b && a > c && b > c )
                printf ( "\nBye" ) ;
}
```

[C] Answer the following:

(1) Can you split the following statement into two statements?

```
char far *scr = ( char far * ) 0xB8000000L ;
```

(2) How would you declare an array of three function pointers where each function receives two **ints** and returns a **float**?

(3) How many bytes are occupied by **near, far** and **huge** pointers?

(4) Can two different **near** pointers contain two different addresses but refer to the same location in memory? <Yes/No>

(5) Can two different **far** pointers contain two different addresses but refer to the same location in memory? <Yes/No>

(6) Why is it that for large memory models NULL has been defined as 0L and for small memory models as just 0?

(7) Can two different **huge** pointers contain two different addresses but refer to the same location in memory? <Yes/No>

(8) In a large data model (compact, large, huge) all pointers to data are 32 bits long, whereas in a small data model (tiny, small, medium) all pointers are 16 bits long. <True/False>

(9) How would you eliminate the warning generated on compiling the following program?

```
main( )
{
```

```
char far *scr ;
scr = 0xB8000000 ;

*scr = 'A' ;
}
```

(10) How would you obtain a **far** address from the segment and offset addresses of a memory location?

(11) A **near** pointer uses the contents of CS register (if the pointer is pointing to code) or contents of DS register (if the pointer is pointing to data) for the segment part, whereas the offset part is stored in the 16-bit **near** pointer. <True/False>

(12) How would you obtain segment and offset addresses from a **far** address of a memory location?

Applications of Pointers

In the previous six chapters we saw how pointers work in different garbs. Let us now put all that theory into practice. I will present here a few applications that use pointers. Let us begin with the first one.

Exploring The Disk

By far the most widely used storage mediums are the floppy disks and the fixed disks (hard disks). Floppy disks and hard disks come in various sizes and capacities but they all work basically in the same way: information is magnetically encoded on their surface in patterns. These patterns are determined by the disk drive and the software that controls the drive.

Although the type of storage device is important, it is the way the stored information is laid out and managed that concerns programmers most. Therefore we would focus our attention on how information is organized and stored on the disk.

The Disk Structure

As most of us know, the disk drives in DOS and Windows are organized as zero-based drives. That is, drive A is drive number 0, drive B is drive number 1, drive C is drive number 2, etc. The hard disk drive can be further partitioned into logical partitions. Each drive consists of four logical parts: Boot Sector, File Allocation Table (FAT), Directory and Data space. Of these, the Boot Sector contains information about how the disk is organized. That is, how many sides does it contain, how many tracks are there on each side, how many sectors are there per track, how many bytes are there per sector, etc. The files and the directories are stored in the Data Space. The Directory contains information about the files like its attributes, name, size, etc. The FAT contains information about where the files and directories are stored in the data space. Figure 7.1 shows the four logical parts of a 1.44 MB disk.

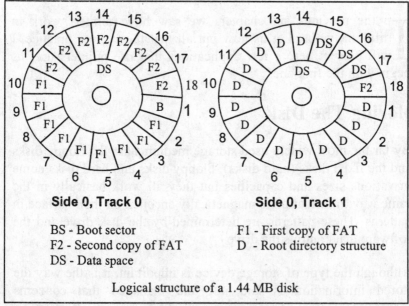

Side 0, Track 0   Side 0, Track 1

BS - Boot sector   F1 - First copy of FAT
F2 - Second copy of FAT   D - Root directory structure
DS - Data space

Logical structure of a 1.44 MB disk

Figure 7.1

When a file/directory is created on the disk, instead of allocating a sector for it, a group of sectors is allocated. This group of sectors is often known as a **cluster**. How many sectors together form one cluster depends upon the capacity of the disk. As the capacity goes on increasing, so also does the maximum cluster number. Accordingly, we have 12-bit, 16-bit or 32-bit FAT. In a 12-bit FAT each entry is of 12 bits. Since each entry in FAT represents a cluster number, the maximum cluster number possible in a 12-bit FAT is 2^{12} (4096). Similarly, in case of a 16-bit FAT the maximum cluster number is 2^{16} (65536). Also, for a 32-bit FAT the maximum cluster number is 2^{28} (268435456. Only 28 of the 32 bits are used in this FAT). All FAT systems are not supported by all versions of Windows. For example, the 32-bit FAT system is supported only in Win 95 OSR2 version or later. There are differences in the organization of contents of Boot Sector, FAT and Directory in FAT12/ FAT16 system on one hand and FAT32 on the other.

The File Allocation Table

The File Allocation Table (FAT) maps the usage of the data space of the disk. It contains information about the space used by each individual file, the unused disk space and the space that is unusable due to defects in the disk. Since FAT contains vital information, two copies of FAT are usually stored on the disk. In case one gets destroyed, the other can be used. A typical FAT entry can contain any of the following:

–   Unused cluster
–   Reserved cluster
–   Bad cluster
–   Last cluster in the file
–   Next cluster number in the file

There is one entry in the FAT for each cluster in the file area. If the value in a FAT entry doesn't mark an unused, reserved or defective cluster, then the cluster corresponding to the FAT entry is part of a file, and the value in the FAT entry would indicate the next cluster in the file.

This means that the space that belongs to a given file is mapped by a chain of FAT entries. Each FAT entry points to the next entry in the chain. The first cluster number in the chain is the starting cluster number in the file's directory entry. When a file is created or extended, a cluster is allocated to the file by searching the FAT for unused clusters and adding them to the chain. Vice versa, when a file is deleted, the cluster that has been allocated to the file is freed by clearing corresponding FAT entries (by setting them to **0**). The FAT chain for a file ends with an entry **FFFFh** in the FAT. Figure 7.2 shows a FAT chain for a file called ICIT.PRG.

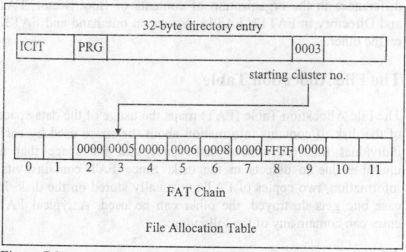

Figure 7.2

This file occupies cluster number **3, 5, 6** and **8** on the disk. Hence the starting cluster number in the directory entry for the file is **3**. Suppose this file is to be loaded into memory then OS would first load starting cluster number—**3**'s contents into memory. To find out the next cluster belonging to this file OS looks at entry number

3 in FAT where it finds a value **5**. Therefore, now it loads the contents of cluster number **5** into memory. Once again OS looks at the FAT and finds in entry number **5** a value **6**, hence it loads the contents of cluster **6** into memory. This process goes on till the OS finds an entry **FFFFh** in FAT, which indicates that there are no more clusters belonging to the file. Hence the process stops.

Now that we have understood how the FAT chain is traversed, let's dig a little deeper into the FAT. The entries present in FAT are 12, 16 or 32 bits long depending on the storage capacity of the disk. Though a 12-bit FAT can handle 4096 clusters only 4078 clusters are available for use since some values are reserved. Similarly, for a 16-bit FAT out of the possible 65536 clusters that it can handle only 65518 are available for use.

In a 12-bit FAT three bytes form two entries. The first two entries (**0** and **1**) in the FAT are reserved for use by the OS. This means that first **3** bytes in a 12-bit FAT, first **4** bytes in 16-bit FAT and first **8** bytes in a 32-bit FAT are not used for storing cluster numbers. Out of these **3** (or **4**, or **8**) bytes, the first byte is the media descriptor byte and the balance contains the value **FFh**. These balance bytes remain unused. The media descriptor byte specifies the type of the disk. It typically has a value **FDh**, **F9h**, **F0h**, **F8h** for a 360 KB, 1.2 MB, 1.44 MB and a hard disk respectively. The contents of a FAT entry are interpreted as shown in Table 7.1.

Values			Meaning
12-bit	**16-bit**	**32-bit**	
000h	0000h	0000000h	Cluster available
FF0h–F6h	FFFFh–FFFF6h	FFFFFFFh–FFFFFF6h	Reserved cluster
FF7h	FFF7h	FFFFFF7h	Bad cluster if not part of chain
FF8h–FFh	FFF8h–FFFFh	FFFFFF8h–FFFFFFh	Last cluster of file
xxx	xxxx	xxxxxxx	Next cluster in file

Table 7.1 Meaning of FAT entries.

As we saw earlier, two identical copies of FAT are maintained on the disk. All copies are updated simultaneously whenever files are modified. If access to a FAT fails due to a read error, the OS tries the other copy. Thus, if one copy of the FAT becomes unreadable due to wear or a software accident, the other copy may still make it possible to salvage the files/directories on the disk.

Here is a program that prints the contents of the first sector of two copies of FAT for a 12-bit or a 16-bit FAT. On similar lines it can be extended to work for a 32-bit FAT.

```
/* Program 82 */
#include <alloc.h>
#include <dos.h>
#include <bios.h>

struct boot
{
    unsigned char jump[3] ;
    char OEMname[8] ;
    short int bps ;
    unsigned char spc ;
    short int reservedsec ;
```

```
        unsigned char fatcopies ;
        short int maxdirentries ;
        short int totalsec ;
        unsigned char mediadesc ;
        short int secperfat ;
        short int secpertrack ;
        short int noofsides ;
        long int hidden ;
        long int hugesec ;
        unsigned char drivenumber ;
        unsigned char reserved ;
        unsigned char bootsignature ;
        long int volumeid ;
        char volumelabel[11] ;
        char filesystype[8] ;
        unsigned char unused[450] ;
} ;

struct boot bs ;
char filetypestr[8] ;

void getfat_12 ( unsigned char *pfat )
{
        int value ;
        int *fatentry ;
        int i, k ;

        for ( k = 2 ; k < 18 ; k++ )
        {
            i = k * 3 / 2 ;

            fatentry = ( int* ) ( pfat + i ) ;

            if ( ( k % 2 ) == 0 )
                  value = ( *fatentry & 0x0fff ) ;
            else
                  value = ( *fatentry >> 4 ) ;
```

```
            printf ( "%03x   ", value ) ;
            if ( k % 9 == 0 )
                printf ( "\n" ) ;
        }
}

void read_fat_info ( long fat_num )
{
    int j, i ;

    unsigned char *p ;

    if ( strncmp ( "FAT12", filetypestr, 5 ) == 0 )
    {
        p = ( unsigned char* ) malloc ( bs.bps ) ;
        absread ( 0, 1, fat_num, p ) ;
        getfat_12( p ) ;
    }

    if ( strncmp ( "FAT16", filetypestr, 5 ) == 0 )
    {
        short int *pfat ;
        p = ( unsigned char* ) malloc ( bs.bps ) ;
        absread ( 2, 1, fat_num, p ) ;
        pfat = ( short int* ) p ;

        for ( j = 0 ; j < 2 ; j++ )
        {
            printf ( "\n%d   ", j * 8 ) ;
            for ( i = 0 ; i < 8 ; i++ )
            {
                printf ( "%04x ", *pfat++ ) ;
            }
        }
    }
}

void fat_info( )
```

```
{
    long int first_fat, second_fat ;

    first_fat = bs.reservedsec ;
    second_fat = bs.reservedsec + bs.secperfat ;

    printf ( "\n%s Fat Information", filetypestr ) ;
    printf ( "\n----------------------------" ) ;

    printf ( "\nFirst FAT Information\n" ) ;

    read_fat_info ( first_fat ) ;

    printf ( "\n\nSecond FAT Information\n" ) ;

    read_fat_info ( second_fat ) ;
    printf ( "\n-------------------------------\n" ) ;
}

main( )
{
    char choice ;

    clrscr( ) ;

    printf ( "A. Drive A" ) ;
    printf ( "\nC. Drive C" ) ;
    printf ( "\n0. Exit" ) ;

    printf ( "\nEnter the drive (A/C): " ) ;
    scanf ( "%c", &choice ) ;

    if ( absread ( choice - 65, 1, 0, &bs ) == -1 )
    {
        printf ( "Error reading sector" ) ;
        exit ( 0 ) ;
    }
    else
```

```
{
    strcpy ( filetypestr, bs.filesystype ) ;
    filetypestr[6] = '\0' ;
}

    fat_info( ) ;
}
```

Each disk contains two copies of FAT. In the function **fat_info( )** the starting sector of each copy of FAT is determined. Next, the function **read_fat_info( )** is called for reading and displaying contents of each FAT copy. Since each copy contains several entries, we have displayed only the first 16 entries for a 12-bit & 16-bit FAT. The organization of the FAT types is shown in Figure 7.3.

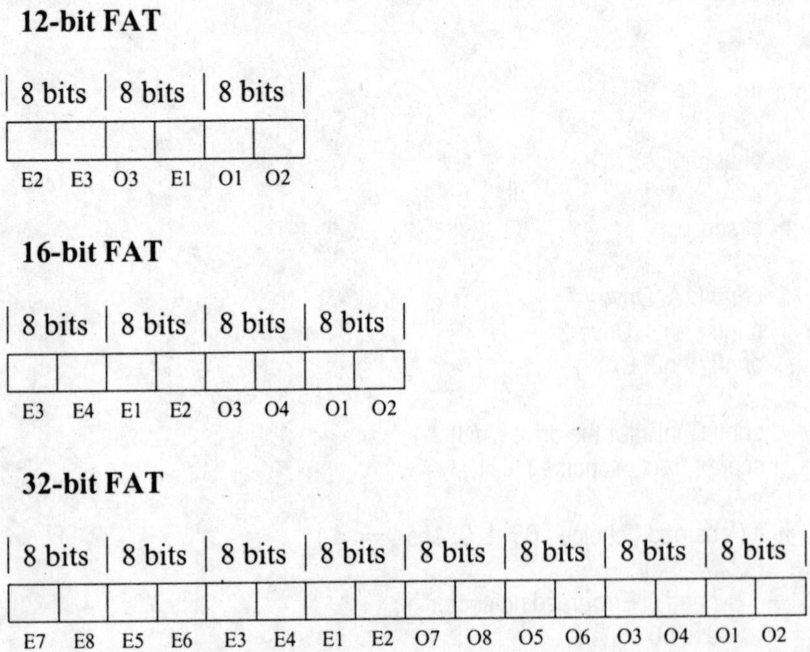

12-bit FAT

| 8 bits | 8 bits | 8 bits |

E2 E3 O3 E1 O1 O2

16-bit FAT

| 8 bits | 8 bits | 8 bits | 8 bits |

E3 E4 E1 E2 O3 O4 O1 O2

32-bit FAT

| 8 bits | 8 bits | 8 bits | 8 bits | 8 bits | 8 bits | 8 bits | 8 bits |

E7 E8 E5 E6 E3 E4 E1 E2 O7 O8 O5 O6 O3 O4 O1 O2

Figure 7.3 Organization of different FAT systems.

For a 32-bit FAT the seven nibbles (a nibble is a group of 4 bits) E1-E2-E3-E4-E5-E6-E7-E8 form the even entry. Note that the arrangement of these nibbles is E7-E8-E5-E6-E3-E4-E1-E2 because the lower byte is always stored in memory earlier than the higher byte. This means if the value of the 4-byte FAT entry is ABCD, it would be stored as DCBA. The odd entry is represented using the set of nibbles O1-O2-O3-O4-O5-O6-O7-O8. In reality the nibble E8 and O8 don't contribute to the cluster number since each entry in the 32-bit FAT is only **28** bits long.

On similar lines in a 16-bit FAT the four nibbles E1-E2-E3-E4 form the even entry whereas the set O1-O2-O3-O4 form the odd entry. Similarly, the even and odd entries in a 12-bit FAT are formed by E1-E2-E3 and O1-O2-O3 respectively. Picking up the values present in odd or even entries from a 32-bit FAT or a 16-bit FAT a relatively simple job. However, to pick up the values from a 12-bit FAT we have to use bitwise operators to discard one nibble out of a group of 4 nibbles. This is done in our program through the functions **getfat_12( )** given below.

```
void getfat_12 ( unsigned char *pfat )
{
    int value ;
    int *fatentry ;
    int i, k ;

    for ( k = 2 ; k < 18 ; k++ )
    {
        i = k * 3 / 2 ;

        fatentry = ( int* ) ( pfat + i ) ;

        if ( ( k % 2 ) == 0 )
            value = ( *fatentry & 0x0fff ) ;
        else
            value = ( *fatentry >> 4 ) ;
```

```
        printf ( "%03x  ", value ) ;

    if ( k % 9 == 0 )
        printf ( "\n" ) ;
    }
}
```

Dictionary

Any computerised dictionary should not only be able to hold all the words but must also be able to search the requested word efficiently. In principle the words can be stored in an array. However, an array suffers from several limitations like:

(a) The size of the array has to be defined while writing the program.

(b) The size of the array cannot be increased or decreased during execution.

(c) Insertion of a new element in the middle of an array is costly since it necessitates movement of existing elements of the array.

(d) Deletion of an element also necessitates movement of array elements.

(e) Since array elements are stored in adjacent memory locations and dictionary contains huge amount of words there is always a possibility that so many adjacent locations may not be available in memory.

We can easily overcome these limitations through usage of linked lists. I would demonstrate this through a program. This program would read a list of countries from a file and maintain them in the order of a dictionary. Later we would receive a country name from the keyboard and report whether it exists in the dictionary or not. If it is not present in the list it gets added to the dictionary at suitable position. Here is a program that achieves this...

```
/* Program 83 */
/* Program to implement a Dictionary */
#include "stdio.h"
#include "string.h"
#include "ctype.h"
#include "alloc.h"

struct clist
{
    char name[20] ;
    struct clist *link ;
} ;

struct clist *a[26] ;

main( )
{
    int sflag, l ;
    char country[20], ch ;
    FILE *fp ;

    clrscr( ) ;
    fp = fopen ( "CNAMES.TXT", "r+" ) ;
    if ( fp == NULL )
    {
        printf ( "\nUnable to Open" ) ;
        exit( ) ;
    }

    while ( fgets ( country, 20, fp ) )
    {
        l = strlen ( country ) ;
        country[ l - 1 ] = '\0' ;

        addtolist ( toupper ( country[0] ) - 65, country ) ;
```

```
    }

    while ( 1 )
    {
        printf ( "\nEnter the Country to Search: " ) ;
        fflush ( stdin ) ;
        gets ( country ) ;

        sflag = search_list ( toupper ( country[0] ) - 65, country ) ;

        if ( sflag )
            printf ( "\n%s is present in the List\n", country ) ;
        else
        {
            printf ( "\nMisspelled\n" ) ;
            printf ( "\nDo you want to Add it in the List (Y/N): " ) ;
            ch = getche( ) ;
            if ( tolower ( ch ) == 'y' )
            {
                fseek ( fp, 0L, SEEK_END ) ;
                fputs ( country, fp ) ;
                fputs ( "\n", fp ) ;
                addtolist ( toupper ( country[0] ) - 65, country ) ;
            }
        }

        printf ( "\nAny More Countries to Search (Y/N): " ) ;
        fflush ( stdin ) ;
        ch = getche( ) ;
        if ( tolower ( ch ) != 'y' )
            break ;
    }

    fclose ( fp ) ;
}

addtolist ( int index, char *str )
{
```

```
    char name[20] ;

    struct clist *q, *r, *temp ;

    temp = q = a[index] ;

    r = malloc ( sizeof ( struct clist ) ) ;
    strcpy ( r -> name, str ) ;

    /* if list is empty */
    if ( q == NULL || strcmp ( q -> name, str ) > 0 )
    {
        q = r ;
        q -> link = temp ;
        a[index] = q ;
    }
    else
    {
        /* traverse the list */
        while ( temp != NULL )
        {
            if ( strcmp ( temp -> name, str ) <= 0 && ( strcmp ( temp -> link
                            -> name, str ) > 0 ) || ( temp -> link == NULL ) )
            {
                r -> link = temp -> link ;
                temp -> link = r ;
                return ;

            }

            temp = temp -> link ;
        }

        r -> link = NULL ;
        temp -> link = r ;
    }
}
```

```
search_list ( int index, char *str )
{
    struct clist *p ;

    p = a[index] ;

    if ( p == NULL )
        return 0 ;
    else
    {
        while ( p != NULL )
        {
            if ( strcmp ( p -> name, str ) == 0 )
                return 1 ;
            else
                p = p -> link ;
        }
        return 0 ;
    }
}
```

To facilitate easy insertion of a new country name in the dictionary we have used linked list to maintain the names of countries. If one linked list is used to store all country names addition of a new country name to it would necessitate searching an appropriate point of insertion starting from the first name. This would involve an exhaustive search. This means if we are to insert a name like 'Zimbabwe', we will have to start the search from the first node. Ideally, we should be able to compare only those names that start with Z. Similarly, once the linked list is built, searching for a specific country in the list would again force us to start our search from the first node. Both these limitations have been overcome in our program. We have maintained 26 linked lists one for each alphabet. Each node in the linked list contains name of a country and pointer to the next node. The starting addresses of each linked list are stored in an array of pointers.

While adding a new country to the dictionary we have called the function **addtolist( )**. This function first picks up the starting address of the appropriate linked list from the array of pointers. Once this has been done it is just a matter of inserting a new node in this linked list. A similar procedure in adopted while searching for a name in the dictionary, the only difference being this time the **search_list( )** function reports the presence or absence of the name in the linked list.

Managing Database

A database file typically contains several records. Each record contains several items of information. Each item of information is known as a field. For creating and maintaining a database the fields are gathered into a structure and then the structure is written/read to/from disk using functions like **fwrite( )** and **fread( )**. Often functions like **addrec( )**, **modirec( )**, **delrec( )** and **listrec( )** are written to perform operations like addition of new records, modification of existing records, deletion of existing records and listing of records respectively. However, all these operations and functions remain specific to the structure at hand. Most DBMS and RDBMS softwares permit us to create database files and perform operations on it in a more generic manner. That is we can create different database files to hold different types of structures and still perform the addition, modification, deletion and listing operations in a more generic way. We too can develop such a system easily. Given below is a program that achieves this.

```
/* Program 84 */
#include "stdio.h"
#include "string.h"
#include "alloc.h"
# include "dos.h"

struct
{
```

```
        char name[11] ;
        int type ;
        int bytes ;
        int dec ;
} f[10] ;

struct header
{
        unsigned long recnum ;
        int fhsize ;
        int byte_rec ;
} ;

struct fhdr
{
        char name[11] ;
        char type ;
        char length ;
        char dec ;
} ;

struct header h ;
struct fhdr fd ;

struct integer
{
        int num ;
        int ind ;
        struct integer *link ;
} ;

struct floatnum
{
        float num ;
        int ind ;
        struct floatnum *link ;
} ;
```

```
struct string
{
    char name[20] ;
    int ind ;
    struct string *link ;
} ;

union fieldlist
{
    struct integer x ;
    struct floatnum n ;
    struct string s ;
} u ;

main( )
{
    char choice ;

    while ( 1 )
    {
        clrscr( ) ,

        gotorc ( 6, 30 ) ;
        printf ( "1. Create Database File and Add Records" ) ;

        gotorc ( 8, 30 ) ;
        printf ( "2. Index Database File" ) ;

        gotorc ( 10, 30 ) ;
        printf ( "3. List Indexed Records" ) ;

        gotorc ( 12, 30 ) ;
        printf ( "0. Exit" ) ;

        gotorc ( 14, 30 ) ;
        printf ( "Enter Choice: " ) ;
        fflush ( stdin ) ;
        choice = getche( ) ;
```

```
        switch ( choice )
        {
            case '1':
                create_dbf( ) ;
                break ;
            case '2':
                create_index( ) ;
                break ;
            case '3':
                list_irec( ) ;
                break ;
            case '0':
                exit( ) ;
        }
    }
}

create_dbf( )
{
    FILE *fp ;
    int i = 0, j = 8, k = 0, num, numoffields = 0, len, totbyte_rec = 0, fh ;
    float decif ;
    char str[20], ch, filename[13] ;

    clrscr( ) ;
    printf ( "\Enter the DataBase File to Create : " ) ;
    fflush ( stdin ) ;
    gets ( filename ) ;
    filename[9] = '\0' ;

    len = strlen ( filename ) ;
    if ( len < 8 )
        filename[ len ] = '\0' ;
    strcat ( filename, ".dbf" ) ;

    fp = fopen ( filename, "wb" ) ;
    if ( fp == NULL )
```

```
{
    puts ( "Unable to Open" ) ;
    exit( ) ;
}

h.recnum = 0 ;
h.fhsize = 0 ;
h.byte_rec = 0 ;

fwrite ( &h, sizeof ( h ), 1, fp ) ;

gotorc ( 6, 32 ) ;
printf ( "DataBase Structure" ) ;

gotorc ( 7, 20 ) ;
printf ( "Name" ) ;

gotorc ( 7, 40 ) ;
printf ( "Type" ) ;

gotorc ( 7, 54 ) ;
printf ( "Bytes" ) ;

gotorc ( 7, 64 ) ;
printf ( "Precision" ) ;

do
{
    gotorc ( j, 20 ) ;
    gets ( f[i].name ) ;

    if ( f[i].name[0] == '\0' )
        break ;

    gotorc ( j, 40 ) ;
    f[i].type = getchar( ) ;

    if ( f[i].type == 'i' )
```

```
        {
            gotorc ( j, 54 ) ;
            printf ( "%d", f[i].bytes = 2 ) ;
        }
        else if ( f[i].type == 'f' )
        {
            gotorc ( j, 54 ) ;
            printf ( "%d", f[i].bytes = 4 ) ;
            gotorc ( j, 64 ) ;
            scanf ( "%d", &f[i].dec ) ;
        }
        else if ( f[i].type == 's' )
        {
            gotorc ( j, 54 ) ;
            scanf ( "%d", &f[i].bytes ) ;
            if ( f[i].bytes > 20 )
                f[i].bytes = 20 ;
        }
        else
        {
            printf ( "Error" ) ;
            exit( ) ;
        }

        totbyte_rec += f[i].bytes ;
        strcpy ( fd.name, f[i].name ) ;
        fd.type = f[i].type ;
        if ( fd.type == 'f' )
            fd.dec = f[i].dec ;
        fd.length = f[i].bytes ;

        fwrite ( &fd, sizeof ( fd ), 1, fp ) ;

        i++ ;
        j++ ;
        fflush ( stdin ) ;
    } while ( i < 10 ) ;
```

```
numoffields = i ;

fseek ( fp, 4L, SEEK_SET ) ;
fh = 14 * i ;

fwrite ( &totbyte_rec, sizeof ( totbyte_rec ), 1, fp ) ;
fwrite ( &fh, sizeof ( fh ), 1, fp ) ;
fseek ( fp, 0L, SEEK_END ) ;

clrscr( ) ;
for ( i = 0 ; i < numoffields ; i++ )
{
    gotorc ( 3, 6 + 20 * i ) ;
    printf ( "%s", f[i].name ) ;
}

j = 0 ;
k = 4 ;
do
{
    for ( i = 0 ; i < numoffields ; i++ )
    {
        gotorc ( k, 6 + 20 * i ) ;
        if ( f[i].type == 'i' )
        {
            scanf ( "%d", &num ) ;
            fwrite ( &num, sizeof ( num ), 1, fp ) ;
        }
        else if ( f[i].type == 'f' )
        {
            scanf ( "%f", &decif ) ;
            fwrite ( &decif, sizeof ( decif ), 1, fp ) ;
        }
        else if ( f[i].type == 's' )
        {
            scanf ( "%s", str ) ;
            if ( f[i].bytes < 20 )
                fwrite ( str, f[i].bytes, 1, fp ) ;
```

```
                      else
                      {
                          * ( str + 19 ) = '\0' ;
                          fwrite ( str, sizeof ( str ), 1, fp ) ;
                      }
                  }
              }
          k++ ;
          j++ ;

          gotorc ( 1, 1 ) ;
          printf ( "Another Record (Y/N): " ) ;
          printf ( " \b" ) ;
          fflush ( stdin ) ;
          ch = getche( ) ;

      } while ( tolower ( ch ) == 'y' ) ;

      h.recnum = j ;
      h.fhsize = numoffields * 14 ;
      h.byte_rec = totbyte_rec ;
      rewind ( fp ) ;
      fwrite ( &h, sizeof ( h ), 1, fp ) ;

      fclose ( fp ) ;
      getch( ) ;
}

create_index( )
{
      FILE *fp, *ft ;
      int i = 0, len, num ;
      unsigned int nfields, bytes, depth = 0 ;
      float decif ;
      char str[20], filename[13], a[4], field[11], type ;

      union fieldlist *p, *temp, *start ;
```

```
clrscr( ) ;
printf ( "\Enter the DataBase File to Read : " ) ;
fflush ( stdin ) ;
gets ( filename ) ;

fp = fopen ( filename, "rb" ) ;
if ( fp == NULL )
{
    puts ( "Unable to Open" ) ;
    exit( ) ;
}

fread ( &h, sizeof ( h ), 1, fp ) ;

/* determine the field and its type */
for ( i = 0 ; i < h.fhsize / 14 ; i++ )
{
    fread ( &fd, sizeof ( fd ), 1, fp ) ;

    strcpy ( f[i].name, fd.name ) ;
    f[i].type = fd.type ;
    f[i].bytes = fd.length ;
    if ( fd.type == 'f' )
        f[i].dec = fd.dec ;
}

printf ( "\nEnter Field Name for Indexing: " ) ;
fflush ( stdin ) ;
scanf ( "%s", field ) ;

fp = fopen ( filename, "rb" ) ;
if ( fp == NULL )
{
    puts ( "Unable to open" ) ;
    return ;
}

strcpy ( filename, field ) ;
```

```
strcat ( filename, ".idx" ) ;

ft = fopen ( filename, "wb" ) ;
if ( ft == NULL )
{
    puts ( "Unable to open" ) ;
    return ;
}

fwrite ( &field, sizeof ( field ), 1, ft ) ;

nfields = h.fhsize / 14 ;

for ( i = 0 ; i < nfields ; i++ )
{
    if ( strcmp ( f[i].name , field ) == 0 )
    {
        type = f[i].type ;
        len = f[i].bytes ;
        break ;
    }

    depth += f[i].bytes ;
}

fseek ( fp, 8L + h.fhsize, SEEK_SET ) ;
switch ( type )
{
    case 'i':
        fseek ( fp, depth, SEEK_CUR ) ;
        fread ( &num, sizeof ( num ), 1, fp ) ;
        fseek ( fp, h.byte_rec - depth - sizeof ( num ), SEEK_CUR ) ;

        p = ( union fieldlist * ) malloc ( sizeof ( struct integer ) ) ;
        p -> x.ind = 1 ;
        p -> x.num  = num ;
        p -> x.link = NULL ;
```

```
            temp = start = p ;
            fseek ( fp, depth, SEEK_CUR ) ;
            bytes = h.byte_rec - sizeof ( num ) ;
            for ( i = 1 ; i < h.recnum ; i++ )
            {
                fread ( &num, sizeof ( num ), 1, fp ) ;

                temp = ( union fieldlist * ) malloc ( sizeof ( struct integer ) ) ;
                temp -> x.ind =  i + 1 ;
                temp -> x.num = num ;
                temp -> x.link = NULL ;

                while ( p -> x.link != NULL )
                    p  = ( union fieldlist * ) p -> x.link ;

                p -> x.link = ( struct integer * ) temp ;
                p = start ;
                fseek ( fp, bytes, SEEK_CUR ) ;
            }

            sort_writeindex ( &start, ft, type ) ;
            break ;

    case 'f':
            fseek ( fp, depth, SEEK_CUR ) ;
            fread ( &decif, sizeof ( decif ), 1, fp ) ;
            fseek ( fp, h.byte_rec - depth - sizeof ( decif ), SEEK_CUR ) ;

            p = ( union fieldlist * ) malloc ( sizeof ( struct floatnum ) ) ;
            p -> n.ind = 1 ;
            p -> n.num  = decif ;
            p -> n.link = NULL ;

            temp = start = p ;
            fseek ( fp, depth, SEEK_CUR ) ;
            bytes = h.byte_rec - sizeof ( decif ) ;
            for ( i = 1 ; i < h.recnum ; i++ )
            {
```

```
                fread ( &decif, sizeof ( decif ), 1, fp ) ;

                temp = ( union fieldlist* ) malloc( sizeof( struct floatnum ) ) ;
                temp -> n.ind = i + 1 ;
                temp -> n.num = decif ;
                temp -> n.link = NULL ;

                while ( p -> n.link != NULL )
                    p = ( union fieldlist * ) p -> n.link ;

                p -> n.link = ( struct floatnum * ) temp ;

                fseek ( fp, bytes, SEEK_CUR ) ;
                fseek ( fp, 0L, SEEK_CUR ) ;
            }

        sort_writeindex ( &start, ft, type ) ;
        break ;

    case 's':
        fseek ( fp, depth, SEEK_CUR ) ;
        fread ( str, len, 1, fp ) ;
        fseek ( fp, h.byte_rec - depth - len, SEEK_CUR ) ;

        p = ( union fieldlist * ) malloc ( sizeof ( struct string ) ) ;
        p -> s.ind = 1 ;
        strcpy ( p -> s.name, str ) ;
        p -> s.link = NULL ;

        temp = start = p ;
        fseek ( fp, depth, SEEK_CUR ) ;
        bytes = h.byte_rec - len ;
        for ( i = 1 ; i < h.recnum ; i++ )
        {
            fread ( str, len, 1, fp ) ;

            temp = ( union fieldlist * ) malloc ( sizeof ( struct string ) ) ;
            temp -> s.ind = i + 1 ;
```

```
                strcpy ( temp -> s.name, str ) ;
                temp -> s.link = NULL ;

                while ( p -> s.link != NULL )
                    p = ( union fieldlist * ) p -> s.link ;

                p -> s.link = ( struct string * ) temp ;

                fseek ( fp, bytes, SEEK_CUR ) ;
            }

            sort_writeindex ( &start, ft, type ) ;
            break ;
        }

    fclose ( fp ) ;
    fclose ( ft ) ;
}

sort_writeindex ( union fieldlist **start, FILE *ft, char type )
{
    union fieldlist *p, *q, *r, *s, *temp, *n, *str ;

    s = NULL ;
    p = *start ;

    /* r precedes p and s for sentinel node for inner loop */
    while ( 1 )
    {
        if ( type == 'i' && s == ( union fieldlist * ) ( *start ) -> x.link )
            break ;
        if ( type == 'f' && s == ( union fieldlist * ) ( *start ) -> n.link )
            break ;
        if ( type == 's' && s == ( union fieldlist * ) ( *start ) -> s.link )
            break ;

        r = p = *start ;
```

```c
if ( type == 's' )
    q = ( union fieldlist * ) p -> s.link ;
else if ( type == 'f' )
    q = ( union fieldlist * ) p -> n.link ;
else
    q = ( union fieldlist * ) p -> x.link ;

while ( ( union fieldlist * ) p -> x.link != s || ( union fieldlist * ) p -> .link
                        != s || ( union fieldlist * ) p -> s.link != s )
{
    if ( type == 'i'  && p -> x.num > q -> x.num )
    {
        if ( p == *start )
        {
            temp = ( union fieldlist * ) q -> x.link ;
            q -> x.link = &( p -> x ) ;
            p -> x.link = ( struct integer * ) temp ;

            *start = q ;
            r = q ;
        }
        else
        {
            temp = ( union fieldlist * ) q -> x.link ;
            q -> x.link = &( p -> x ) ;
            p -> x.link = ( struct integer * ) temp ;

            r -> x.link = &( q -> x ) ;
            r = q ;
        }
    }
    else if ( type == 'f' && p -> n.num > q -> n.num )
    {
        if ( p == *start )
        {
            temp = ( union fieldlist * ) q -> n.link ;
            q -> n.link = &( p -> n ) ;
            p -> n.link = ( struct floatnum * ) temp ;
```

```
                *start = q ;
                r = q ;
        }
        else
        {
                temp = ( union fieldlist * ) q -> n.link ;
                q -> n.link = &( p -> n ) ;
                p -> n.link = ( struct floatnum * ) temp ;

                r -> n.link = &( q -> n ) ;
                r = q ;
        }
}
else if ( type == 's' && strcmp ( p -> s.name, q -> s.name ) > 0 )
{
        if ( p == *start )
        {
                temp = ( union fieldlist * ) q -> s.link ;
                q -> s.link = &( p -> s ) ;
                p -> s.link = ( struct string * ) temp ;

                *start = q ;
                r = q ;
        }
        else
        {
                temp = ( union fieldlist * ) q -> s.link
                q -> s.link = &( p -> s ) ;
                p -> s.link = ( struct string * ) temp ;

                r -> s.link = &( q -> s ) ;
                r = q ;
        }
}
else
{
        r = p ;
```

```
                    if ( type == 'i' )
                        p = ( union fieldlist * ) p -> x.link ;
                    if ( type == 'f' )
                        p = ( union fieldlist * ) p -> n.link ;
                    if ( type == 's' )
                        p = ( union fieldlist * ) p -> s.link ;
                }
            if ( type == 'i' )
                q = ( union fieldlist * ) p -> x.link ;
            if ( type == 'f' )
                q = ( union fieldlist * ) p -> n.link ;
            if ( type == 's' )
                q = ( union fieldlist * ) p -> s.link ;

            if ( q == NULL || q == s )
            {
                s = p ;
                break ;
            }
        }
    }

p = *start ;
if ( type == 's' )
{
    while ( p != NULL )
    {
        fwrite ( &p -> s.ind, sizeof ( p -> s.ind ), 1, ft ) ;

        p = ( union fieldlist * ) p -> s.link ;
    }
}
else if ( type == 'f' )
{
    while ( p != NULL )
    {
        fwrite ( &p -> n.ind, sizeof ( p -> n.ind ), 1, ft ) ;
```

```
                p = ( union fieldlist * ) p -> n.link ;
        }
    }
    else
    {
        while ( p != NULL )
        {
            fwrite ( &p -> x.ind, sizeof ( p -> x.ind ), 1, ft ) ;

            p = ( union fieldlist * ) p -> x.link ;
        }
    }
}

list_irec( )
{
    FILE *fp, *ft ;
    int i = 0, j = 8, k = 0, len ;
    int num, ind ;
    float decif ;
    char str[20], ch, filename[13] ;

    clrscr( ) ;
    printf ( "\Enter the DataBase File to Read : " ) ;
    fflush ( stdin ) ;
    gets ( filename ) ;

    fp = fopen ( filename, "rb" ) ;
    if ( fp == NULL )
    {
        puts ( "Unable to Open" ) ;
        exit( ) ;
    }
    printf ( "\nEnter the Index File to Use: " ) ;
    fflush ( stdin ) ;
    gets ( filename ) ;
    ft = fopen ( filename, "rb" ) ;
    if ( ft == NULL )
```

```
{
    puts ( "Unable to Open" ) ;
    exit( ) ;
}

fseek ( ft, 11L, SEEK_SET ) ;

fseek ( fp, 0L, SEEK_CUR ) ;
fread ( &h, sizeof ( h ), 1, fp ) ;

for ( i = 0 ; i < h.fhsize / 14 ; i++ )
{
    fread ( &fd, sizeof ( fd ), 1, fp ) ;

    strcpy ( f[i].name, fd.name ) ;
    f[i].type = fd.type ;
    f[i].bytes = fd.length ;

    if ( fd.type == 'f' )
        f[i].dec = fd.dec ;
}

clrscr( ) ;
for ( i = 0 ; i < h.fhsize / 14 ; i++ )
{
    gotorc ( 3, 6 + 10 * i ) ;
    printf ( "%s", f[i].name ) ;
}

j = 0 ;
k = 4 ;
fseek ( fp, 8L + h.fhsize, SEEK_SET ) ;

while ( fread ( &ind, sizeof ( ind ), 1, ft ) == 1)
{
    fseek ( fp, ( ind - 1 ) * h.byte_rec, SEEK_CUR ) ;
```

```
            for ( i = 0 ; i < h.fhsize / 14 ; i++ )
            {
                gotorc ( k, 6 + 10 * i ) ;
                if ( f[i].type == 'i' )
                {
                    if ( fread ( &num, sizeof ( num ), 1, fp ) )
                        printf ( "%d", num ) ;
                }
                else if ( f[i].type == 'f' )
                {
                    if ( fread ( &decif, sizeof ( decif ), 1, fp ) )
                        printf ( "%.*f", f[i].dec, decif ) ;
                }
                else if ( f[i].type == 's' )
                {
                    if ( fread ( &str, f[i].bytes, 1, fp ) == 1 )
                        printf ( "%s", str ) ;
                }
            }
            fseek ( fp, 8L + h.fhsize, SEEK_SET ) ;
            k++ ;
            j++ ;
        }
    getch( ) ;
    fclose ( fp ) ;
    fclose ( ft ) ;
}

gotorc ( int x, int y )
{
    union REGS i, o ;

    i.h.ah = 2 ;
    i.h.dl = y ;
    i.h.dh = x ;
    i.h.bh = 0 ;

    int86 ( 0x10, &i, &i ) ;
```

}

On executing the program a menu containing the following items pops up:

1. Create Database File and Add Records
2. Index Database File
3. List Indexed Records
0. Exit

On selecting the first item we are asked to build the structure of the records to be stored in the file. While building this structure we can create fields of types string, integer, or float. For the sake of programming convenience we have restricted the number of fields that can be added to the structure to 10. Each time you add a field you are prompted to enter its name, type, size and precision. If field type is integer or float the size of the field is assumed to be 2 and 4 bytes respectively. Precision indicates number of places after the decimal point and hence is relevant only for a field of the type float. To indicate the type of the field you must type 's' for string, 'i' for integer and 'f' for float. To indicate that you are through with entry of fields you should simply hit enter in the field **Name**. Once the structure has been created you are asked to enter records.

After this we can create an index file for the database by selecting the second menu option. While indexing the records we have the choice of creating an index based on any one field. Once the index file has been created we can list the records indexed according to the index file.

To help maintain a generic structure we have stored in the database file the information about the fields and a header containing the total number of records and the record size. The index file contains the name of the field on which the database has been indexed. This is followed by the positions of records in the database file had they been sorted according to the index field.

As the user enters the records they are written to the database file on a record-by-record basis. While creating the index file the records are read and a linked list is created. This linked list doesn't contain the entire record read from the database file. Instead, every node contains only the field value on which database is being indexed and position of the record in the database. While creating the index file the linked list is sorted and then the indexes are stored in an index file along with the field name on which the database has been indexed.

While listing the records firstly the database file and the index files are opened. Then one by one the positions of the records are picked up from the index file and the appropriate records are read from the database file. Every record read from the database file is then displayed on the screen.

The Keyboard Queue

Every key we type first goes to a place called keyboard buffer before it gets processed. This buffer is 32 bytes big and occupies addresses 41Eh to 43Dh. As keys get collected in this buffer, they get processed on a first come first serve basis. This means that the keyboard buffer is nothing but a queue. The head and tail of this queue are stored at locations 41Ch and 41Ah respectively (refer Figure 7.4). The head and tail are really pointers, and therefore occupy 2 bytes each. Each of these pointers contains addresses that are offsets into the 32-byte buffer. When there is no key in the keyboard buffer both these pointers contain the offset address 1Eh. Note that this offset is from address 400h. This indicates that the queue is empty. Suppose we key in a Z. The ASCII code and the scan code of this key will get stored in bytes 41Eh and 41Fh respectively.

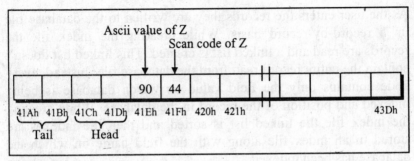

Figure 7.4

Since an element has been inserted in the queue, the tail pointer's value should be incremented to reflect this. Hence the value in 41Ah and 41Bh will now be 20h (1Eh + 2), i.e. the offset of the next byte in the buffer. As we key in more characters, they would get stored beyond Z in the buffer. Each time a character is stored in the buffer the tail pointer would be suitably incremented. In the meanwhile, as we type characters, they would even get processed. Out of all the characters present in the buffer (queue), the one present at the head of the queue gets processed first. As each character gets processed, the head pointer (41Ch, 41Dh) is incremented to reflect this. As each character in the queue gets processed, the head moves towards the tail. If the buffer becomes full, the tail will wrap around to the beginning of the buffer (41Eh, 41Fh). Since the characters were also being processed, the character in the beginning of the buffer may have already been displayed on the screen. So these bytes can be re-utilized. You can notice that this is a circular queue at work. In conclusion we can say that the tail always points to the next free slot in the buffer, whereas, the head always points to the character to be processed/displayed. With this much knowledge we can now write a program to print the contents of the queue and the values of head and tail pointer, as each key is hit.

Here is the program...

```
/* Program 85 */
#include <stdio.h>

unsigned char far *kb = ( unsigned char far* ) 0x41e ;
unsigned int far *tail = ( unsigned char far* ) 0x41a ;
unsigned int far *head = ( unsigned char far* ) 0x41c ;

void disp_key_buffer ( void ) ;

void main( )
{

    unsigned char ch = 0 ;

    fflush ( stdin ) ;
    clrscr( ) ;
    printf( "hit q to exit" ) ;
    while ( ch != 'q' )
    {
        disp_key_buffer( ) ;
        ch = getch( ) ;
    }
}

void disp_key_buffer ( void )
{
    int i ;

    clrscr( );
    printf ( "head = %x tail = %x\n\n", *head + 0x400, *tail + 0x400 ) ;

    printf ( "Address Contents\n" ) ;
    for ( i = 0 ; i < 32 ; i += 2 )
        printf ( "%7x %d %c %d\n", 0x41e + i, *( kb + i ), *( kb + i ),
                                   *( kb + i + 1 ) ) ;

    printf ( "\n\nPress 'q' to exit or any key to continue" ) ;
}
```

The program begins with a call to **fflush( )** to clear the keyboard buffer. The **disp_key_buffer( )** function is used to print the buffer contents and the head and tail pointer values.

Infix to Postfix

When higher level programming languages came into existence one of the major hurdles faced by the computer scientists was to generate machine language instructions that would properly evaluate any arithmetic expression. To convert a complex assignment statement such as:

$$X = A / B + C * D - F * G / Q$$

into a correct instruction sequence was a formidable task. That it is no longer considered so formidable is a tribute to the elegant and simple solutions that the computer scientists came out with. As of today, this conversion is considered to be one of the minor aspects of compiler writing.

To fix the order of evaluation of an expression each language assigns to each operator a priority. Even after assigning priorities how can a compiler accept an expression and produce correct code? For this the expression is reworked into a form called 'postfix' notation. If **e** is an expression with operators and operands, the conventional way of writing **e** is called infix, because the operators come in between the operands. (Unary operators precede their operand.) The postfix form of an expression calls for each operator to appear after its operands. For example, the postfix for of the infix expression A * B / C is A B * C /.

If we study the postfix form we see that the multiplication comes immediately after its two operands A and B. Now imagine that A * B is computed and stored in T. Then we have the division operator (/), coming immediately after its two operands T and C.

Notice three features of the postfix expression:

−   The operands maintain the same order as in the equivalent infix expression.
−   Parentheses are not needed to designate the expression unambiguously.
−   While evaluating the postfix expression the priority of the operators is no longer relevant.

Given below is a program that converts an infix expression into its postfix form.

```
/* Program 86 */
#define MAX 1000

void push ( char *stk, int *sp, char item ) ;
char pop ( char *stk, int *sp ) ;

main( )
{
    static char target[MAX], stack[MAX] ;
    char *t, str[MAX], *s, n1, n2, item, nn :
    int p1, p2, i, top = -1 ;

    printf ( "\nEnter the infix expression: " ) ;
    gets ( str ) ;

    s = str ;
    t = target ;

    while ( *s )
    {
        if ( *s == ' ' || *s == '\t' )
        {
            s++ ;
            continue ;
        }
```

```
if ( isdigit ( *s ) || isalpha ( *s ) )
{
    while ( isdigit ( *s ) || isalpha ( *s ) )
    {
        *t = *s ;
        t++ ;
        s++ ;
    }
}

if ( *s == '(' )
{
    push ( stack, &top, *s ) ;
    s++ ;
}

if ( *s == ')' )
{
    n1 = pop ( stack, &top ) ;
    while ( n1 != '(' )
    {
        *t = n1 ;
        t++ ;
        n1 = pop ( stack, &top ) ;
    }
    s++ ;
}

if ( *s == '+' || *s == '*' || *s == '/' || *s == '%' )
{
    if ( top == -1 )
        push ( stack, &top, *s ) ;
    else
    {
        n1 = pop ( stack, &top ) ;

        while ( priority ( n1 ) >= priority ( *s ) )
        {
```

```
                            *t = n1 ;
                            t++ ;
                            n1 = pop ( stack, &top ) ;
                        }

                    push ( stack, &top, n1 ) ;
                    push ( stack, &top, *s ) ;
                }
                s++ ;
            }
        }

    while ( top != -1 )
    {
        n1 = pop ( stack, &top ) ;
        *t = n1 ;
        t++ ;
    }
    *t = '\0' ;

    t = target ;

    while ( *t )
    {
        printf ( "%c", *t ) ;
        t++ ;
    }
}

/* checks the priority of the operators */
int priority ( char ele )
{
    int pri ;
    char a, b, c ;

    if ( ele == '*' || ele == '/' || ele == '%' )
        pri = 2 ;
    else
```

```
    {
        if ( ele == '+' || ele == '-' )
            pri = 1 ;
        else
            pri = 0 ;
    }
    return pri ;
}

void push ( char *stk, int *sp, char item )
{
    if ( *sp == MAX )
        printf ( "\nStack is full" ) ;
    else
    {
        *sp = *sp + 1 ;
        stk[ *sp ] = item ;
    }
}

char pop ( char *stk, int *sp )
{
    int item ;
    if ( *sp == -1 )
    {
        printf ( "\nStack is empty" ) ;
        return ( -1 ) ;
    }
    else
    {
        item = stk[ *sp ] ;
        *sp = *sp - 1 ;
        return ( item ) ;
    }
}
```

Evaluation of Postfix Expression

In the last section we saw a program that could translate an infix expression to the postfix form. The virtue of postfix notation is that it enables easy evaluation of expressions. To begin with, the need for parentheses is eliminated. Secondly, the priority of the operators is no longer relevant. The expression can be evaluated by making a left to right scan, stacking operands, and evaluating operators using as operands the correct numbers from the stack and finally placing the result onto the stack. This evaluation process is much simpler than attempting a direct evaluation of infix notation. The following program implements the postfix expression evaluation algorithm.

```
/* Program 87 */
#define MAX 25

void push ( int * , int * , int ) ;
int pop ( int *, int * ) ;

main( )
{
    char str[MAX], *s ;
    int n1, n2, n3, nn ;
    int stack[MAX], top = -1 ;

    clrscr( ) ;
    printf ( "\nEnter the postfix expression to be evaluated: " ) ;
    gets ( str ) ;

    s = str ;
    while ( *s )
    {
        /* skip whitespace, if any */
        if ( *s == ' ' || *s == '\t' )
        {
            s++ ;
```

```
        continue ;
    }

    /* if digit is encountered */
    if ( *s >= 48 && *s <= 57 )
    {
        nn = *s - '0' ;
        push ( stack, &top, nn ) ;
    }
    else
    {
        /* if operator is encountered */
        n1 = pop ( stack, &top ) ;
        n2 = pop ( stack, &top ) ;

        switch ( *s )
        {
            case '+' :
                n3 = n2 + n1 ;
                break ;
            case '-' :
                n3 = n2 - n1 ;
                break ;
            case '/' :
                n3 = n2 / n1 ;
                break ;
            case '*' :
                n3 = n2 * n1 ;
                break ;
            case '%' :
                n3 = n2 % n1 ;
                break ;
            default :
                printf ( "Unknown operator" ) ;
                exit ( 1 ) ;
        }
        push ( stack, &top, n3 ) ;
    }
```

```
            s++ ;
        }
        printf ( "\nResult is : %d", pop ( stack, &top ) ) ;
}

void push ( int *stk, int *sp, int item )
{
    if ( *sp == MAX )
        printf ( "\nStack is full" ) ;
    else
    {
        *sp = *sp + 1 ;
        stk[ *sp ] = item ;
    }
}

int pop ( int *stk, int *sp )
{
    int item ;

    if ( *sp == -1 )
    {
        printf ( "\nStack is empty" ) ;
        return ( -1 ) ;
    }
    else
    {
        item = stk[ *sp ] ;
        *sp = *sp - 1 ;
        return ( item ) ;
    }
}
```

Locating Duplicate Filenames

When the hard disk is new the files and directories are properly organized. As the hard disk grows old, some laxity sets in and one tends to create files with duplicate names in different directories. We can write a program to locate these duplicate filenames. Here it is...

```
/* Program 88 */
/* program to find files with duplicate names using binary search tree */
#include <dos.h>
#include <dir.h>
#include <string.h>
#include "alloc.h"

struct btreenode
{
    struct btreenode *leftchild ;
    char data[13] ; /* file name */
    char *loc ; /* location of filename */
    struct btreenode *rightchild ;
} *bt = NULL ;

void disktree ( void ) ;

main( )
{
    char current_dir[32] ;

    clrscr( ) ;
    getcwd ( current_dir, 32 ) ;
    chdir ( "\\" ) ;
    disktree( ) ;
    chdir ( current_dir ) ;
}

void disktree( )
{
    struct ffblk file ;
    int flag ;
    char loc[80] ;
```

```
        getcwd ( loc, 80 ) ;
        flag = findfirst ( "*.*", &file, FA_NORMAL | FA_RDONLY | FA_HIDDEN |
                        FA_SYSTEM | FA_LABEL | FA_DIREC | FA_ARCH )
        while ( flag == 0 )
        {
            if ( file.ff_name[0] != '.' )
            {
                if ( file.ff_attrib == FA_DIREC && file.ff_fsize == 0 )
                {
                    chdir ( file.ff_name ) ;
                    disktree( ) ;
                    chdir ( loc ) ;
                }
                else
                    insert ( &bt, loc, file.ff_name ) ;
            }
            flag = findnext ( &file ) ;
        }
    }

    /* inserts a new node in a binary search tree */
    int insert ( struct btreenode  **sr, char* l, char* f )
    {
        char *p ;
        int flag ;

        if ( *sr == NULL )
        {
            *sr = ( char * ) malloc ( sizeof ( struct btreenode ) ) ;

            if ( *sr == NULL )
            {
                printf ( "\nout of memory" ) ;
                exit ( 1 ) ;
            }

            ( *sr ) -> leftchild = NULL ;
            ( *sr ) -> rightchild = NULL ;
```

```
        strcpy ( ( *sr ) -> data, f ) ;
        p = ( char * ) malloc ( ( strlen ( l ) + 1 ) ) ;

        if ( p == NULL )
        {
            printf ( "\nout of memory" ) ;
            exit ( 1 ) ;
        }

        strcpy ( p, l ) ;
        ( *sr ) -> loc = p ;
    }
    else
    {
        flag = strcmp ( ( *sr ) -> data, f ) ;

        if ( flag == 0 )
        {
            printf ( "org : %s", ( *sr ) -> loc ) ;

            if ( strlen ( ( *sr ) -> loc ) > 4 )
                printf ( "\\" ) ;

            printf ( "%s\n", ( *sr ) -> data ) ;
            printf ("dup : %s", l ) ;

            if ( strlen ( l ) > 4 )
                printf ( "\\" ) ;

            printf ( "%s\n\n", f ) ;
        }
        else if ( flag < 0 )
            insert ( &( ( *sr ) -> leftchild ), l, f ) ;
        else
            insert ( &( ( *sr ) -> rightchild ), l, f ) ;
    }
    return ;
}
```

To locate duplicate names we have created a binary tree. As each directory on the disk is visited, the files present in it are inserted one by one into the binary tree. During this insertion if it is found that the filename already exists in the tree then its original and new path both are displayed.

The **btreenode** structure is used to represent a node in the binary tree. The data field of the node is used for storing the file name and a character pointer (**char *loc**) to store the path name or location of the file.

For searching the filename we would be required to frequently switch between directories. Once the execution of the program is finished it should correctly restore the current directory to the same value as it was at the beginning of the program. So before we call any functions we have stored the current directory in a buffer by calling **getcwd( )** (get current working directory). This buffer is used (just before **main( )** ends) to restore the current directory by calling **chdir( )** (change directory).

The heart of the program is the recursive function **disktree( )**. It recursively traverses all the directories present in the disk. The function first gets the current directory and stores it in a buffer. This buffer will be later required for passing the value to the **insert( )** function and also to switch back to the parent directory after all the sub-directories have been traversed.

The standard library functions **findfirst( )** and **findnext( )** have been used to search files. If the attribute of a directory entry is FA_DIREC and the size is zero then it signifies that it is a directory. The program switches to this directory using **chdir( )** and calls **disktree( )** again. When the control returns to this point again, **chdir( )** is called to change the directory to the parent. On the other hand, if a file is found, it is inserted in the binary tree using the **insert( )** function. The **insert( )** function inserts a new node in a binary search tree. The first parameter passed to it is a pointer to pointer. We initially pass the only global pointer **bt** which holds the entire tree. Note that **bt** is initialized to NULL at the beginning of program. The second parameter is a pointer to string containing the location of the filename, whereas, the third is a pointer to the name of the file itself.

The statement **if (*sr == NULL)** tests whether the tree is empty or not. If the tree is empty, memory is allocated for a node using **malloc( )**. The **leftchild** and **rightchild** are set to NULL. The filename is copied in the **data** part of the node by **strcpy( )**. The location of the filename can't be simply copied to the node as the data member **loc** of **btreenode** isn't an array but a pointer. So using a character pointer firstly memory equivalent to the string's length is allocated. The string is then copied inside the **loc** pointer.

If the tree is non-empty the filename contained in **f** is compared with the data of the first node using **strcmp( )**. If the return value of **strcmp( )** is zero it means that filename is already present so we print the already existing node's data i.e. filename and location and report it as original file. We also print the current filename **f** and location **loc** and report it as duplicate. These being duplicates they aren't inserted in the tree. If the return value of **strcmp( )** is less than zero we call **insert( )** function with the first parameter as **(*sr) -> leftchild** to add this new file as a child of the current node. On the other hand if the return value of **strcmp( )** is greater than zero then the new file is added as right child of the current node.

Thus using a binary search tree we are able to quickly locate files with duplicate names while building the tree.

Hashing

Suppose you want to write an application that generates 1000 random numbers in the range 1 to 32,767. All the random numbers are required to be unique. For example, once the number 511 is generated, it can't be generated again. You propose to use a random number generating function **rand( )** that doesn't generate unique numbers and devise a scheme to reject the previously generated random numbers. Hence you need to remember the random numbers that you generate. It is wasteful to use a 32,767-element boolean array for this purpose. And if you use linked list, the amount of time to figure out if the number is already generated increases as the linked list grows. In such a situation a technique **hashing** can be used. Here we will partition the hash table into 32 buckets. Each bucket will hold numbers in a specific range. For example, random numbers in the range 0 to 1000 would be stored in bucket 0, numbers in the range 1001 to 2000 would be stored in bucket 1, etc. We will store these numbers in a linked list attached to each bucket. This arrangement is shown in the following Figure 7.5.

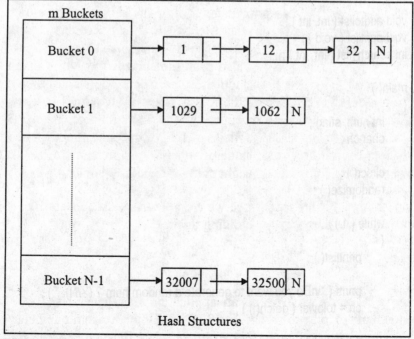

Figure 7.5

While searching a number first we would reach an appropriate bucket and then search the number in the linked list associated with it. Given below is a program that implements this hashing technique.

```
/* Program 89 */
/* program to generate unique random no's using hashing */
#include "alloc.h"
#include "stdlib.h"

struct node
{
    int data ;
    struct node *link ;
};

struct node *bucks[33] ;

void addtolist ( int, int ) ;
void printlist ( void ) ;
int search_list ( int, int ) ;

main( )
{
    int num, sflag ;
    char ch ;

    clrscr( ) ;
    randomize( ) ;

    while ( 1 )
    {
        printlist( ) ;

        printf ( "\nDo you want to generate a random num ? (Y/N): " ) ;
        ch = tolower ( getch( ) ) ;

        if ( ch != 'y' )
```

```
            break ;

        num = random ( 32767 ) ;
        printf ( "\nRandom no. is %d", num ) ;

        sflag = search_list ( num / 1000, num ) ;

        if ( sflag )
            printf ( "\n%d is present in the List", num ) ;
        else
        {
            printf ( "\n%d not present", num ) ;
            printf ( "\nAdd it in the List (y/n):" ) ;
            ch = getche( ) ;

            if ( tolower ( ch ) == 'y' )
                addtolist ( num / 1000, num ) ;
        }
    }
}

void addtolist ( int index, int data )
{
    struct node *q, *r, *temp ;

    temp = q = bucks[ index ] ;

    r = malloc ( sizeof ( struct node ) ) ;
    r -> data = data ;

    /* if list is empty */
    if ( q == NULL || q -> data > data )
    {
        q = r ;
        q -> link = temp ;
        bucks[ index ] = q ;
    }
    else
```

```
    {
        /* traverse the list */
        while ( temp != NULL )
        {
                if ( ( temp -> data < data ) && ( temp -> link -> data > data )
                                            || ( temp -> link == NULL ) )
                {
                    r -> link = temp -> link ;
                    temp -> link = r ;
                    return ;
                }
                temp = temp -> link ;
        }
        r -> link = NULL ;
        temp -> link = r ;
    }
}

int search_list ( int index, int data )
{
    struct node *p ;

    p = bucks[ index ] ;

    if ( p == NULL )
        return 0 ;
    else
    {
        while ( p != NULL )
        {
            if ( p -> data == data )
                return 1 ;
            else
                p = p -> link ;
        }
        return 0 ;
    }
}
```

```
void printlist ( void )
{
    struct node *p ;
    int i ;

    printf( "\nlist: " ) ;
    for ( i = 0 ; i < 33 ; i++ )
    {
        p = bucks[i] ;

        while ( p != NULL )
        {
            printf ( "%d ", p -> data ) ;
            p = p -> link ;
        }
    }
}
```

We have generated random numbers using the standard library function **random( )**. The statement **struct node* bucks[33]** defines an array of pointers. Each pointer in this array points to the linked list associated with that bucket. Thus **bucks[0]** will point to the linked list holding numbers in range of 0 to 1000, **bucks[1]** will point to the linked list holding numbers in range of 1001 to 2000, and so on. The array is declared global so that initially the all elements point to NULL.

While storing the random number we first go to the appropriate hash bucket and then search the number in the linked list associated with the bucket.

Function Calls and Stack

A stack is used by programming languages for implementing function calls. Let us see how this is done with the help of a sample program.

```
/* Program 90 */
main( )
{
    display( ) ;
    show( ) ;
    puts ( "a" ) ;
}

display( )
{
    puts ( "inside show" ) ;
}
```

Let us see how this program gets executed. On being run it is loaded in its entirety into memory. Let us assume that the two functions **display( )** and **show( )** are stored from memory location 1000 and 2000 respectively. While executing any program the computer stores the address of the next instruction to get executed in registers CS (code segment) and IP (instruction pointer). The CS register holds the segment address, whereas IP holds the offset address. Thus when the execution of **main( )** begins and the call to the function **display( )** is encountered, CS:IP would hold the address 510 (refer Figure 7.6). Being a called function the control should now reach **display( )**. However, if it were to go directly to **display( )** to execute the function it would not know where to return after executing the function. That's where the stack comes in. The computer first pushes the address of the next executable instruction (in our case 510) on the stack and then only transfers the control to the function **display( )**. While executing statement in **display( )** CS:IP would contain the address of the next executable instruction within the function. Once all instructions in the function **display( )** have been executed the control returns back to **main( )**. But where in **main( )**? At the next instruction from where **display( )** was called. That is at location number 510. But how would the computer know that the control should come back to 510 and not 515? Remember we earlier stored 510 on the stack? This value is now popped from the stack into CS:IP. Thus the control comes back to address 510 after executing the function **display( )**. Exactly similar procedure takes place when the function **show( )** is called. The entire process is shown in Figure 7.6.

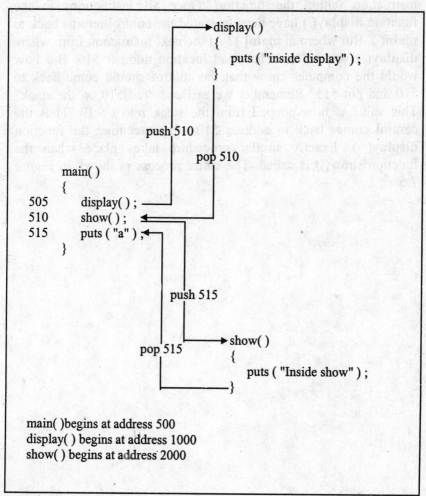

```
                              ┌────────► display( )
                              │          {
                              │              puts ( "inside display" ) ;
                              │          }
                      push 510
                      pop 510
              main( )
              {
        505       display( ) ;
        510       show( ) ;
        515       puts ( "a" ) ;
              }


                      push 515

                                 ┌──────► show( )
                      pop 515     │       {
                                  │           puts ( "Inside show" ) ;
                                  │       }
```

main( ) begins at address 500
display( ) begins at address 1000
show( ) begins at address 2000

Figure 7.6

Let us now confirm this with the help of a program. Here is the program...

```
/* Program 91 */
/* to show the use of stack in function calls */
#include "dos.h"
```

```
unsigned int far *ptr ;
void ( *p )( void ) ;

void f1 ( void ) ;
void f2 ( void ) ;

main( )
{
    clrscr( ) ;

    f1( ) ;
    f2( ) ;

    printf ( "\nback to main..." ) ;
    exit ( 1 ) ;
}

void f1 ( void )
{
    ptr = ( unsigned int far * ) MK_FP ( _SS, _SP + 2 ) ;
    printf ( "\n%x", *ptr ) ;

    p = ( void ( * )( ) ) MK_FP ( _CS, *ptr ) ;
    ( *p )( ) ;
    printf ( "\nI am f1( ) function " ) ;
}

void f2 ( void )
{
    printf ( "\nI am f2( ) function" ) ;
}
```

In **main( )** we have called two functions **f1( )** and **f2( )**. Before control is transferred to **f1( )** the address of instruction following the call to **f1( )** would be pushed on to the stack. In our case the address of the instruction where **f2( )** is called is saved on the stack. On saving this address on the stack, the stack pointer (SP) register would be decremented by 2. Note that SP always points to the top of stack. Whenever a function is called, to facilitate referencing of arguments of a function the C compiler pushes the value of the BP (Base Pointer) register to the stack. Hence the stack pointer (SP) would once again be decremented by 2.

We have used the macro **MK_FP** to construct a **far** pointer from the segment address (_SS) and offset address (_SP+2). This **far** pointer would point to the location in the stack where address of **f2( )** is stored. This address can be retrieved through the expression ***ptr**. This retrieved address would be an offset address. This is then combined with the code segment address (stored in _CS) to create a **far** pointer. Finally, using this **far** pointer the function **f2( )** is called.

Solved Problems

[A] Attempt the following:

(1) Suppose Fundu Parking Garage contains 10 parking lanes. each with a capacity to hold 10 cars at a time. As each car arrives/departs, the values A/D (representing arrival /departure) is entered along with the car registration number. If a car is departing the data should get updated. If a new car is arriving then on the screen a message should be displayed indicating suitable parking slot for the car. Cars arrive at the south end of the garage and leave from the north end. If a customer arrives to pick up a car that is not the nothernmost, all cars to the north of the car are moved out, the car is driven out, and the other cars are restored in the same order that they were in originally. Whenever a car leaves, all cars to the south are moved forward so that at all times all the empty spaces are in the south part of the garage. Write a program that implements this parking system.

Program

```
/* a car garage simulation using de-queue (link list implementation) */
#include "stdio.h"
#include "alloc.h"

#define TOP 1
#define BOT 2

struct node
{
    char plate [15] ;
    struct node *link ;
} *front[5], *rear[5] ;

char plate[15], temp[15] ;
```

```
int i ;
void add_dq (struct node**, struct node**, int, char*) ;
char* del_dq ( struct node**, struct node**, int ) ;
void push ( struct node**, char*) ;
char* pop ( struct node** ) ;

main( )
{
    char ad ;
    int s, lane = -1, min, lc ;

    clrscr( );
    while ( 1 )
    {
        for ( i = 0 ; i < 5 ; i++ )
        {
            printf( "lane %d: ", i ) ;
            q_display ( front[i] ) ;
        }
        printf( "\nArrival/Departure/Quit? ( A/D/Q ): " ) ;
        ad = getch( ) ;

        if ( ad == 'Q' )
            exit ( 1 ) ;

        printf ( "\nEnter license plate num:" ) ;
        gets ( plate ) ;
        ad = toupper ( ad ) ;

        if ( ad == 'A' ) /* arrival of car */
        {
            lane = -1 ; /* assume no lane is available */
            min = 10 ;
            for ( i = 0 ; i < 5 ; i++ )
            {
                s = count ( front[i] ) ;
                if ( s < min )
```

```
                        {
                            min = s ;
                            lane = i ;
                        }
                    }

                    if ( lane == -1 )
                        printf ( "\nNo room available" ) ;
                    else
                    {
                        add_dq ( &front[ lane ], &rear[ lane ], BOT, plate ) ;
                        printf ( "\npark car at lane %d slot %d\n", lane, s ) ;
                    }
                }
                else if ( ad == 'D' ) /* departure of car */
                {
                    for ( i = 0 ; i < 5 ; ++i )
                    {
                        s = search ( front[i], plate ) ;
                        if ( s != -1 )
                        {
                            lane = i ;
                            break ;
                        }
                    }

                    if ( i == 5 )
                        printf ( "\nno such car!!\n" ) ;
                    else
                    {
                        printf ( "\ncar found at lane %d slot %d\n", lane, s ) ;
                        del_dq ( &front[ lane ], &rear[ lane ], s ) ;
                    }
                }
                else if ( ad == 'Q' )
                    exit ( 1 ) ;
        }
    }
```

```
/* adds a new element at the end of queue */
void add_dq ( struct node **f, struct node **r, int tb, char *p )
{
    struct node *q ;
    /* create new node */
    q = malloc ( sizeof ( struct node ) ) ;
    strcpy ( q -> plate, p ) ;
    q -> link = NULL ;

    /* if the queue is empty */
    if ( *f == NULL )
        *f = q ;
    else
    {
        if ( tb == BOT )
            ( *r ) -> link = q ;
        else
        {
            q -> link = *f ;
            *f = q ;
            return ;
        }
    }
    *r = q ;
}

char* del_dq ( struct node **f, struct node **r, int n )
{
    struct node *q, *top = NULL ;
    /* if queue is empty */
    if ( *f == NULL )
        printf ( "queue is empty" ) ;
    else
    {
        if ( n == 0 )
        {
            strcpy ( temp, ( *f ) -> plate ) ;
```

```
                q = *f ;
                *f = ( *f ) -> link ;
                free ( q ) ;
                return temp ;
        }

        /* locate node */
        for ( i = 0 ; i < n ; i++ )
        {
                /* drive out cars */
                push ( &top, ( *f ) -> plate ) ;

                /* delete the node */
                q = *f ;
                *f = q -> link ;
                free ( q ) ;
        }

        /* delete the nth node */
        q = *f ;
        *f = q -> link ;
        free ( q ) ;

        for ( i = 0 ; i < n ; i++ )
        {
                strcpy ( temp, pop ( &top ) ) ;

                /* add the node */
                add_dq ( f, r, TOP, temp ) ;
        }
    }
}

count ( struct node *q )
{
    int c = 0 ;

    /* traverse the entire linked list */
```

```
        while ( q != NULL )
        {
            q = q -> link ;
            c++ ;
        }
        return c ;
}

search ( struct node *q, char *p )
{
    int s = -1, c = 0 ;

    while ( q != NULL )
    {
        if ( strcmp ( p, q -> plate ) == 0 )
        {
            s = c ;
            break ;
        }
        else
        {
            q = q -> link ,
            c++ ;
        }
    }
    return ( s ) ;
}

/* adds a new element to the top of stack */
void push ( struct node **s, char* item )
{
    struct node *q ;
    q = ( struct node* ) malloc ( sizeof ( struct node ) ) ;
    strcpy ( q -> plate, item ) ;
    q -> link = *s ;
    *s = q ;
}
```

```
/* removes an element from top of stack */
char* pop ( struct node **s )
{
    struct node *q ;

    /* if stack is empty */
    if ( *s == NULL )
    {
        return NULL ;
    }
    else
    {
        q = *s ;
        strcpy ( temp, q -> plate ) ;
        s = q -> link ;
        free ( q ) ;
        return ( temp ) ;
    }
}

q_display ( struct node *q )
{
    while( q != NULL )
    {
        printf ( "%s", q -> plate ) ;
        q = q -> link ;
    }
    printf ( "\n" ) ;
}
```

If you search for an entry in this index and cannot find it, you will earn yourself a place in Indexer's heaven!

Index

READER'S EVALUATION

It is our sincere endeavour to publish books which are specifically designed to meet your requirements. Your feedback on our titles would be of crucial help to us in this endeavour. Please spare some of your valuable time to fill the form given below and mail it to:

Publishing Manager,

BPB Publications,

20, Ansari Road, Daryaganj, New Delhi 110002

Looking forward to receiving your valuable comments and suggestions.

Title: UNDERSTADING POINTERS IN C   (THIRD REVISED EDITION)

Author: Yashavant K. Kanetkar   ISBN 81-7656-358-7

Please tick the appropriate box below each question as per the following rating code:

1.   COVERAGE (have all relevant topics been included in the book?)

Excellent	Good	Average	Bad

2.   PRESENTATION (have the topics been clearly explained?)

Excellent	Good	Average	Bad

3.   DEPTH (have the topics been explained in sufficient detail.?)

Excellent	Good	Average	Bad

4.   EXAMPLES/SAMPLE PROGRAMS/EXERCISES (Are these clear and illustrative?)

Excellent	Good	Average	Bad

5.   Is there any other topic which you would like to be included in the book?
   (i)
   (ii)
   (iii)

6   Is there any topic which you feel should be explained in a better manner?
   (i)
   (ii)
   (iii)

7.   Is there any other book on this subject which you have been using? If yes, please state title, author and publisher.

8.   How does this book compare with the other one?
   (i)   Coverage in this book is better/much better/same/worse.
   (ii)   Presentation in this book is better/much better/same/worse.
   (iii)   Depth in this book is more/much more/same/lesser.
   (iv)   Examples/sample programs in this book are better/much better/same/worse.

9.   Did you experience any difficulty in obtaining this book in your town? Yes/No

10.   How did you come to know about this book?
   (i)   From friends/fellow students
   (ii)   From teacher/instructor
   (iii)   Saw it in the bookshop
   (iv)   Through an advertisement/book reviews in magazine(s).

Name: _____

Affiliation: _____

Qualification: _____

Address: _____
_____